Rowing Faster

Volker Nolte

editor

Library of Congress Cataloging-in-Publication Data

Rowing faster / Volker Nolte, editor.
  p. cm.
  Includes bibliographical references and index.
  ISBN 0-7360-4465-5 (soft cover)
  1. Rowing. I. Nolte, Volker, 1952-
  GV791.R66 2005
  797.123--dc22   2004016933

ISBN-10: 0-7360-4465-5
ISBN-13: 978-0-7360-4465-3

Acquisitions Editor: Ed McNeely; **Developmental Editor:** Leigh Keylock; **Assistant Editor:** Cory Weber; **Copyeditor:** Alisha Jeddeloh; **Proofreader:** Julie Marx Goodreau; **Indexer:** Betty Frizzéll; **Permission Manager:** Toni Harte; **Graphic Designer:** Robert Reuther; **Graphic Artist:** Kim McFarland; **Photo Manager:** Dan Wendt; **Cover Designer:** Keith Blomberg; **Photographer (cover):** Harry Howe/Getty Images; **Photographer (interior):** Photos on pages 1 and 227 © Joel W. Rogers; all other photos by Volker Nolte, unless otherwise noted; **Art Manager:** Kareema McLendon; **Illustrators:** Brian McElwain, Kim McFarland, Denise Lowry, and Roberto Sabas; **Printer:** United Graphics

Human Kinetics books are available at special discounts for bulk purchase. Special editions or book excerpts can also be created to specification. For details, contact the Special Sales Manager at Human Kinetics.

Printed in the United States of America   10   9   8

Human Kinetics
Web site: www.HumanKinetics.com

United States: Human Kinetics
P.O. Box 5076
Champaign, IL 61825-5076
800-747-4457
e-mail: humank@hkusa.com

Canada: Human Kinetics
475 Devonshire Road, Unit 100
Windsor, ON N8Y 2L5
800-465-7301 (in Canada only)
e-mail: info@hkcanada.com

Europe: Human Kinetics
107 Bradford Road
Stanningley
Leeds LS28 6AT, United Kingdom
+44 (0)113 255 5665
e-mail: hk@hkeurope.com

Australia: Human Kinetics
57A Price Avenue
Lower Mitcham, South Australia 5062
08 8372 0999
e-mail: info@hkaustralia.com

New Zealand: Human Kinetics
Division of Sports Distributors NZ Ltd.
P.O. Box 300 226 Albany
North Shore City, Auckland
0064 9 448 1207
e-mail: info@humankinetics.co.nz

Rowing
Faster

contents

PREFACE   vii

PART I   *Training*

CHAPTER 1   THE ART OF ROWING 3
Volker Nolte

CHAPTER 2   ROWING PHYSIOLOGY 9
Ulrich Hartmann and Alois Mader

CHAPTER 3   MONITORING ATHLETES' PHYSIOLOGY 25
Kurt Jensen

CHAPTER 4   MANAGING ROWERS' MEDICAL CONCERNS 31
Richard Backus and Kristine Karlson

CHAPTER 5   DEVELOPING AN AEROBIC BASE 49
Marty Aitken

CHAPTER 6   IMPROVING ANAEROBIC THRESHOLD 63
Wolfgang Fritsch

CHAPTER 7   SPRINTING AND SPEED WORK 77
Declan A.J. Connolly

CHAPTER 8   BUILDING STRENGTH 87
Ed McNeely

CHAPTER 9   DESIGNING YOUR TRAINING PLAN 99
Ed McNeely

PART II   *Technique*

CHAPTER 10   ROWING BIOMECHANICS 111
Margaret McBride

CHAPTER 11   RIGGING 125
Volker Nolte

CHAPTER 12   BLADEWORK 141
Mike Spracklen

CHAPTER 13   THE CATCH 155
Brian Richardson

CHAPTER 14   LEG DRIVE 165
Richard Tonks

CHAPTER 15   RECOVERY 177
Volker Nolte

CHAPTER 16   INSIDE THE ROWER'S MIND 185
Volker Lippens

CHAPTER 17   ERGOMETER TECHNIQUE 195
Larry Gluckman

CHAPTER 18   TECHNOLOGY FOR TECHNIQUE IMPROVEMENT . . 209
Valery Kleshnev

PART III   *Racing*

CHAPTER 19   SELECTING ATHLETES AND CREWS 229
Thor Nilsen

CHAPTER 20   SETTING RACE PLANS AND TACTICS 237
Mike Teti and Volker Nolte

CHAPTER 21   RELAXING AND FOCUSING ON RACE DAY 249
James Joy

CHAPTER 22   COXING 261
Lesley Thompson-Willie

BIBLIOGRAPHY   275

INDEX   284

ABOUT THE EDITOR   289

ABOUT THE CONTRIBUTORS   291

preface

Rowing, one of the original sports in the modern Olympics, has a long, rich history. Rowing has evolved a great deal over the past 100 years, but one thing remains the same: the spirit of innovation and teamwork that is part of every winning crew. In this book we have tried to keep these traditions.

Over the past decade rowing has experienced a resurgence in popularity. The efforts of the International Federation of Rowing Associations (FISA) to bring rowing to less developed countries and the growth of rowing as a National Collegiate Athletic Association (NCAA) sport make this an exciting time for the sport. Advances in boat building, training methods, stroke biomechanics, and team building allow crews to go faster than ever before. In fact, the art and science of rowing are advancing so fast that it is difficult to keep up. While the world's top coaches and athletes are privy to the newest innovations in rowing, very little of this information filters down to clubs or colleges. *Rowing Faster* bridges this gap between elite coaches and the rest of the rowing world.

A finely tuned crew pulling together is an impressive sight. Rowing is about cooperation and teamwork, and nowhere is this more obvious than in coaching. Over the past decade hiring international coaches has become the norm for countries looking to take advantage of new ideas and training methods. *Rowing Faster* continues this tradition of teamwork: This book is a compilation of the best rowing information available from around the world. Together the crew of contributing authors has coached or competed for a total of 10 different countries, making this a truly international look at rowing.

Rowing Faster is divided into three parts. Part I focuses on physical preparation and training and what it takes physically to be a great rower. Each chapter in part I provides guidance and sample programs for developing rowing fitness. Some of the top sport scientists and rowing coaches show you how to improve aerobic base, increase anaerobic threshold, and improve race speed. The final chapter in this section brings it all together, showing you how to develop a winning training program.

Part II teaches the finer points of rowing technique. The chapters in this section examine the catch, leg drive, recovery, and bladework. Master technicians discuss the details that make the difference between a good rower and a great rower, sharing their favorite drills for perfecting each phase of the stroke. Part II also includes chapters on rigging and technology to help you set up your boat to get the most out of training and racing.

Part III prepares you to race. It covers precompetition tapering to help you put the finishing touches on your physical preparation, focusing and relaxation techniques for dealing with competitive stress and changing race conditions, and race plans for 1000-meter, 2000-meter, and head races. There is even a chapter on the coxswain.

Rowing Faster is for serious rowers or rowing coaches who are looking to take their rowing to the next level. It is for anyone who is willing to toil in the early morning hours to gain a couple of tenths of a second per 500 meters. Whether you are junior or masters, club or elite, *Rowing Faster* has something to offer you. The contributors to this book are some of the finest minds in the world of rowing today, and they present the best information and advice available to the rowing community. It is our hope that this book will help you achieve your rowing goals.

part I

Training

chapter 1

The Art of Rowing

Volker Nolte

"Rowing is an art as well as a science!" (Alexander 1922-1926). When I learned to row as a 14-year-old in 1969, the coach strictly forbade us from drinking any cold water before, during, or shortly after training. Even after a hot summer day's training, the coach would watch us to make sure we didn't take a drink. Only after a shower were we allowed to drink some juice, but it had to be at room temperature. We were warned of stomach cramps and poor performance if we broke the rules.

A few years later, my undergraduate physical education classes introduced me to ballistic stretching. Holding a stretch was an absolute no-no, and rhythm and swing were the keys to success.

During my years in international rowing between 1970 and 1972, I was invited to Germany's national team center in Ratzeburg, where the famous coach Karl Adam emphasized interval training. His basic training plan was Friday afternoon 6 × 560 meters, Saturday morning 6 × 500, Saturday afternoon 4 × 1000, Sunday morning 4 × 1000, and Sunday afternoon 6 × 500.

Backed by scientific research, coaches and athletes once believed that lukewarm liquids, ballistic stretching, and high-intensity intervals were the way to go. Since then we've learned that it is vital to rehydrate during training and that the body absorbs cool water the best. Stretching methods have gone 360 degrees, from ballistic to static back to ballistic stretching (Sands and McNeal 2000). Similarly, after rejecting intervals in favor of long, low-intensity endurance training, experts once again advocate using intervals.

Rowing has seen many more developments over the years, including basic endurance training, on-water resistance training, high-altitude training, carbon fiber boats, and Big Blades. Some of these changes will be around for years to come, some will be the start of new developments, and some will simply pass. These changes are normal and certainly nothing to worry about. Some rowers even argue that such developments are a stimulating part of high-performance sport, and coaches and athletes have to keep up with the times. Indeed, coaches and athletes are most often the ones who discover such developments in their search to improve rowing performance.

Rowing Development

Without a doubt, rowing performance has improved over the years. Schwanitz (1991) studied the race times of all Olympic gold medalists from 1948 to 1988 and found that with each Olympic Games, race times improved 1.3 percent for all boat classes. However, more detailed studies show that each boat class improves at a different speed. Schwanitz (1995), for example, saw the men's pair (M2-) improve at 1.8 percent, while the men's eight (M8+) increased its speed 0.9 percent from 1992 to 1996. These significant improvements suggest that the Olympic champions one year would not win a medal at the following Olympic Games if they performed at the same level as they did at the previous Games.

Figure 1.1 shows the race times of the winners in the men's eight at the International Lucerne Regatta from 1970 to 2003. The race times improve 1.8 seconds or 0.5 percent every four years (trend 70-03). The Lucerne Regatta is ideal for this kind of comparison since it has the same racing conditions from year to year: the same race course, world-class competition, and similar weather conditions.

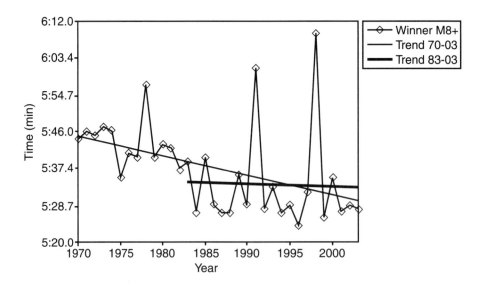

FIGURE 1.1   Race times for the men's eight (M8+) at the International Lucerne Regatta, 1970 to 2003.

Such increases in sport performance are astounding. In the Lucerne Regatta, the men of 2003 rowed about 15 seconds faster than their counterparts 34 years earlier. How is this possible? There are three ways to row faster:

1. Rowers can produce more energy.
2. Rowers can use their energy more efficiently.
3. Rowers can produce more energy *and* use their energy more efficiently.

Several factors affect energy production and efficiency:

- Biomechanics (rowing technique, race analysis)
- Equipment (boat and oar developments)
- Physiology (training concepts, fitness monitoring)
- Psychology (goal setting, motivation)
- Sociology (team cohesion, team support)
- Sports medicine (injury prevention, rehabilitation)

Physiology, psychology, sociology, and sports medicine allow the rower to produce more energy, while biomechanics and equipment are responsible for more efficient energy usage. However, it is difficult to pinpoint specific factors behind the performance peak. For example, the maximal oxygen uptake ($\dot{V}O_2$max) of top athletes does not show significant improvements from 1970 to 2003, nor do race times indicate a sudden increase after 1992, when rowers started using Big Blades. In addition, rowing is already very energy efficient, so large improvements in efficiency are difficult to come by (Nolte 1984; Affeld, Schichl, and Ziemann 1993; Kleshnev 2004).

So, what caused these improvements? It seems obvious that such speed development is possible only when all the influencing factors progress. Psychology in particular seems to have a significant influence. It's possible that rowers only push as hard as the performance standard demands. The standard for the men's eight in 1980 was 6:40 minutes for the Lucerne race, and perhaps coaches and athletes geared their training to reach or just surpass this level.

It could be that rowers can only train at a load that the equipment allows. This would mean that the rowing equipment of 1980 did not permit the high loads required for rowing faster, since oars and boats were not stiff enough to respond properly. Or, perhaps rowers only excel when they have the analysis technology to detect weaknesses. In 1980 coaches and athletes did not have the technology to measure physiological and biomechanical parameters on a sophisticated level.

In any case, athletes and coaches competing at the highest level of performance must accept the challenge of ever-improving standards. To keep up with the times, athletes must make rowing the center of their lives for many years and have professional support from experienced coaches and consultants. For a system to produce elite performances while developing athletes with fulfilled lives beyond rowing, it must be based on the philosophy, "Athletes first, winning second" (Martens 2004, 22). It has to focus on the development of the athletes as individuals, not just as rowers.

Excellence is only possible in an environment of trust, respect, open communication, and high standards. Add scientific knowledge about the sport and you have a complete program: This is the art of rowing.

The art of rowing encompasses high standards in learning and training as well as knowledge of the science of rowing.

Becoming a World-Class Rower

Every competitive rower's objective is to improve performance. For a young beginner, the goal is to take the first steps properly. For masters rowers, the goal is to strive for improvements in a healthy way. For high-performance rowers, the goal is to become the best athletes they can possibly be.

This book contains information that all rowers need in order to improve, from beginners to world champions. Internationally renowned rowing experts present their views on different areas of the sport. All of these experts have been directly involved with performances on the highest level. The coaches have been behind numerous medals at the world championships and Olympic Games, and the researchers have worked on internationally acknowledged studies. Some of these experts have also rowed on national teams and won international medals. Every one of them knows the demands, circumstances, and facts of rowing at all levels. In addition, this book presents the most up-to-date knowledge about rowing that is available. It is the current standard of information, and it invites rowers, coaches, and scientists to excel and succeed.

As you read, it will become clear that there are many ways to approach improvement. Although each of these experts has a unique perspective, they all combine practical experience and theoretical science. They also all reach for the highest achievement in the sport. You can take something special from each expert and create your own philosophy.

You can read the chapters in order, but each chapter stands alone, so you can also select the chapters that most capture your interest. However you choose to proceed, the experts will give you exciting insights into the newest ideas in rowing and include their personal experiences. Take ideas from our experts and use them in your daily rowing practice. They are sure to improve your knowledge about the sport and ultimately your performance.

A Glimpse Into the Future

Schwanitz (1995) predicts 0.9 percent speed improvement for the men's eight every four years. However, figure 1.1 indicates that the actual improvements from 1970 to 2003 fall short of this prediction by about 10 seconds—the eights of 2003 were 10 seconds behind their forecast. A closer look reveals that the performance of the men's eight between 1983 and 2003, in fact, statistically stagnates (see figure 1.1, trend 83-03).

What conclusions could we draw from these findings? How likely is it that the following conditions are true?

- Rowers reached the highest level of performance, and no further development is possible.
- Performance improvement is occurring at a lower pace. Instead of 0.9 percent every four years, we'll see improvements of less than 0.1 percent.
- This study is only based on statistical value, and it is only a matter of time until the winner of the men's eight at the Lucerne Regatta will row significantly faster than ever before.

That rowers have reached a maximal performance is doubtful; we see continuous performance improvements in other sports as well as in other boat classes. It is also unlikely that performance improvements have slowed. For example, other boat classes have experienced unbroken speed increases.

It's very possible that environmental conditions played a role; rowing associations favored other boat classes over the men's eight, leading some programs to prioritize the men's coxless pair or men's coxless four; and training and technique of the men's eight fell behind that of other boat classes. If this is the case, we will likely see a dramatic decrease in the winners' times of the men's eight in the near future.

This is an exciting possibility, and perhaps this book will help speed this progress. Think of this book as a stimulating training camp that includes top coaches, scientists such as physiologists and biomechanists, and experienced team leaders. As a participant in our special training camp, you can draw from the combined knowledge of forerunners in the field of international rowing. Go out, strengthen what you already do well, and be open and apply new ideas. Every author of this book has a proven record of success, so we know that it works.

chapter 2

Rowing Physiology

Ulrich Hartmann and Alois Mader

Rowing is a strength-endurance sport that demands superior technique. It requires individual discipline as well as teamwork, years of rigorous technique and conditioning training that emphasizes endurance and power, and certain physical characteristics. In this chapter we discuss optimum body size and physiological performance for elite rowers. As we do so, keep in mind that there are many rowers who only meet some of these requirements—you can still be a rower even if you aren't the perfect size or don't have the greatest physical ability. Above-average physical capability and perfect body type are useless if you don't have the technique to row the boat.

In spite of changes in rowing equipment, modern trends in training, and changes in body-size requirements, many experts agree that the improvement in rowing performance over the last 30 years is for the most part due to an improvement in physical conditioning. In particular, in the mid-1970s the German Democratic Republic athletes demonstrated dramatically superior conditioning that led to dramatic racing results.

Physiological Conditions

For the most part, metabolic performance determines physiological, rowing-specific performance. In a rowing race that lasts 5 minutes and 30 seconds, the average mechanical power output of elite male athletes is about 420 to 450 watts on the Gjessing ergometer (475 to 525 watts on the Concept2, type C ergometer), with a heart rate of about 190 beats per minute; a maximal oxygen uptake of 6000 to 6500 milliliters per minute ($\dot{V}O_2$max of 65 to 70 milliliters per kilogram body weight); postexercise lactate (lactic acid) levels of 16 to 21 millimoles per liter in the arterial blood; and a blood pH between 7.0 and 6.85, the limit of physiologically tolerable acidosis.

The majority of the rower's energy supply comes from the aerobic energy system. Therefore, in order to estimate a rower's performance, it is necessary to determine exactly how much energy the aerobic energy system provides. The more energy rowers can obtain aerobically, the better their basic conditions can be determined.

The most significant criterion for determining aerobic energy production is maximal oxygen uptake ($\dot{V}O_2$max). Hagerman and Lee (1971) measured a $\dot{V}O_2$max uptake of 4686 ± 130 milliliters per minute during tests in a rowing tank, and Hagerman et al. (1975) found 5434 and 5362 milliliters per minute and 5806 milliliters per minute. When measuring $\dot{V}O_2$max in national team members over 10 years, Hagerman et al. (1978, 1979) found values of 5950 ± 326 milliliters per minute and 6100 milliliters per minute. Carey et al. (1974) found a $\dot{V}O_2$max of 5320 ± 110 milliliters per minute in university club rowers, Jackson et al. (1976) found between 6130 and 6454 milliliters per minute in world champions according to the boat class, Strømme et al. (1977) found a $\dot{V}O_2$max of 5710 ± 610 milliliters per minute in Norwegian elite rowers, and Secher et al. (1982) registered a $\dot{V}O_2$max of 5600 ± 100 milliliters per minute in top rowers. In accordance to our own findings, an oxygen uptake above 6500 milliliters per minute must correlate with the associated mechanical output and can be attained only in exceptional cases.

Figure 2.1 describes the metabolic performance of elite male rowers during a six-minute maximal test. During the first minute of the race, mechanical power increases to its highest value, then it decreases until the fifth minute, and finally it increases briefly with a last spurt. Oxygen uptake reaches its highest value after about 90 seconds and then plateaus for the remaining 4 minutes. Heart rate increases greatly until the third minute, and then it increases gradually but continuously to its maximal value toward the end of the race. Stroke frequency is highest through the start phase, then decreases slightly to a medium frequency, and then increases significantly during the final spurt. Finally, blood lactate concentration has a mean value of 8 to 10 millimoles per liter after 240 seconds, 12 to 13 millimoles per liter after 180 seconds, approximately 14 millimoles per liter after 240 seconds, and 16 to 18 millimoles per liter at the end of the load.

Figure 2.2 demonstrates the importance of the $\dot{V}O_2$ uptake in a top rowing performance. It describes the power output on a rowing ergometer for male elite, club, and junior rowers during a six-minute test. They reached their highest values for $\dot{V}O_2$ uptake after 60 to 90 seconds, after which $\dot{V}O_2$ changes little. $\dot{V}O_2$ values at the end of the six-minute test are not much higher than in the second or fifth minute.

Figure 2.3 shows the contribution of $\dot{V}O_2$ to the total energy supply of a rowing performance. The dark area represents the $\dot{V}O_2$ during the six-minute test. The area

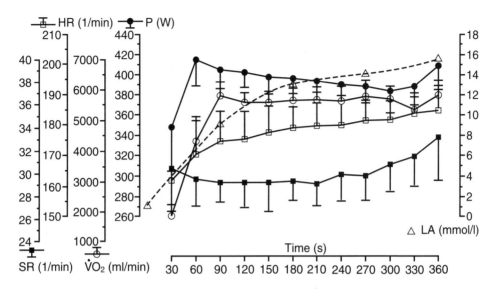

FIGURE 2.1 Time course for power output (P), oxygen uptake (V̇O₂), heart rate (HR), and stroke rate (SR) during a six-minute maximal load on a Gjessing rowing ergometer. The mean values for blood lactate (LA) are also marked.

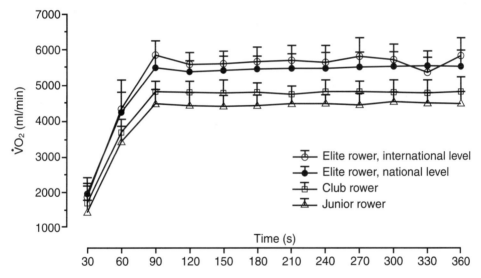

FIGURE 2.2 Oxygen uptake of male international, national, club, and junior rowers during a six-minute ergometer test.

covered by the V̇O₂ uptake describes the portion of energy that is aerobic. It is clear that aerobic energy makes up a large portion of the necessary energy requirement in rowing.

Admittedly, energy recruited through oxygen uptake (figure 2.3a, dark area) is not enough to meet the energy needs of the whole competition (figure 2.3b, overall area). Rowers need an enormous amount of energy, especially at the start, when oxygen uptake is still increasing and an energy deficit exists. Part of the energy supply has to be covered by anaerobic lactic (figure 2.3b; medium-shaded area) and anaerobic alactic (light area) metabolic systems.

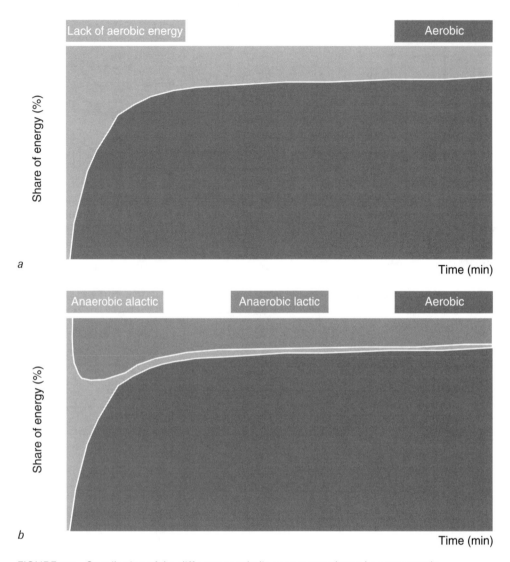

FIGURE 2.3   Contribution of the different metabolisms to a rower's total energy supply.

As we've discussed, figure 2.1 shows the behavior of lactate during simulated racing loads. Just as high oxygen uptake represents aerobic energy, a high postexercise lactate value (16 to 18 millimoles per liter) is evidence of anaerobic energy, because the anaerobic energy system produces lactic acid. However, these lactate values may be limited evidence for the glycolytic, or anaerobic lactic, influence on the energy supply for the rowing performance.

Contrary to popular belief, blood lactate levels alone do not provide reliable information on the anaerobic lactic share of energy supply. Studies have found a maximum of 14 to 17 millimoles per liter to be normal after typical rowing exercise. However, variables such as body size, muscle composition, and so on may be significant influencing factors, as we'll discuss later.

Because of physiological reasons, the glycolysis, or anaerobic lactic, share of the energy supply is not immediately available (there is a delay time of two to four seconds in the beginning), so energy must come predominantly from high-energy phosphates (ATP/CRPH; approximately the light area in figure 2.3b).

Body-Size Requirements

The average elite male heavyweight rower is approximately 197 centimeters tall (185 for women) and weighs 95 kilograms (85 for women). Ideally, his percentage of body fat does not exceed 8 percent or 7.6 kilograms (14 percent or 11.9 kilograms for women). In practice, further data may only be determined through indirect procedures and therefore are estimates only.

Based on height, weight, and body-fat percentage, the optimal body cell mass (muscles, brain, inner organs) of elite male heavyweights is about 52 percent of body mass. Of this, 85 percent is muscle mass. Of the muscle mass, only 75 percent (30 kilograms or one-third of body mass) is used in rowing. Optimal body cell mass is the result of body growth and training. If training starts at age 16 and lasts 10 to 15 years, the athlete will acquire most of the physical fundamentals for high-performance rowing during the first 3 or 4 years of training.

According to studies on the development of successful rowers, the average height for males at age 16 is 187 centimeters and the average weight is no more than 82 kilograms. Based on height and weight, the body cell mass of these rowers is about 48 percent, not far from the optimum 52 percent. Until the end of growth at about age 19, height increases about 10 centimeters and body mass increases about 12 kilograms. Approximately 85 percent of the increase in body mass is muscle, so from ages 16 to 20, muscle mass increases from one-fourth to one-third of body mass. Relative power based on body mass increases little, but the absolute strength and power increase greatly.

Figure 2.4 shows that performance requirements are the same for C-squad and A-squad rowers, based on the ratio of body mass to muscle mass. The existing differences in performance result from talent and training rather than near-equal muscle mass.

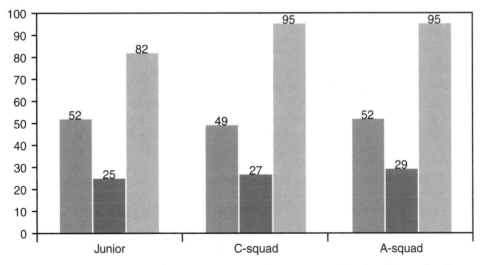

FIGURE 2.4 Development of body mass in kg (light bar), percentage of body cell mass (medium-shaded bar), and percentage of active muscle mass (dark bar).

Muscular Requirements

The strength of a single muscle can be more a function of muscle fiber than mass. There are two types of fibers, fast twitch (FT) and slow twitch (ST). ST fibers (red, slow oxidative fibers) rely on aerobic energy and are fatigue-resistant. They produce large amounts of energy at a relatively slow pace, making them good for endurance activities.

FTa fibers (white, fast oxidative fibers) contract more quickly than ST fibers. They also fatigue more quickly, but the faster contractions result in greater power. FTb fibers (white, fast glycolytic fibers) have little resistance to fatigue but contract extremely fast. FTb fibers produce energy extremely quickly and have a low percentage of aerobic energy supply, so they are good for short bursts of activity as in sprinting and jumping, or very fast and heavy forces during peak strokes in rowing.

In rowing, primarily the first two fiber types, ST and FTa, are important. The flexor muscles of arms and trunk, like the biceps, consist mostly of ST fibers (50 to 90 percent) and FTa fibers (10 to 30 percent). Extensors, like the triceps and the quadriceps, consist of fast or slow twitch fibers. The ratio depends on genetic predisposition but is usually about 50 percent FT fibers and 50 percent ST fibers. In elite rowers, the extensors contain mostly FTa fibers. The large number of capillaries found in FTa fibers means these elite rowers generate aerobic energy more easily than most other athletes, even when they have a given percentage of FTa fibers.

Because rowing requires a great deal of strength, FTa fibers have an essential advantage over ST fibers. Let's say you have a muscle that consists solely of FTa fibers and a muscle that consists solely of ST fibers. The FTa muscle is one-third as big as the ST muscle, but it generates the same amount of power. With more capillaries and a smaller cross section, the FTa muscle gets a much greater supply of oxygen, and therefore it is more efficient than the muscle that needs three times the cross section for the same amount of power.

No muscle, however, consists of only one fiber type. Because of that, strength comes down to the ratio of fiber types. Rowers with a high stroke power and slim physique most likely have more FTa fibers than rowers with the same stroke power but larger, more developed muscles.

It is possible to calculate the essential differences in strength per square centimeter of muscle mass. For a muscle that is 95 percent ST fibers and 5 percent FTa fibers, a relative power factor referring to 100 percent ST fibers can be calculated as:

$$0.95 \times 1.0 + 0.05 \times 3 = 1.1$$

If the muscle is 30 percent FTa fibers, the power factor is calculated as:

$$0.7 \times 1.0 + 0.3 \times 3 = 1.6$$

Given the same cross section, this muscle has an isometric maximal power that is 1.45 (1.6 divided by 1.1) times higher than the first, so it is capable of proportionally higher stroke power (in this case 45 percent more power output).

Unfortunately, it seems that extensive endurance training converts FTa fibers into ST fibers, resulting in decreased speed and stroke power. This conversion also occurs in highly talented rowers, especially those in the fast boat categories. Most coaches and rowers avoid endurance training of more than 7500 kilometers per year.

Metabolic Conditions for Rowing-Specific Energy

In rowing, power is measured on an ergometer. $W_{Gjessing}$ refers to the power output measured in watts on a Gjessing ergometer, and $W_{Concept2C}$ refers to power output measured by a Concept2, type C ergometer. An elite rower can generate about 450 $W_{Gjessing}$, or 520 $W_{Concept2C}$, of effective power to row through a six-minute period. The duration of the rowing stroke is 0.6 seconds, so the average power per stroke is 450 / 0.6 = 750 $W_{Gjessing}$ per stroke. A 95-kilogram rower can achieve up to 1500 $W_{Gjessing}$ per stroke. Note that comparing power output on a Gjessing ergometer versus a Concept2, type C ergometer can be done by using the following equation:

$$P_{Concept2C} \; (W) = 1.33 \times P_{Gjessing} - 83 \; (W)$$

However, overall power is distinctly higher than this measurement. In addition to the measured 450 $W_{Gjessing}$ of apparent power, there are 80 more $W_{Gjessing}$ of power that are not measured but are necessary to move the mass of the rower. That is, an elite 95-kilogram rower has a total power output of 530 $W_{Gjessing}$ (620 $W_{Concept2C}$) for six minutes on a rowing ergometer during a maximal power test.

An elite rower's high absolute metabolic capacity and stroke power result from active muscle mass, which consists of three components: anaerobic alactic energy, anaerobic lactic energy, and aerobic energy (oxygen uptake capacity, mitochondria volume).

Alactic anaerobic expenditure depends on the amount of available adenosine triphosphate (ATP) and creatine phosphate (CRPH) in the muscles. This stored energy fuels rowers during the first 6 to 10 seconds when they need a lot of power to accelerate the boat. In those few seconds rowers spend 60 to 80 percent of that small energy supply system. The power that rowers generate during this period is two to three times higher than the power they generate in the second to sixth minutes. Figure 2.5 clarifies the relationships between power, CRPH, and ATP during rowing-specific loading.

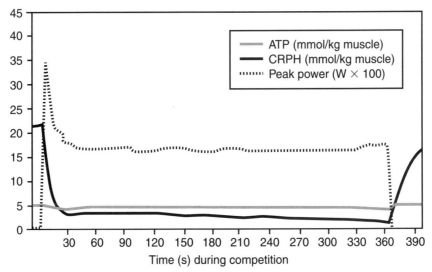

FIGURE 2.5 Dynamics of the anaerobic alactic energy supply during a rowing competition in terms of power output, creatine phosphate (CRPH), and adenosine triphosphate (ATP).

In addition to maximal glycolytic power (anaerobic lactic energy supply), the body can generate large amounts of energy through the anaerobic lactic energy metabolism over a short time. When the body does this, it produces lactate at a high rate. In sprinting, for instance, maximal glycolytic power can only be maximally mobilized between the 4th and 10th seconds (equal to 7 to 12 maximal strokes in rowing). The anaerobic lactic (work) capacity complies with the accumulated lactate up to the physiologically highest possible acidosis in the muscle cell (pH less than 6.95) when the body reaches complete exhaustion. This means that it is physiologically not possible to repeat multiple actions in the same manner in a short period of time.

A maximal lactate formation rate of approximately 1.2 millimoles per second × kilogram of muscle mass would result in very high power output per stroke while stroke frequency is more than 36 strokes per minute. That power could theoretically be maintained for 20 to 25 seconds. In practice, however, such high power and stroke frequency are only advisable for a few seconds because there is still a great deal of time left in the rowing race. More precise estimates of lactate formation can only be done via computer simulation. Figure 2.6 shows the lactate formation rate, or VLAmax, and blood pH over a six-minute rowing load.

For longer load durations, such as during competition, glycolytic power is restricted to the lactic work capacity, or accumulated lactate. A hint about the lactic work capacity is the maximal blood lactate (< 25 millimoles per liter). A maximal afterload concentration of 22 millimoles per liter in blood during the seventh through twelfth minutes complies with a peak concentration of muscle lactate of 35 millimoles per kilogram just after termination of the test. During loading the pH drops as a consequence of accumulated muscle lactate.

Available glycolytic power during a six-minute rowing competition is 8 to 10 percent of total glycolytic power. This complies with the mechanical power of only 17 percent (one-sixth) of the mean mechanical power during a rowing competition respective to the overall energy conversion over the distance, resulting from the net lactate forma-

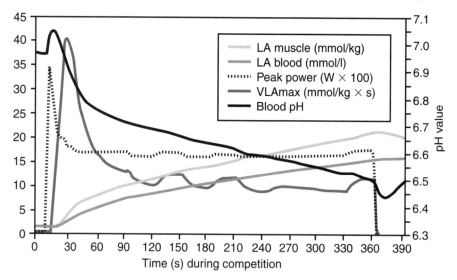

FIGURE 2.6   Dynamics of the anaerobic lactic energy supply during a maximum load in a rowing competition in terms of power output, lactate formation rate (VLAmax), lactate in muscle (LA muscle), lactate in blood (LA blood), and pH value.

tion. This shows that the anaerobic lactic energy supply has only a small influence on the total power output. This also means that the amount of anaerobic training in practice should be reviewed.

Additionally, naturally high glycolytic power that exists without specific training is not advantageous. At power demands greater than 70 percent of $\dot{V}O_2$max, high glycolytic power capability reduces the aerobic energy supply to lower than 80 percent of $\dot{V}O_2$max. However, extensive endurance training of low intensity over long periods of time reduces excessive glycolytic power to a rowing-specific optimum lactate formation rate of not more than 0.6 millimoles per second $\times$ kilogram.

It is a popular fallacy that training can greatly increase anaerobic lactic capacity. There is no measurable difference in the lactic capacity between trained and untrained athletes. The secret of power in rowing is not to try and increase glycolytic power, but rather to decrease it while at the same time increasing oxidative performance, as we'll soon discuss.

Another fallacy is that interval training enhances staying power. During the second half of a rowing competition it is possible to achieve cellular pH values of less than 6.6 because of the large amount of glycolytic energy production during the first half of the race. Though glycolytic energy production lessens, it continues to increase acidosis. With increasing acidosis, however, a glycolysis enzyme called phosphofructokinase increasingly blocks the anaerobic lactic energy supply to stop further lactate production, thus preventing an even lower pH. If not for this enzyme, the low pH would lead to destruction of body protein and mitochondria in the body's cells. Therefore, the only way to enhance staying power is to enhance aerobic power in order to keep lactate within tolerable limits.

Before moving on, let's clarify the terms *aerobic capacity* and *anaerobic capacity* and discuss endurance in general. In sports the following terms are often used simultaneously:

- Aerobic-anaerobic threshold and the oxidative or aerobic energy supply
- Maximum tolerable lactate acidosis during maximal performance and glycolytic or anaerobic energy supply

Again, endurance (aerobic capacity) is only part of the total oxidative energy supply mechanism. It dominantly supplies energy until the body reaches the anaerobic threshold or, better, the maximum lactate steady state.

Figure 2.7 describes the effect of an increase in endurance. The saturation area (percentage value of $\dot{V}O_2$max where in addition to the aerobic energy supply, a further increasing share of anaerobic lactic energy supply is used) of $\dot{V}O_2$ of an untrained individual is 65 percent (figure 2.7a), compared to nearly 85 percent in an athletically-trained individual (figure 2.7b). At the same time, the accumulation of blood lactate, which marks a greater contribution of glycolytic energy, shifts to the right (figure 2.7b, see dotted extension of lactate line). In a better-trained individual, lactate accumulation leads to a 50 percent higher performance output (figure 2.7b). This is the result of an increased oxidative influence (a better aerobic performance) and a later, less intensive beginning glycolytic energy supply.

When aerobic training is excessive (more than 7000 kilometers of rowing per year), the glycolytic energy supply (anaerobic capacity) becomes less usable (figure 2.7b). Anaerobic capacity is the production of high lactate values in a short time and the maintenance of those values over some time. This is also called lactate tolerance.

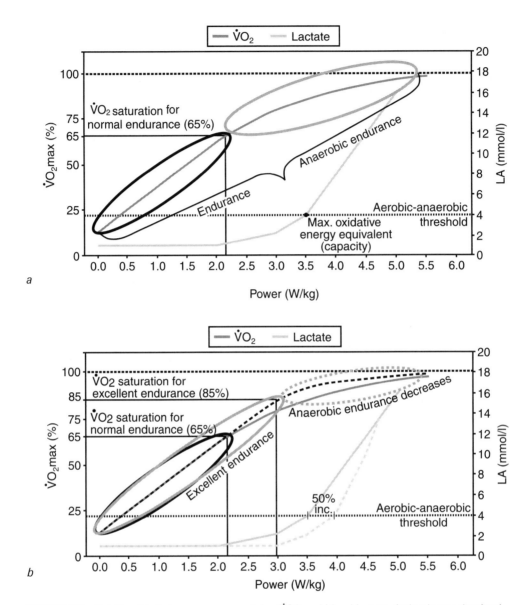

FIGURE 2.7   Relationship between oxygen uptake ($\dot{V}O_2$) and blood lactate during increasing load.

Here is a summary:

- A high anaerobic (glycolytic) performance means a low endurance performance (low aerobic capacity, as in the 100-meter sprint).
- A high aerobic performance means a low glycolytic performance (or low lactate formation rate, as in the marathon run).
- The secret for success in a sport such as rowing is the development of the different patterns of energy supply.

The number and volume of mitochondria determine a muscle's aerobic performance. A rower needs a mitochondria volume of about 5 percent cell mass for a performance of 450 W$_{Gjessing}$ (520 W$_{Concept2C}$). Not every muscle gets the same load in rowing, and muscles that are especially stressed, like the leg extensors and arm flexors, can develop 10 to 12 percent more mitochondria. Such muscles fatigue less during six-minute loading because this kind of performance relies almost solely on aerobic energy.

Another factor in high endurance performance is applicable muscle mass. In most rowers this is about 30 kilograms. In ST fibers, the average mitochondria volume is 3.5 percent, or 35 milliliters of volume per kilogram of muscle. An average untrained individual with 82 kilograms body mass and 30 percent applicable muscle mass has a power output of about 328 watts and a $\dot{V}O_2$max of about 4000 milliliters per minute. A trained individual (same body mass, higher applicable muscle mass) has a higher percentage of mitochondria volume (about 5 percent) and a $\dot{V}O_2$max of 6500 milliliters per minute and a power output of 510 watts. For elite rowers this means a performance range of 450 to 420 watts on the Gjessing ergometer for a six-minute period or 520 to 475 watts on the Concept2, type C ergometer.

Figure 2.8 shows oxygen uptake ($\dot{V}O_2$max) during a maximal load in a simulated rowing competition.

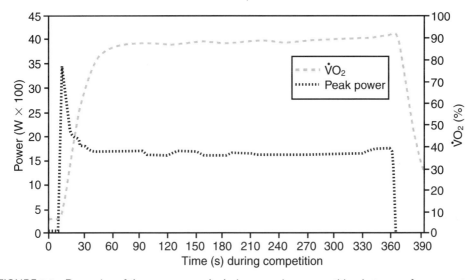

FIGURE 2.8 Dynamics of the energy supply during a rowing competition in terms of power output and oxygen uptake ($\dot{V}O_2$).

Figure 2.9 gives a summary and an overview of metabolism during a race. Because of the high performance in the first few seconds (first to fifth seconds approximately 1000 watts, sixth to tenth seconds 800 watts), the CRPH reserves of 20 millimoles per kilogram decrease by 15 percent within 25 seconds. During this period ATP decreases by about 17 percent. VLA (lactate formation) reaches 40 percent, and then after about 70 seconds it decreases to 12 percent and holds steady until the end. Because of the initial short-term activation, muscle lactate concentration rises to about 7 millimoles per liter, or about 30 percent of the final concentration. The increase in blood lactate follows the increase in muscle lactate. After an initial delay of 4 seconds there is a steep rise, which comes to an end after about 90 seconds. The slight increase in $\dot{V}O_2$ results from the slight decrease in CRPH, which, especially at the end of the load, leads to a further increase in lactate concentration.

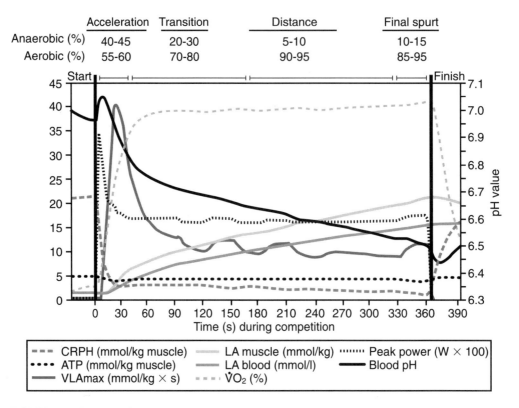

FIGURE 2.9   Theoretical energy supply during rowing competition in terms of power output, oxygen uptake (V̇O₂), creatine phosphate (CRPH), adenosine triphosphate (ATP), lactate in muscle (LA muscle), lactate in blood (LA blood), and lactate formation rate (VLAmax).

The rower did not reach the maximum performance possible (because he had to row six minutes and not just 250 meters and thus tried to save some energy), fully utilizing neither V̇O₂ (only by 90 percent; see figure 2.10 on page 22) nor VLA (16 millimoles per liter postexercise blood lactate; see figures 2.1 and 2.6). The reason for this lies in the contribution of the different energy supplies.

Figure 2.9 shows the theoretical contributions of energy supply in a rowing performance. In the acceleration phase, 40 to 45 percent of total energy is anaerobic and 55 to 60 percent is aerobic. In the transition phase, 20 to 30 percent of total energy is anaerobic and 70 to 80 percent is aerobic. In the distance phase, 5 to 10 percent of total energy is anaerobic and 90 to 95 percent is aerobic. In the final spurt phase, 10 to 15 percent of total energy is anaerobic and 85 to 90 percent is aerobic. Clearly, aerobic energy dominates.

During a competition of 5:30 to 7:00 minutes, a well-trained rower's aerobic energy system produces 80 to 85 percent of the total energy, the anaerobic lactic system produces 11 to 15 percent, and the anaerobic alactic system produces 5 to 9 percent of the energy.

It is impossible to directly infer competition speed from metabolic performance. To some extent, elite athletes can use excellent rowing technique to compensate for low metabolic performance, so although high metabolic performance is necessary, it alone does not result in success.

Simulation of Different Energy Systems

Table 2.1 shows the results of a computer calculation of the energy requirements in rowing on the basis of the assumption of different metabolic conditions. It is possible to quantify the influence of VLA (anaerobic lactic energy) based on the results of a six-minute maximal rowing performance.

TABLE 2.1 Energy Supply During Six Minutes of Maximal Performance

METABOLIC CONDITIONS		PERCENTAGE OF ENERGY SUPPLY			COMMENTS		
$\dot{V}O_2$max (ml/min)	VLAmax (mmol/ kg × s)	Aerobic (%)	Anaerobic lactic (%)	Anaerobic alactic (%)	$\dot{V}O_2$ (%)	pH	Lactate accumulation (mmol/l)
6000	1.40	80.0	15.6	4.4	<90	6.4	18.0
6000	0.70	82.6	13.1	4.3	=90	6.6	16.0
6000	0.35	85.0	10.8	4.2	>90	6.7	13.0
6300	1.40	82.5	13.4	4.1	<85	6.6	16.0
6300	0.70	85.1	10.9	4.0	=85	6.7	13.5
6300	0.35	87.5	8.6	3.9	>85	6.8	11.0
5400	1.40	76.2	18.9	4.9	>95	<6.40	23.0
				ATP depleted; breakdown			
5400	0.70	78.3	16.7	5.0	>95	<6.45	21.0
				ATP nearly depleted; limit			
5400	0.35	80.1	14.8	5.1	>95	=6.55	18.0
				Glycolytic capacity too low			

Test performed on 500-watt cycle ergometer.

Power output depends on different ratios of glycolytic (VLA) or oxidative ($\dot{V}O_2$) capacities.

Summary based on a high (6000 milliliters per minute), very high (6300), and low (5400) $\dot{V}O_2$max or a high (1.40 millimoles per liter per second), medium (0.70), and low (0.35) VLAmax.

Comments include the calculated proportions of energy provision (%) as well as the cellular pH values and PBLC. The assumed performance is 430 W$_{Gjessing}$ and 490 W$_{Concept2C}$.

If a high $\dot{V}O_2$max of 6300 milliliters per minute and the different assumptions of VLAmax, as in table 2.1, are taken as a basis, the partial or complete utilization of individual proportions of energy metabolism is not necessary.

If athletes have an oxygen uptake below 5400 milliliters per minute, they can realize the given performance of 430 W$_{Gjessing}$ (490 W$_{Concept2C}$) if they use their $\dot{V}O_2$max to a high degree and have a VLAmax of 0.7 millimoles per liter per second. However, if they have a high VLA of 1.4, the resulting high blood lactate concentration as well as the pH will prevent athletes from performing to the end because of a lack of ATP for further muscle contraction. If they have a low VLA (0.35), postexercise lactate concentration will be tolerable; however, they would not be able to perform to the end of the load because of a generally too low oxygen uptake combined with a too low glycolytic capacity for the given performance.

Figure 2.10 shows the possible energy supply distribution. With an increasing glycolytic performance, the anaerobic lactic supply of about 10 percent of a well-trained rower (figure 2.10a) can increase to 15 percent (figure 2.10b) at the cost of a decreased aerobic supply (from 85 to less than 80 percent) of total energy supply. This in itself does not directly affect a single competition, but with an increasing amount of high glycolytic loads (higher number of interval repetitions) the individual's load tolerance will decrease dramatically.

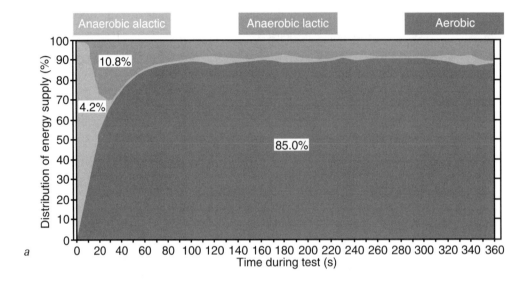

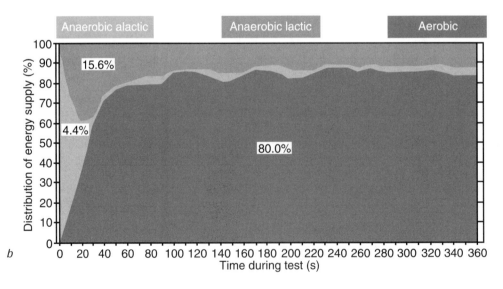

FIGURE 2.10   Possible distribution of energy supply.

Conclusion

The physiology of high-performance rowing is the result of several components:

- An optimized active muscle mass (one-third of body mass). This is based on individual body growth and strength training.
- A highly developed metabolism, based on the aerobic performance of the active muscle mass and a reduction of glycolysis to half of its maximum. Note that it is necessary to develop the aerobic and anaerobic metabolisms together over a period of years under the individual aspects of load tolerance and adaptation.
- A 60 percent increase in aerobic performance of the muscle mass due to an increase in mitochondria from 3.0 percent to 5.5 or 6.0 percent per kilogram active muscle mass. This is the result of extensive endurance training.
- A lactate formation rate of less than 0.6 millimoles per second per kilogram during an all-out test of 10 to 12 seconds.

chapter 3

Monitoring Athletes' Physiology

Kurt Jensen

Competitive rowing involves a 2-kilometer, all-out performance that depends on boat class, wind, and water conditions. Obviously, rowing is an aerobic sport, and rowers are among the athletes with the highest maximal oxygen uptake. However, anaerobic energy supply is also important, accounting for 25 to 30 percent of the rower's total energy supply (Secher 1993). Because anaerobic energy metabolism depends on muscle mass, strength training is an important part of the training schedule. Rowers often have limited hours for training but still want to optimize their physical performance. Everyone has an opinion on how to do this, including how much muscle mass is enough, how much time rowers should spend in the weight room and in the boat, and how much strength training lightweight rowers and women should do.

There is no single answer to these questions, especially because different classes have different physical requirements. In the open class there are no weight limits, so rowers might increase muscle in order to increase strength and anaerobic power. Lightweight rowers, on the other hand, need to stay a certain weight, so increasing muscle mass isn't really an option. These rowers depend more on aerobic power and capacity.

Although there's no one right answer, there is a golden standard based on world-class rowers that can help athletes determine the path they want to take in their training. This chapter outlines a practical test, or golden standard, for monitoring athletes' physiological capacity. Such monitoring can help answer these questions about balanced training.

Developing the Test Method

I developed the golden standard from the performances of 21 elite Danish rowers in a series of physical tests (see table 3.1). During the preparation season, the rowers participated in a four-day test series involving all-out performance over fixed time or fixed distance on a Concept2, type C rowing ergometer (see table 3.2). You can take more than four days to run the series of tests as long as the range is constant and you follow the same protocol each time.

The first test is always the 10-second test. This is the most intensive test, but it is also the least exhausting, so rowers can repeat it two or three times to be sure they get the best results. After 30 minutes of active rest, do the 6-kilometer test. This test is exhausting, but if rowers are well trained, they will be able to recover for the next day, when they perform the intensive 2-kilometer test. On the third day do the 60-second test. This test is also intensive, but again, if rowers are well trained, they will be ready for the next day and their last, most exhaustive performance: the 60 minute test.

TABLE 3.1 Physical Characteristics of Rowers

Mean (SD)	Height (m)	Body mass (kg)	$\dot{V}O_2max$ (ml × kg$^{-0.73}$ × min^{-1})
Men, open class, N = 4	1.94 (0.06)	87.8 (2.8)	232 (8)
Men, lightweight, N = 8	1.83 (0.05)	76.7 (3.4)	238 (18)
Women, open class, N = 5	1.82 (0.05)	79.0 (6.0)	185 (7)
Women, lightweight, N = 4	1.72 (0.04)	61.1 (2.4)	186 (7)

TABLE 3.2 Four-Day Test Series

Test series	Stroke rate*	Day to perform	Test focus	Reference values (%)
1. 10 s**	Max	Day 1	Muscle power	173 ± 22
2. 6 km	26-28	Day 1***	Aerobic capacity	85 ± 3
3. 2 km	30-36	Day 2	Aerobic power	100 (defined)
4. 60 s	Max	Day 3	Anaerobic capacity	153 ± 10
5. 60 min	22-24	Day 4	Aerobic capacity, endurance	76 ± 4

* On a slide ergometer the stroke rate should be two to four strokes faster.

** Best of three trials.

*** After 30 minutes of active rest.

To achieve optimal performance in the 10-second and 60-second tests, go as fast as possible from the start, trying to keep the intensity high until the end—although the intensity during the 60-second test will drop significantly anyway. In the 6-kilometer and 60-minute tests, you will have to find the highest (almost) constant power that you are able to keep the entire duration.

The tests measure average power in watts, which you can read on the small computer on the ergometer. Figure 3.1a shows the rowers' average power against time in a power-endurance curve, indicating anaerobic (10 and 60 seconds) and primary aerobic power (2 kilometers, 6 kilometers, and 60 minutes). Figure 3.1b shows power relative to average power during the 2-kilometer test. The 2-kilometer test was taken as a reference because it simulates the race and will correspond to 100 percent of the maximal oxygen uptake of rowers or slightly above.

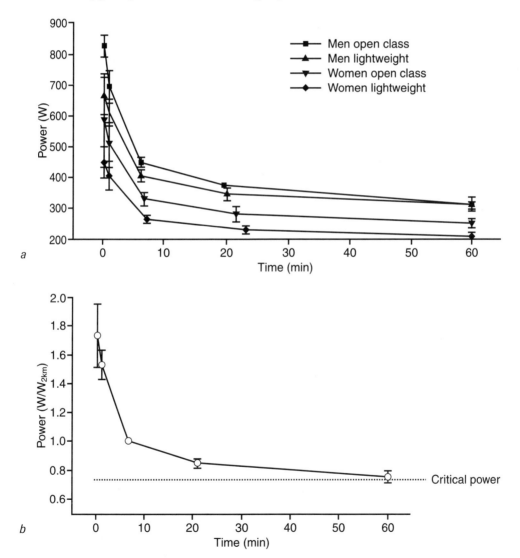

FIGURE 3.1 *(a)* Average power in the test series for the four categories of rowers; *(b)* relative power compared with power in the 2-kilometer test for all rowers.

Analyzing the Results

The power-endurance curves include specific physical performance over distances typically used to quantify training . Each group has a specific profile (figure 3.1a). When the power is expressed relative to the power during the 2-kilometer performance and plotted against time (figure 3.1b), there is no significant difference between open class and lightweight or between men and women ($P > 0.05$). A single curve thus represents men and women in the open and lightweight class. We calculated critical power, or the lower limit of endurance work, to be 274 watts or 74 percent of average power during the 2-kilometer performance (figure 3.1b).

We can analyze the results by either comparing maximal oxygen uptake of heavyweights and lightweights or by comparing their power-endurance curves.

• Comparison of maximal oxygen uptake. Body mass is within the normal range for the season. Because aerobic power is expressed in units that are independent of body mass, we can make comparisons between groups. Instead of expressing maximal oxygen uptake in liters per minute, which will always be higher for heavier rowers, we can express maximal oxygen uptake relative to body mass. To compare maximal uptake between rowers of different sizes, divide $\dot{V}O_2$max by the body weight lifted in the 0.73 power (Jensen, Johansen, and Secher 2001). Table 3.1 (page 26) shows no significant difference in aerobic power between open class and lightweights. However, the women have 20 percent less aerobic power than the men, as commonly observed in athletes (Jensen, Johansen, and Secher 2001).

• Comparison of power-endurance curves (figure 3.1a and b). In absolute terms, work efficiency is different between lightweights and heavyweights due to differences in body dimensions and gender. Surprisingly, however, we observed no difference between groups in any of the four performance tests when power was expressed relative to average power in the 2-kilometer race performance.

This indicates that the power-endurance curve can be used as a reference, or golden standard, for open class and lightweights, men and women.

Anaerobic performance parameters: Power taken as a percentage of the average power over the 2-kilometer performance is 173 percent during the 10-second test and 153 percent during the 60-second test (table 3.1). In other words, the rowers were able to increase their performance by 73 and 53 percent in the 10-second and 60-second tests, respectively, compared with the 2-kilometer performance test.

Aerobic performance parameters: The rowers maintained power at 85 percent of the 2-kilometer performance during the 6-kilometer performance and 76 percent during the 60-minute performance.

These values serve as a golden standard for rowers trying to evaluate an optimal balance between anaerobic and aerobic training. The critical power serves as the lower limit for aerobic quality training.

Carry out the four-day series at least once a year, at the beginning of the preparation period, in order to plan individual training intensity and relative load. Then you can repeat it at the end of the preparation period (after several months) in order to see if the training has had the appropriate effect. Don't use the four-day test series too often, as it takes a lot of motivation for rowers to put forth their full effort for a series of its length and intensity. You can, however, sometimes use one of the tests in a weekly training program.

Applications in Rowing Training

Assuming that the data from this study reflects optimal adaptation for rowing performance, rowers can use the same general training preparation whether they're open class or lightweights, men or women. Divide the training according to the power-endurance curve for each rower. If a rower does poorly in the anaerobic tests, he might do more strength and power training. On the other hand, if an individual rower is too strong in relation to her aerobic endurance, she should focus on aerobic training.

Quality training is that which rowers perform at a higher intensity than what they can sustain for one hour of maximal rowing. Quality training can be divided into intensities (figure 3.2).

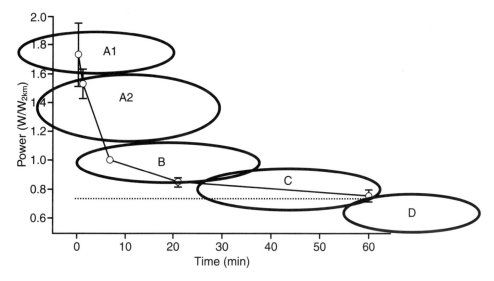

FIGURE 3.2 Relative power of the different training intensities compared with power in the 2-kilometer test.

Quality Training

A1—Muscle power training at the intensity of the 10-second test

A2—Muscle capacity training at the intensity of the 60-second test

B—Aerobic power training less than, but close to, the intensity of a 2-kilometer rowing competition

C—Aerobic capacity training at an intensity less than that of the 6-kilometer race but higher than that of the 60-minute test

D—Aerobic endurance training at an intensity at or slightly lower than the intensity of the 60-minute test

Sample Training Models

A1—10 × 10 seconds with 50 seconds in between

A2—5 × 40 seconds with 120 seconds in between

B—5 × 5 minutes with 5 minutes in between

C—2 × 20 minutes with 10 minutes in between

D—Continuous rowing for 40 to 80 minutes

Conclusion

It seems that the muscular and respiratory systems of men and women, and of light-weight and open class rowers, adapt in the same way to training. However, the test results might be related to the uniformity of the national training program. Further research based on international medal winners from other nations is necessary to confirm that the described physical adaptations are optimal. In the meantime, rowers can use these standards to determine the best training for their performance goals.

chapter 4

Managing Rowers' Medical Concerns

Richard Backus and Kristine Karlson

In 1988 at the Lucerne Regatta, one-third of the Canadian boats were unable to start because of upper respiratory infections among the rowers. One-third of the competition budget was spent in vain. In Canada, funding depends on performance, so it took Canadian rowing two years to recover from this medical disaster.

One night at the world championships in the Czech Republic, one country's male single sculler developed chest pain. The team didn't have a doctor, so a doctor from another team examined the sculler. The doctor diagnosed him with viral pericarditis, or inflammation of the sac around the heart. The sculler returned home the next morning instead of competing, and it was three months before he could train again. That team now always travels with a doctor. The medical team is an integral part of the sport of rowing, because a crew never knows what might come up.

Preparticipation Examination

Every rower should have a full physical examination at least once a year, more often if the budget allows. Because rowing requires great exertion, every medical condition has to be fully investigated before the competitive season. For example, if an athlete has asthma that requires inhaled medication, this is the time to prove the asthma with formal pulmonary function testing and file the appropriate therapeutic use exemption (TUE) form with FISA. Rowers with such conditions must file this form annually.

Laboratory screening tests should include at least a hematocrit and a ferritin test, useful for assessing the oxygen-carrying system. The hematocrit is the percent of blood that is comprised of red blood cells. A long testing history that shows a rower has a high hematocrit is the best defense against charges of blood doping or erythropoietin (EPO) use. Ferritin testing assesses the amount of iron in the blood. Males may have too much iron and should not take iron supplements. Females often have chronically low ferritin, the correction of which is often difficult, and it is not clear that correction significantly improves performance.

Certain physical screening tests are helpful. An assessment of core strength is necessary, and double straight-leg lowering is one way to assess this. Lying on their back, the rowers should be able to lower their legs all the way down without the pelvis rolling. Dividing the arc into thirds is an accurate enough assessment. This exercise is also a good way to assess hamstring tightness. The shoulders should be stable. The rest of the musculoskeletal examination is straightforward.

Skin assessment is important. Rowers are often exposed to sunlight, so they should have regular mole inspections. The physician should examine hand calluses, saddle sores on the buttocks, slide bites, and hand warts.

Cardiovascular health is also important. In addition to the usual examination, the physician should look for thoracic in-and-out flow problems (blood flow through the chest to the arms and back again).

Finally, the physician should review each rower's immunization records, including travel immunization for future regattas and immunization against water-borne illnesses. Rowers should certainly be immunized against hepatitis A and possibly cholera, typhus, and enteropathic E. coli as well.

These are rowing-specific concerns that the physician should address in addition to a typical medical examination. Coaches should develop a working relationship with a physician who has rowing interests and ideally is trained in sports medicine.

Training Considerations

Medical considerations during the training phase are characterized by complete examinations, and this is the time for more invasive therapies that may require more time away from rowing. The objective is correction of the underlying problem rather than amelioration.

Overuse Injuries

Training consists of work followed by recovery, forcing the body to adapt to higher loads. It is best to progress the training program at a rate similar to the body's ability to adapt. If the training program progresses much more slowly than the ability to adapt, your athlete is undertrained and competitors enter competition fitter than your athletes. If the training program progresses much faster than the body's ability to adapt, overtraining is inevitable, leading to injury and poor performance.

Because rowing is a team sport, the coach deals with several athletes each of whom has a unique rate of adaptation to training loads. It isn't fair to train the athlete who adapts the fastest with the progressions appropriate for the athlete who adapts the slowest. Even rowers in elite training squads have different adaptation rates due to rigging, posture, technique, inherent strength balances, and external stressors. If the elite training squad is similar enough in adaptation ability, it is reasonable to train them with the progressions of the least adaptable member. The art of coaching is to find the ideal rate of development for the entire crew.

The most cynical way to determine that rate is to use progressions that keep the weakest athlete hurting or injured. Even with the best of intentions, this may occur simply by overshooting slightly in the training schedule. This is due to the nature of overuse injuries—they do not occur suddenly. Athletes only recognize an overuse injury when they have pain, and nerves that detect pain have a threshold. If you hit your finger gently with a hammer and gradually hit it harder and harder, from one stroke to the next the sensation changes to pain. The hammering, or inflammation, goes on for some time before you feel pain. Once the nerves transmit pain, they release substances that increase inflammation.

Muscle adaptation to stress involves breakdown followed by a mild inflammatory reaction that stimulates hypertrophy, so ongoing inflammation is part of training. Adaptation to training stress occurs in all tissues, and overuse injury occurs in the tissue that adapts the slowest. The effects of overtraining vary from mild decrease in function such as ongoing cramps in back muscles, to mechanical disruption such as tears in the hamstring and acute tenosynovitis (inflammation of the tendon and tendon sheath), to more serious injuries such as stress fractures, some of which may become full fractures.

When injured, athletes adapt less quickly, and once they've recovered they aren't always able to make up the lost time. Some injured rowers might use the recovery time as a taper and come back stronger, but this doesn't happen often. Figure 4.1

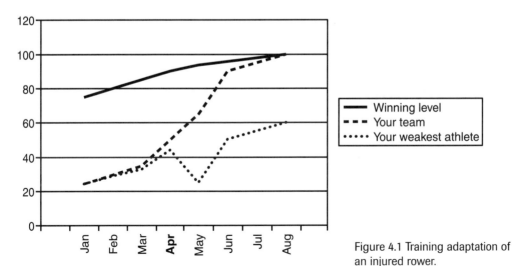

Figure 4.1 Training adaptation of an injured rower.

illustrates an athlete injured in April who cannot catch up with the team even though after the injury he can adapt at the same rate as the rest of the team.

Because overuse injuries can cause so much trouble, the best strategy is prevention. Early in the season or at the end of the previous season, rowers should work on problems with strength (especially core strength), rigging, and technique. Every change requires adaptation, including rigging changes designed to improve performance, so the overall level of training should drop to accommodate adaptation.

When athletes develop an overuse injury, they need to analyze all contributing factors. They should change elements of technique, rigging, or training that seem to have contributed to the injury to give the injured part of the body some rest. These possible changes will be discussed in greater detail with the individual injuries, beginning on page 35.

Medical Team

The coach should assemble a competent medical team. Even with the best medical care, however, there will still be problems. Many of these problems stem from the fact that each member of the medical team has a different treatment philosophy. For example, many overuse injuries aren't due to tissue damage, so they aren't really injuries. Instead, they are poor or altered function of the tissue. Muscle cramping is a classic example and may be the major cause of back pain in rowers. To have a therapist talking about "torn muscles" or "working out scar tissue" in this situation does nothing to help an athlete's confidence; it is making up a catastrophe where there is none.

Different therapists use different terminology to describe an athlete's source of pain. A malrotation L4 on L5 sounds like a different diagnosis than paralumbar muscle spasm, but they are both descriptions of the same problem. The athlete interprets each description as a different diagnosis, and if the descriptions are always changing, she loses confidence in her caregivers. She believes the previous caregiver misdiagnosed her, therefore nobody knows what is wrong, therefore she has a serious injury that nobody knows anything about. This diagnostic confusion is best avoided by establishing a single leader of the therapeutic team who is sensitive to this problem.

All manual therapies are addictive. Any handling of muscle, from simple stretching to massage to manipulation, induces temporary relaxation of the muscle through feedback inhibition—the stretch reflex. The more often manual therapy occurs, the more likely it is to become part of the athlete's self-concept of health. If you are a habitual finger popper, for example, your fingers feel stiff until they are popped. Your popped fingers feel more flexible, even though there is no measurable difference in flexibility. This addiction also occurs when manual therapy becomes part of the precompetition routine. This isn't a problem if you have unlimited access to manual therapy. However, once an athlete is used to the therapy, withdrawal may decrease performance. Your therapeutic team must be sensitive to this double-edged sword, especially since there is no concrete evidence that manual therapy improves performance.

Avoid therapists who promote their own skills or techniques over others. When therapists compete for the bodies of the athletes it may be flattering for the athletes, but it does not help their performance.

Wrist Injuries

DeQuervain's tendinosis   This tendinosis involves the inflammation of the tendons at the base of the thumb.

- Causes. Excessive or repetitive rotation of the hand when feathering. Occurs in either wrist in sculling, in the inside wrist in sweeping.
- Treatment. Immobilization, rest, ice, systemic and topical anti-inflammatories, early physiotherapy with modalities, early assessment by physician; should have significant improvement in one week, then consider steroid injection or surgery in resistant cases.
- Coaching considerations. Assign alternative exercise for lower body to maintain fitness.
- Prevention. Graduated resistance exercises for grip, wrist flexion, and wrist extension; ergometer work on relaxation at finish (going around the corner) and during recovery; early identification by athlete; work on confidence in rough-water rowing.

Intersection syndrome (crossover tendinosis)   This syndrome is the inflammation of the back of the wrist where the tendons that pull the thumb upward cross over the tendons that extend the wrist.

- Causes. Excessive or repetitive rotation of the hand when feathering. Occurs in either wrist in sculling, in the inside wrist in sweeping.
- Treatment. Immobilization, rest, ice, systemic and topical anti-inflammatories, early physiotherapy with modalities, early assessment by physician; should have significant improvement in one week, then consider steroid injection or surgery in resistant cases.
- Coaching considerations. Assign alternative exercise for lower body to maintain fitness.
- Prevention. Graduated resistance exercises for grip, wrist flexion, and wrist extension; ergometer work on relaxation at finish (going around the corner) and during recovery; early identification by athlete; work on confidence in rough-water rowing.

Forearm compartment syndrome   An inelastic fascial compartment encloses the muscles that extend the wrist. In forearm compartment syndrome, the muscles swell from overuse and the fascial compartment is unable to expand, putting pressure on the muscles. Swelling of the entire arm is an emergency, as this may mean that there are blood clots in the vein that drains the arm. In the last 15 years there have been three such emergencies in Canadian rowing.

- Causes. Poor relaxation during recovery, unstable boat, rough water.
- Treatment. Rest, massage, graduated resistance training, surgery in resistant cases. If the entire arm swells after a workout, the athlete should go directly to the emergency room.

- Coaching considerations. Work on relaxation during the recovery phase of the stroke, avoid exercises that destabilize the boat, row in larger boats with better rowers.
- Prevention. Graduated resistance exercises for grip, wrist flexion, and wrist extension; ergometer work on relaxation at finish (going around the corner) and during recovery; early identification by athlete; work on confidence in rough-water rowing.

Elbow Injuries

Lateral epicondylosis (tennis elbow)   This injury is the irritation of the bone on the outside of the elbow where the wrist and finger extensors attach.

- Causes. Overuse, weak grip.
- Treatment. Early referral to physiotherapy, topical anti-inflammatories, steroid injection in resistant cases.
- Coaching considerations. Rarely affects rowing, but if it does, check grip dimension. The larger the handle's diameter, the less likely the athlete is to use an encircling grip and the less stress on the extensor tendon. Consider switching sides in sweep rowing.
- Prevention. Resistance exercises for grip strength, work on rowing technique.

Medial epicondylosis (golfer's elbow)   This injury is the irritation of the bone on the inside of the elbow where the wrist and finger flexors attach.

- Causes. Overuse, weak grip.
- Treatment. Same as for lateral epicondylosis, but more difficult to treat.
- Coaching considerations. Rarely affects rowing, but if it does, check grip dimension. The larger the handle's diameter, the less likely the athlete is to use an encircling grip and the less stress on the flexor tendon. Consider switching sides in sweep rowing.
- Prevention. Resistance exercises for grip strength, work on rowing technique.

Biceps tendinosis   Biceps tendinosis is the irritation of the biceps tendon where it attaches to the radius bone in the forearm.

- Causes. Overuse, weak elbow flexion.
- Treatment. Early referral to physiotherapy, topical anti-inflammatories, steroid injection in resistant cases.
- Coaching considerations. Uncommon, but requires time off and alternative activities. Consider switching sides in sweep rowing.
- Prevention. Resistance exercises for the biceps, including high-speed eccentric exercises.

Triceps tendinosis   This tendinosis is the irritation of the triceps tendon, which covers the entire back of the elbow.

- Causes. Overuse, weak elbow extension.
- Treatment. Same as for biceps tendinosis, but more difficult to treat. Eccentric exercises to the point of pain offer some help for chronic triceps tendinosis.
- Coaching considerations. Uncommon, a problem with pain rather than performance, but very difficult to treat once established.
- Prevention. Resistance exercises for the triceps.

Shoulder Injuries

Rotator cuff dysfunction   This is a spectrum of injuries that ranges from tendinosis and bursitis to partial tearing to a complete tear in one or more of the tendons of the rotator cuff.

- Causes. Excessive movement of the head of the humerus (upper-arm bone). This pinches the rotator cuff or its bursa (the small serous sac between tendon and bone) between the head of the humerus and the overlying bone, the acromion (the outer end of the scapula), or the coracoacromial ligament. The looser the shoulder, the weaker the muscles, the farther forward the scapula is carried, and the more likely it is to occur. Ligament laxity is genetic and is more common in young people. Laxity in the anterior capsule is often due to stretching of the capsule in bench presses, flys, and dips, which allows pinching of the rotator cuff. It also occurs at the catch when the athlete tries to extend too far, stretching the scapula forward and putting power through the shoulder without bracing the scapular and rotator cuff muscles.
- Treatment. Local icing; anti-inflammatories; strengthening of the core muscles, scapular muscles, and rotator cuff through high-speed eccentric exercises such as "beer can emptying." Avoid provocative exercises in the weight room—pull, don't push.
- Coaching considerations. During treatment, rowers shouldn't go for length at the catch. They should apply power at the catch through a strongly supported shoulder rather than pulling through a fully relaxed shoulder. Avoid benching, flys, dips, and shoulder presses.
- Prevention. Work on technique in the weight room and on the water, particularly at the catch. Identify athletes with multidirectional instability of the shoulder (done with a simple clinical test) and have them perform scapular-platform and rotator cuff exercises early and frequently.

Tendinosis of the long head of the biceps   This type of tendinosis is rare in rowing. The long head of the biceps starts in the shoulder joint and travels over the humeral head and through a tight, bony groove, where it can become irritated.

- Causes. Weight training, long-standing ligament laxity (see causes of rotator cuff dysfunction).
- Treatment. Local icing and anti-inflammatories in the acute phase, high-speed eccentric exercises such as "catching the baby" (hold arms out in front with palms up and bounce them).

- Coaching considerations. Don't go for length at the catch during treatment. Apply power at the catch through a strongly supported shoulder rather than pulling through a fully relaxed shoulder. Pull, don't push, in the weight room. Avoid benching, flys, dips, and shoulder presses.
- Prevention. Work on technique in the weight room and on the water, particularly at the catch. Identify athletes with multidirectional instability of the shoulder (done with a simple clinical test) and have them perform scapular-platform and rotator cuff exercises early and frequently.

Rib Injuries

Rib stress fracture   Bone always remodels with exercise, but the breakdown occurs slightly faster than the rebuilding. Without enough recovery time, the bone doesn't have a chance to rebuild, resulting in a stress fracture. In high-volume training programs, this injury occurs in 10 percent of rowers per year regardless of gender, weight, or boat category. The combination of rib pain at night, pain with chest compression, and inability to row is an almost certain sign of a rib fracture.

- Causes. Overuse, high training volume with insufficient recovery, occasionally associated with coughing.
- Treatment. Time—on average, six weeks. The first two weeks (until night pain disappears) do alternative exercises such as biking. The next two weeks work on the ergometer gently. The last two weeks gradually return to the water. In very important situations such as the world championships or Olympics, consider an anaesthetic block of the nerves in the rib. However, there is a small risk of lung puncture with the needle in this procedure.
- Coaching considerations. Work on technique, especially keeping the back straight. Encourage athletes to watch for symptoms so they can report any injury as early as possible.
- Prevention. There have been few studies on prevention; however, bench pulls stress the ribs to lay down new bone. Be careful not to overdo it. Inspiratory muscle training may train athletes to take longer breaths during workouts. Make sure that other sources of cough such as exercise-induced asthma are treated (if treatment requires inhaled steroids or beta-adrenergics, athletes need a therapeutic use exemption [TUE] form).

Intercostal strain   This is a spasm or strain of the rib muscles. Rib stress fractures are often misdiagnosed as intercostal strain, so always check for stress fractures first. Intercostal strain may be a prestress fracture condition in the rib.

- Causes. Overuse.
- Treatment. Physician review to rule out stress fracture, therapy for rib mobilization.
- Coaching considerations. Work on technique, especially keeping the back straight. Encourage athletes to watch for symptoms so they can report any injury as early as possible.

- Prevention. There have been few studies on prevention; however, bench pulls stress the ribs to lay down new bone. Be careful not to overdo it. Inspiratory muscle training may train athletes to take longer breaths during workouts. Make sure that other sources of cough such as exercise-induced asthma are treated (if treatment requires inhaled steroids or beta-adrenergics, athletes need a TUE form).

Costochondritis   This is the inflammation of the joint between the sternum and the rib.

- Causes. Overuse, trauma from the oar striking the costal margin, possibly a viral infection.
- Treatment. Anti-inflammatories, possibly corticosteroid injection (requires a TUE form).
- Coaching considerations. Work on technique, especially keeping the back straight. Encourage athletes to watch for symptoms so they can report any injury as early as possible.
- Prevention. Little is known about preventing this condition. Consider flu shots annually and use strategies to prevent upper respiratory infections. Make sure that other sources of cough such as exercise-induced asthma are treated.

Back Injuries

Spondylolisthesis   In spondylolisthesis, stress fractures that occur in childhood in parts of the spine allow a vertebra to slip forward onto the one below. This injury is present in 2.7 percent of the North American population, and rowing is probably the only sport that can increase the amount of slippage.

- Causes. Usually unknown, in a small percentage of cases due to exercise that combines back extension with impact, as in gymnastics or figure skating.
- Treatment. Improve core stabilization, emphasizing flexion exercises (sit-ups). Monitor progression with X-rays.
- Coaching considerations. Monitor progression, work on core strength, have the athlete do alternative activities with a flexion bias such as cycling or even running.
- Prevention. This injury usually occurs before the athlete is old enough to row. Core stabilization cannot be stressed enough for preventing further slippage. X-ray rowers with back pain.

Intervertebral disk lesion   An intervertebral disk lesion results from protrusion of the disk into the spinal canal, which causes inflammation and local swelling. This can put pressure on the nerve root, causing pain and occasionally some nerve deficiency. As long as nerve deficiency isn't worsening, this is a benign condition that heals on its own. Rowers who experience back pain with bladder or bowel control problems should see a doctor immediately.

- Causes. Usually unknown, occasionally due to heavy loading of the lower spine in flexion, as in deadlifts, or flexion-rotation, as in lifting a boat from the water.

- Treatment. Improve core stabilization, emphasizing extension exercises and extension stretches; on rare occasions, surgery.
- Coaching considerations. Assign alternative activities with an extension bias like swimming or even running until pain lessens; return to water using fastidious technique. This is the athlete's opportunity to focus on technique.
- Prevention. Limit weight-room progressions such as squats, good mornings, and deadlifts. Core stabilization cannot be stressed enough.

Mechanical back pain   This refers to irritation of the small joints of the back or a muscle cramp, which results in muscle spasm. Because of the richness of the nerve supply in this area, the pain is particularly distressing. This is the most common form of back pain.

- Causes. Triggered by a muscle contraction when the muscle is already shortened and the athlete has muscle weakness, fatigue, stress, nutritional deprivation, or overheating. Think of what causes a hamstring cramp and translate this to the back. Because of the number and complexity of the muscles in the back, the specific muscle can never be known. The muscle spasm causes changes in the movement of the back. These changes are a result rather than a cause of the back pain. Mechanical back pain is rarely if ever due to muscle tearing or scarring.
- Treatment. Early therapy to trigger the stretch receptors (stretching and all manual therapies inhibit muscle contraction, thereby relieving spasm), but the results are often temporary and should be repeated often; measures to reduce muscle irritability such as ice and anti-inflammatories. Because a muscle that has gone into spasm remains irritable and prone to spasm again, and because during spasm there is little opportunity to strengthen the muscle, mechanical back pain often becomes a recurring theme for a year or longer.
- Coaching considerations. Because strength is an issue, rowers should return early to rowing, very gradually increase loads, emphasize training recovery, make sure boats are stable, keep the back warm, and do core-stabilization exercises and stretching before and after rows. Avoid on-water strength training like bucket rows or full-pressure rowing at very low stroke rates; it's better to do these in a more controlled environment like the weight room.
- Prevention. Core stabilization cannot be stressed enough and has to be maintained throughout the year every year. Follow each row with stretching, keep the back warm, pay attention to training recovery.

Hip Injuries

Piriformis syndrome   This syndrome is a rare condition involving inflammation of the piriformis muscle, a small muscle in the buttock that rotates the hip. The inflammation places pressure on the sciatic nerve. May result in some sensory changes in the leg.

- Causes. Pressure on the buttocks, occasionally because the steering foot angle is too great.

- Treatment. Seat pad, piriformis stretching program.
- Coaching considerations. Adjust the steering cable to change the foot angle if relevant, make slight rigging changes such as lowering the footstretcher, add seat pad.
- Prevention. Seat pad.

Ischial bursitis   Inflammation of the bursa on the sitting bones of the pelvis.

- Causes. Pressure from the seat.
- Treatment. Seat pad.
- Coaching considerations. Slight rigging changes may help, such as lowering the footstretcher.
- Prevention. Seat pad.

Meralgia paresthetica   Compression of the lateral cutaneous nerve of the thigh, usually at the pelvis, resulting in numbness or a tingling or burning sensation.

- Causes. Weight gain, pressure on the waist.
- Treatment. Lose weight, avoid waist constrictions, steroid shots if painful.
- Coaching considerations. None—pain problem only, should not interfere with rowing.
- Prevention. Avoid waist constriction.

Hip flexor tendinosis   Uncommon irritation of the iliopsoas tendon or the underlying bursa in the front of the hip joint.

- Causes. Overuse, too much layback.
- Treatment. Stretch and build strength in the hip flexor; chronic pain in older rowers may require steroid injections.
- Coaching considerations. Work on technique, reduce layback.
- Prevention. Work on core stabilization and strengthening the hip flexor. Athletes with a snapping hip should avoid activities that make it snap.

Knee Injuries

Anterior knee pain   This category of knee pain includes patellofemoral pain (runner's knee), quadriceps tendinosis (cyclist's knee), and patellar tendinosis (jumper's knee). Although each is quite different, in rowing treatment is the same.

- Causes. Too much running, excessive pronation (flattening of the foot), poor form when doing squats.
- Treatment. Local therapy, eccentric high-speed dips in controlled alignment, strengthening of the quadriceps, strengthening of the hamstrings (should be 70 percent as strong as the quadriceps). Consider orthotic management even in the boat. Patellar tendinosis responds to low-speed eccentric exercises with the foot flexed 30 degrees (Hakan Alfredson protocol).

- Coaching considerations. Reduce running or change to stop–start running; consider alternatives such as in-line skating, skipping, or swimming; assure adequate footwear; consider lowering the footstretcher (reducing knee flexion).
- Prevention. Strengthen quadriceps and hamstrings, watch for alignment problems, recommend suitable shoes, consider orthotic management, gradually increase running (no long downhills).

Posterior knee pain   This category of knee pain includes hamstring tendinosis and intersection tendinosis between the hamstring tendon and the head of the gastrocnemius. There are many more knee pathologies, but they aren't usually seen in rowers.

- Causes. Bunching of the fleece tights behind the knee. Also, some boats have no deck under the thigh or calf, so the hamstrings may activate late to change the body's direction at the finish (this is speculation, but worth considering).
- Treatment. Local therapy, strengthening of the hamstring muscles. Posterior knee pain is most common in lightweight males. When fleece tights bunch up, look for impingement of the distal hamstring tendons. Inspection of many rowers' popliteal (back of knee) areas reveals a change in skin color over the medial hamstring tendons, consistent with increased skin pressure.
- Coaching considerations. Cut a hole in the tights behind the knee, inspect the length of the deck under the legs of the rower, strengthen quadriceps and hamstrings.
- Prevention. Check clothing and boat decks.

General Hygiene and Illness Prevention

Rowing involves people spending a considerable amount of time together, which significantly increases the risk for infectious diseases. In temperate climates the winter months in particular are bad because workouts are indoors and athletes have to share limited workout space.

Viral upper respiratory infections (URIs) are common in the general population and probably are no more or less common in athletes. Some research suggests that athletes who exercise very strenuously put their immune system at risk, increasing their susceptibility to infectious diseases. In general, however, athletes tend to be healthier than the general population.

Most URIs are spread by hand-to-mouth contact and inhaled droplets. Infection-control principles suggest that washing the hands frequently is the best way to prevent transmission. During travel, using a waterless sanitizer every two hours dramatically reduces infections. Cleaning handles and weight equipment as much as possible, especially during the peak cold season, also helps.

Mononucleosis, also known as mono, is a common viral infection in young people. It is spread by close direct contact. It results in significant fatigue for several weeks and occasionally more severe illness. Athletes should be cautious about close contact with persons with mononucleosis.

Vaccines can also prevent some illnesses. Athletes should stay up-to-date with routine vaccines such as tetanus. The flu vaccine may be a good idea for teams and individuals who cannot afford time off. Vaccination for hepatitis A may be necessary for travel to countries with a high prevalence of this disease. Rowers should also consider immunization against meningitis, another devastating disease. There is now a vaccine for enteropathic E. coli, which causes travelers' diarrhea. The vaccine is oral, lasts for three months, and should be required for all athletes traveling abroad.

Oar and ergometer handles are often shared, and athletes may break blisters during rowing. Disinfect handles regularly to avoid the spread of wart viruses and blood-borne diseases such as HIV and hepatitis B (washing the oar with a fresh mixture of one part bleach to nine parts water, followed by a soap and water wash, is an effective disinfectant).

Never share water bottles. This alone can significantly cut disease transmission.

At some training sites, the docks are covered with goose excrement. Remember that animals can transmit viruses—ever heard of avian flu or SARS?

Environmental Exposure

Rowing is an outdoor sport, and protection against environmental exposure is an important part of assuring the health and safety of rowers and coaches. Heat, cold, water quality, sun exposure, and lightning are all important exposure threats.

A highly aerobic sport such as rowing exposes athletes to the risk of heat-related illness when practices and races are held in hot weather. Whenever possible, avoid scheduling training sessions during the hottest part of the day. Athletes should stay hydrated, as dehydration worsens the effects of heat-related illness. Heat exhaustion is relatively benign, characterized by clammy skin, nausea, and headache. Athletes suffering from heat exhaustion need to get out of the heat, rehydrate, and cool down with ice packs, water mist, or cold baths. Heat stroke is much more dangerous than heat exhaustion: It carries significant risk of death. It is characterized by very high body temperatures and decreased mental function. Athletes suffering possible heat stroke need to get to a hospital quickly.

Exposure to cold is also potentially dangerous. The body loses heat faster when wet. Rowers get wet from the splash that occurs when the oars enter the water, which

Keeping rowers healthy and knowledgeable about possible injuries is essential in training and racing.

© Joel W. Rogers

increases the risk of hypothermia. Athletes should make every attempt to stay as dry as possible. Dressing in noncotton layers and wearing a hat help prevent hypothermia, as does changing out of wet clothing as soon as possible after the training session or race.

Splash from oars can also expose rowers to infectious diseases when they row in water of poor quality. Rowers who train or race on questionable bodies of water might consider immunization against hepatitis A, a virus associated with poor sanitation. Showering after rowing is important, as is proper care of open wounds such as blisters. Rowers should never drink from the water where they row, since even water that looks clean can be contaminated.

Rowers and coaches face more intense sunlight because they train on water. The water reflects the sun's rays, increasing exposure to harmful solar radiation. Again, avoid training during the hottest part of the day as much as possible. Sunscreen, hats, and sunglasses can help. Rowers and coaches should watch their skin carefully for development of spots that could be skin cancer.

Participants in any boating sport must be vigilant about stormy weather. Skipping a practice or training inside is a small price to pay for avoiding potentially life-threatening storms. Stormy weather can involve lightning strikes and dangerously high water that could swamp small boats. When in doubt, it is best to err on the side of caution and cancel or postpone events.

Women's Health

Not long ago, women raced only 1000 meters while men raced 2000 meters. This was probably the result of concerns about women being athletes. An increase in the number of women athletes and studies on women and sports have disproved these concerns. Still, the female athlete does face some gender-specific concerns.

The female athlete triad was first formally described in the early 1990s. It consists of three interrelated problems: eating disorders, amenorrhea (loss of menstrual periods), and osteoporosis. The concern is that female athletes may develop unusually low bone density, leading to significant fractures later in life.

The two main eating disorders are anorexia nervosa (excessive calorie restriction and excessive exercising) and bulimia nervosa (bingeing and purging by exercise, laxatives, and vomiting). Less extreme eating behaviors that cannot be completely diagnosed as either anorexia or bulimia are known as disordered eating. The person most at risk for disordered eating is the driven and accomplished young woman who has a desire to achieve and please others such as parents and coaches. Disordered eating can also be due to psychological concerns such as poor self-esteem, which seems paradoxical given the accomplishments of many of these individuals.

Amenorrhea, or loss of menstrual periods, is the second leg of the triad. When menstrual periods stop for several months, athletes should be concerned. Because the most common reason for missing periods is pregnancy, this should be ruled out with a pregnancy test. Beyond pregnancy, amenorrhea indicates decreased estrogen, which can lead to decreased bone density.

Many female athletes see missing menstrual periods as an indicator that they are training hard enough. However, recent evidence suggests that it is not training volume but rather calorie deficit that leads to amenorrhea. Athletes who lose their periods during intense training are probably suffering from a calorie deficit. Cutting back on training volume may not always be a viable option, but increasing calorie intake is. When an athlete who is trying to lose weight, such as a lightweight, experiences amenorrhea, she should revisit weight goals and training options. There is still no real evidence, however, that athletes who miss a few menstrual periods during the most intense part of the season are putting themselves at risk.

Some women who are unwilling to change training volume or diet to reverse amenorrhea turn to birth control pills. Research has shown no significant effects of oral contraceptives on athletic performance. Birth control pills come in many different formulations and the athlete and her clinician can deal with any problematic side effects by changing to a different pill.

Osteoporosis is the third part of the female athlete triad. People who have osteoporosis, or low bone density, may not be aware of it until it is too late. Bone fractures from osteoporosis often occur late in life. When a young athlete experiences recurrent stress fractures or a fracture resulting from minimal trauma, she may be at risk for future problems and should consider having her bone density measured. Prevention of osteoporosis involves addressing amenorrhea, if present, and getting enough calcium. Female athletes should consume 1200 to 1500 milligrams of calcium daily.

Precompetition Considerations

Right before the competitive season begins, the medical emphasis shifts from helping the athlete cope with the stress of training and exhaustive diagnosis and treatment to keeping the athlete as healthy as possible and controlling injuries. This is the time of the training taper, and most of the medical team's work should be done; as Dr. Bill Webb of Australia says, "The only good doctor is an idle doctor." However, rowers do face a few specific medical concerns during this time.

Making Weight

Lightweight rowing, like any sport with weight classes, imposes a weight limit on athletes. For many lightweights this means losing weight for competitions. Weight loss can be fine for the right individuals when done in a safe fashion. Making weight is not right for everyone, however.

In the United States, the national governing body of collegiate sports recently imposed a system to limit weight loss for collegiate wrestlers. This was in response to the 1997 deaths of three wrestlers who were trying to lose large amounts of weight in short periods of time. In the new system, wrestlers are weighed and have their body fat measured preseason, and their body fat at their competitive weight is projected. Athletes are certified to wrestle only if they have more than 6 to 8 percent body fat (the corresponding body-fat percentage for women is 12 to 15 percent), so this determines their weight class early in the season. Weigh-ins are held no earlier than two hours before the wrestler's first match (before, weigh-ins were held the previous day), so the wrestler cannot undertake extreme weight change immediately prior to the match. This system has resulted in safer weight loss among wrestlers.

Similarly, only those rowers who will have a body fat level of at least 6 percent (male) or 12 percent (female) at weight should attempt to row lightweight. Measurement of hydrated body fat may help athletes decide if they should try to make weight. Body fat should be measured by experienced personnel using skinfold calipers and an appropriate mathematical formula. Scales that measure body fat are available, but they are fairly inaccurate. The most precise test, underwater weighing, is impractical in anything other than a research setting.

Once an athlete and coach have determined that body fat at weight won't be too low, they need to plan for the necessary weight loss. Weight loss should be gradual, about 0.5 kilograms per week. Losing weight gets harder as more is lost, so the athlete and coach need to allow for this. In general, lightweights should plan to dehydrate no more than 2 percent before weigh-in and rehydrate immediately after. Weight loss by dehydration of greater than 2 percent will probably affect performance regardless of attempts to rehydrate.

Losing weight usually means calorie restriction. Fasting, like dehydration, affects performance and is not recommended. Athletes should cut calories from all three calorie types—carbohydrates, fat, and protein. Eliminating all fat is difficult, and because fat provides a sense of fullness, athletes who eliminate fat often end up eating more calories because they are hungry. Athletes should also avoid eliminating specific foods because this can lead to cravings. Instead they should cut back on serving sizes and eat a balanced diet.

Diet pills are potentially dangerous, and many contain stimulants banned by the WADA (World Anti-Doping Agency), which tests rowers for illegal substances. Other drastic weight-loss measures such as vomiting and laxatives result in dehydration and impaired performance. Fad diets are also usually bad ideas for athletes. Low-carbohydrate diets, for example, do not provide enough energy for working muscles.

Severe calorie restriction can lead to general unhappiness and may lead susceptible individuals to eating disorders. Coaches and rowers should be aware of warning signs such as excessive weight loss, maintaining a very low weight off-season, and secretive eating.

Staying Hydrated

Water is the most important nutrient. Dehydration affects performance more than any other nutritional deficiency. Athletes, especially those in hot climates, need to stay ahead of dehydration, drinking the right amount of fluids even if they don't feel thirsty. Making up a water deficit is difficult to do during a workout once performance has been affected.

The consequences of dehydration range from decreased performance to death from heat stroke. Dehydration of 2 percent or less usually does not affect performance. Dehydration of 3 to 4 percent can diminish athletic performance. More significant dehydration is dangerous and can lead to death from heat stroke or multiple organ failure.

Athletes can regulate their hydration in two easy ways. Weighing themselves before and after training gives a good idea of fluid deficit in kilograms. They should replenish this deficit as quickly as possible. In some sports, athletes are not allowed to train on the following day if they have not recovered their water weight. The other measure of hydration is urine color and urination frequency. Some vitamins can affect urine color, but in general urine should be a pale yellow. Urination should occur at least once every four hours.

Recovering from dehydration using plain water can sometimes be a problem. Electrolytes (mostly sodium) are lost in sweat and should be replaced. In addition, replacing with water alone may increase urination frequency but still not help the body recover from dehydration, since the body needs salt to retain the water. Sports drinks, which have added salt and electrolytes, may be an option. Alternatively, drinking plain water and eating a small amount of salty food is just as efficient and is cheaper.

Research shows that the body absorbs water more easily in relatively large volumes. Rehydration is better accomplished by drinking a large amount at once rather than sipping small amounts over a longer period of time. Athletes may have difficulty tolerating large volumes of fluid during training and racing, so they should practice drinking their replacement volume all at once.

On the other hand, some athletes enter competition with too much water in the body. This is often due to creatine supplementation and carbohydrate loading. Carbohydrate or glycogen loading is not a common practice in rowing, but creatine usage is, particularly among heavyweight men. Creatine is hydrated to dissolve in the muscle, where it is surrounded by water molecules, making the muscle heavier and more swollen than usual. This feeling is much like being pumped after a good workout, and it is probably the reason that rowers are often reluctant to discontinue its use. However, the extra water contributes weight without power. A good way to shave up to eight kilograms from the weight of your eight is to have the rowers stop taking creatine supplements one week before competition. They will strenuously object, stating that their muscles feel flabby. Creatine in the muscle doesn't return to the original level for four weeks after discontinuing, so there is no metabolic reason not to stop.

Avoiding Travel-Related Illnesses

Much has been written about jet lag. It affects all rowers, and there's no mystery about it. Rowers should help the body adapt to the new time zone as soon as possible and as long as possible before competition. A rule of thumb is one day of adaptation for every hour of time difference. It helps if the athletes already have a strict routine for waking and going outside, eating, and exercising at the same time every day. They should follow the same routine in the new time zone on the day of arrival, avoiding snacking or sleeping outside of the routine. Some travelers advocate the use of melatonin, but it is not clear that this helps, and it exposes athletes to unregulated drugs.

Upper respiratory tract and gastrointestinal infections are also possibilities during travel. Air travel dries the respiratory tract and exposes rowers to the respiratory infections carried by other travelers. These illnesses are transmitted from hand to mouth, so if rowers do not touch their faces with their hands, they greatly reduce their chance of getting sick. People usually touch their faces every three minutes on average, so rowers may want to wear surgical masks or a hydrating breathing mask designed specifically for air travel.

Rowers should also wash their hands frequently to reduce disease transmission. American military recruits cut their rate of colds in half simply by washing their hands with soap and water five times a day according to a schedule. An alternative is to use a waterless sanitizer, which appears to be just as effective in reducing hand bacterial counts but has not been tested for cold prevention. Rowers must take special care after using the washroom (where every sneeze collects) or if they are unfortunate enough to be close to a sick passenger. In addition, maintaining hydration during the flight is very important, and all fluids and foods must be clean. If a rower gets sick in spite of these precautions, he should be isolated from the other rowers. An extra hotel room is useful as an isolation ward, and rowers must be prepared to shift rooms with all their gear to meet this requirement.

Competition Considerations

The medical team must take care of administrative and legal concerns as well as the athlete during the competition phase.

- **Drug Notification.** All FISA regattas have doping control. Part of this process is the preregistration of all restricted drugs on a FISA therapeutic use exemption (TUE) form, usually well before the regatta. It is worthwhile to have every athlete fill out a form, listing supplements, herbs, and over-the-counter remedies as well as all medications. The individual from the medical team who will accompany the athlete to doping control should keep this form. If the team is not traveling with medical personnel, it is usually the team manager who gets this duty. Make sure that any TUE forms covering restricted drugs are presented to the control commission before that athlete's race.

- **Doping Control.** Someone who is familiar with the doping control process should accompany the athlete. This is the only opportunity to register any objections and the only opportunity to question the doping control officials about the process. This person is often the team doctor, but the team manager should also be familiar with the process, as she may well be the designated person. The doping control process along with the list of restricted and banned drugs are available on the FISA, IOC (International Olympic Committee), WADA, and CCES (Canadian Centre for Ethics in Sport) Web sites. Remember that supplements are the cause of most inadvertent doping infractions.

- **Substitutions.** If one of the rowers is ill, FISA rules allow a substitute for that race. You must contact the medical commission at the regatta; they will assign a FISA physician to examine the athlete. If the FISA physician agrees, the coach can substitute another rower for the race or races. Details are available at the regatta site.

Postcompetition Considerations

Rowers enjoy the party at the end of each regatta. Although the coach is not responsible for every aspect of the athlete's life, it is reasonable to suggest prudence about alcohol, particularly in relation to violence or driving. An accessible supply of condoms is also recommended.

In multisport events such as the Olympics, rowing finishes in the first week and rowers are on holiday when the rest of the village is still in competition. This is the time for rowers to be considerate of competition requirements of other sports.

The medical team's responsibility for the athlete does not end at the finish line. The postcompetition phase is an opportunity to reevaluate an athlete's physical status, and it is a time for the athlete to work on problems without the stress of training or competition. All injured athletes should leave the competition phase with a corrective training program to follow during their time off. If the medical team and athletes have done their job, the athletes will return next season healthier than ever.

chapter 5

Developing an Aerobic Base

Marty Aitken

Developing an aerobic base is vital for high performance in modern rowing. It was once believed that the 2000-meter race involved 70 percent aerobic activity and 30 percent anaerobic activity. Today we know it to be 80 percent or more aerobic and 20 percent or less anaerobic. Most programs reflect these percentages over the year's training, which means that building the aerobic base has become increasingly important.

During the 1970s we concentrated on Fartlek training, which included 500- and 1000-meter pieces and very little steady-state work. I remember a training session in Australia where the famous New Zealand coach Rusty Robinson had the crew doing 10 × 1000 meters with one minute of rest between each set. None of the athletes were pulling more than 70 percent by the end of the session, so the training was probably more in the midrange speed rather than what he set out to achieve. In the 1980s we did less high-speed work as 20- to 30-minute pieces became more popular.

The East Germans (GDR) were a rowing powerhouse during the 1970s and 1980s, and we all wanted to know the secret of their success. At the 1978 world championships we couldn't figure out what the GDR men's quad was doing. During practice it seemed that they paddled down the lake at Karipiro, went around the corner out of sight of the boathouse, then sat around for an hour before coming back again. It seems the reason for this unorthodox training was that they had done enough steady-state training by that point. It wasn't until the collapse of the GDR in 1989 that we learned that the East Germans were doing an enormous volume of steady-state training at a stroke rate of 18 strokes per minute. For most of us this was the beginning of the realization that there was another way to train—by performing a large amount of steady-state training to build the aerobic base—and today it is common practice.

Most aerobic training is divided into two intensity levels. The bulk of the training occurs at the lower intensity. Training at the higher intensity is called utilization training 1 (UT_1), and training at the lower intensity is called utilization training 2 (UT_2). There is still a debate over the ideal lactate levels for aerobic training because physiologists have conducted very little on-water testing to determine the best levels. Some suggest that UT_2 lactate levels range from 1.0 to 2.0 millimoles of lactate per liter of blood and UT_1 lactate levels range between 2.0 and 4.0 (Jensen, Nilsen, and Smith 1990). For the past eight years I have used an Eppendorf lactate analyzer to assess training levels, and I have found that that the transition between the two intensities occurs at about 1.5 millimoles per liter. I have used 1.5 as the upper limit for UT_2 training for some time now. However, because everyone is different, 1.5 may be too high for some rowers and too low for others. If you have the time and resources, it is best to assess each athlete individually.

Because our athletes do so much aerobic training, we carefully specify how hard we want them to train. Fortunately, rowing takes place on a level surface, making it easier to maintain the same heart rate for a long period of time. Most outdoor aerobic sports, such as cycling, cross-country skiing, and running, take place on courses that often have hills and other variations, making it difficult to maintain a specific heart rate. Although in rowing we have headwinds and tailwinds to contend with and we have to turn the boat around, we can control training intensity by prescribing a heart rate and maintaining it with little variation for a long period of time. This is a significant advantage.

Photo by Marty Aitken

Swiss 2000 Olympic quad scull.

Before training, most athletes have a lactate concentration of about 1.6 millimoles per liter. Once they start aerobic work, the concentration decreases to below 1.0, and as they reach steady-state work it levels off to above 1.0. I ask the athletes to work at an intensity that requires a concentration of 1.0 to 1.5 millimoles per liter for UT_2 training (1.5 to 2.0 for UT_1). These ranges are the result of experience more than scientific experimentation. The athletes can recognize the transition between the two intensities, so I have tested the ranges by asking athletes to train at what they consider to be their ideal training heart rate, taking several lactate samples over the course of a typical 90-minute aerobic session. I have found that almost all the athletes work at an intensity of 0.8 to 1.6 millimoles per liter of lactate.

Determining Training Effectiveness

You need to assess the lactate range and associated heart rate for each athlete for two reasons: to determine the appropriate training intensity level for each individual, and to evaluate whether the training program is working.

The most common way to measure an athlete's adaptation to training is maximum oxygen uptake, or $\dot{V}O_2$max. This test is done in the laboratory and consists of a step test with lactate samples and gas analysis, or a combination of the step test and an all-out $\dot{V}O_2$max test.

The best way to determine the appropriate intensity level is to use a portable VO_2-analyzer in the boat and measure lactate levels as you increase the load. This simulates the training environment better than any other method, but it is often neither possible nor practical. The results achieved on the ergometer are not the same as in the boat, so testing on the ergometer is less than ideal; however, I have found the most practical test is the simple step test on the ergometer.

The test consists of four to six submaximal steps, or workloads, that increase lactate levels from 0.8 up to 6.0 or 7.0 millimoles per liter. Since each individual achieves a steady lactate concentration at different times, the longer the step, the more accurate the test. To accurately assess the effect of training you must use the same test in a consistent manner.

The test consists of five steps that last 4 minutes, with 45 seconds of rest between steps. Take a lactate sample between each step. Because the athletes need to grip the handle, it is more practical and easier on the athletes to take blood from the ear. Figure 5.1 shows one athlete's results over a season.

The load increases with each step, as does the amount of lactate the athlete produces. The exception is at the lowest levels, where the lactate level remains the same until the athlete reaches 1.0 millimoles per liter, at which point lactate begins to increase. Conduct this test once every two months during a season. If the training is effective, the graph will shift to the right because the athlete is producing less lactate for a given work output, which is the goal of aerobic training. If the graph is not shifting, you should look at the training loads and intensity. I have found that large volumes of UT_2 training (between 1.0 and 1.5 millimoles per liter) move the graph farther to the right than more intense forms of training.

The pattern should be similar to that in figure 5.2, which shows an athlete's best test for each year. The best result each year should be farther right than that of the previous year. This test is invaluable for determining if the aerobic training is having the desired effect.

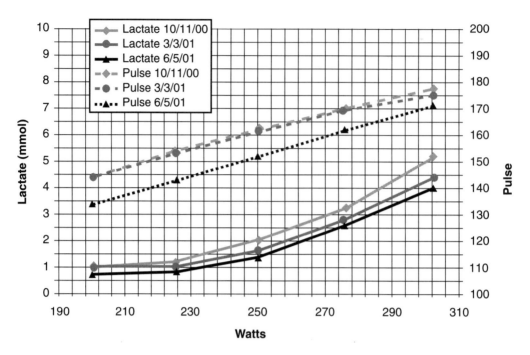

FIGURE 5.1   Step test on the Concept2 ergometer.

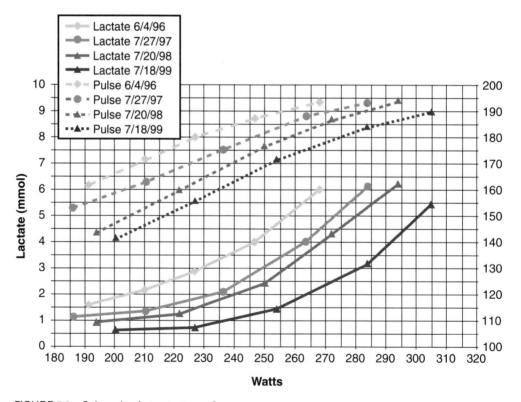

FIGURE 5.2   Submaximal step test over four years.

Determining Heart Rate

Some physiologists and coaches use the ergometer step test described in the last section to determine a heart rate for all aerobic training. However, I have found that this is not always accurate. For 60 percent of athletes it is a good indicator, but for the other 40 percent it is incorrect. I use the step test only to determine the athletes' aerobic fitness. To determine training heart rate based on lactate production, I conduct a test in the boat. I developed this test through trial and error over two years.

For the first test I ask the athletes to train at a heart rate that is 10 beats below the rate indicated by the step test. After 30 minutes I take a lactate sample. They train for 10 more minutes at 5 beats below that heart rate and I take another sample. Next I ask the athletes to row for another 10 minutes at the pulse rate indicated by the step test, and then I take another sample. In the last stage the athletes train for 10 minutes at 5 beats above the previous heart rate and I take a final sample. After the test I graph the results, which gives me a good idea of how much lactate the athletes produce at a given heart rate. Figure 5.3 is a sample graph of this test.

I test the athletes again a few days later, asking them to train at the heart rate determined by the first test. I take a lactate sample every 20 minutes. Table 5.1 shows typical results from the second test.

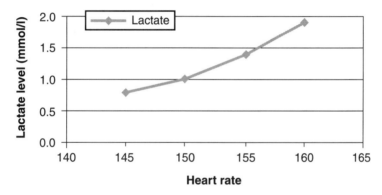

FIGURE 5.3   On-water lactate test.

The first sample, 1.72, is a little above my target range of 1.5 millimoles per liter, and the rest fall below 1.5. This is typical for most athletes, indicating that lactate concentration takes a short time to lessen after the athletes reach steady-state work and slightly increases while they are warming up. I have taken many samples using this method and these results are common.

TABLE 5.1   Lactate Concentrations During Steady-State Training

Total training time (minutes)	25:00	46:00	63:00	85:00
Heart rate (beats per minute)	156	155	154	156
Lactate (millimoles per liter)	1.72	1.46	1.48	1.47

I have also found it necessary to reassess athletes at regular intervals, as the body adapts fairly quickly to increases in workload. Over time the lactate level at a given heart rate decreases and you must set a new training heart rate. For example, you may find an athlete who has been training at a heart rate of 145 beats per minute who only produces 0.8 millimoles of lactate per liter of blood. After testing the rower on the water you find the training heart rate should be 150 beats per minute if he is to reach 1.5 millimoles per liter. To determine the new heart rate, you only need to repeat the second on-water test.

You need to reassess the athletes once every 10 weeks and in most cases increase the heart rate slightly. Using this method I've seen excellent improvements in the step test and therefore the aerobic base. Figure 5.4 is an example of periodic adjustment of the heart rate to achieve the same lactate levels.

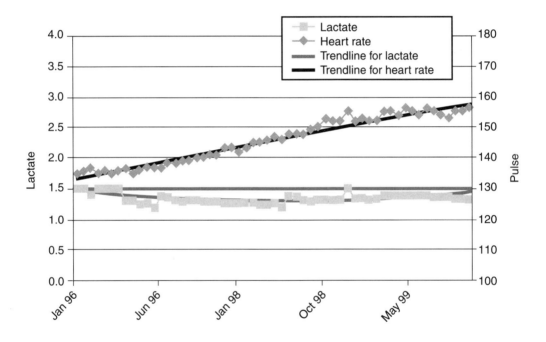

FIGURE 5.4   Steady-state heart rate and lactate levels over four years.

Cross-Training

Cross-training is becoming increasingly popular and can include many different sports. Cross-training has worked well for me as a training substitute for rowing. I use cross-training for several reasons, the most obvious of which is that I don't want my athletes to feel like the 1978 GDR quad. Giving the athletes a break from the boat relieves the tedium of hours and hours of steady-state rowing. It also enables me to increase aerobic training volume without increasing the risk of overuse injuries. I use two main forms of cross-training—cycling and cross-country skiing.

Cycling

Cycling is by far the easiest type of cross-training, and it requires only a bike and helmet. I include cycling in weekly training and in cross-training camps.

I like cycling for several reasons. First, it duplicates the leg-drive action that occurs in the boat. Second, rowers can only row for about two hours at a time in the boat whereas on the bike it is easy to ride for extended periods of time, from two to four or five hours. Cycling allows rowers to further develop the aerobic base because it enables them to do large volumes of steady-state work without increasing the risk of overuse injuries that can occur from sessions in the boat lasting more than two hours at a time.

Xeno Müller, the 1996 men's single Olympic champion, supplements his rowing program with cycling. He is fortunate enough to live in southern California where the weather is ideal for bike riding all year round, so in the winter he does three or four sessions a week on the bike. These training sessions last from two and a half to three hours and make up about a third of his weekly training. As the racing season approaches he needs to do mostly rowing-specific work, so he reduces the number of cycling sessions and replaces them with sessions in the boat that last up to two hours.

In cross-training camps I regularly use cycling in the afternoon session. I have the rowers spend two and half to three and a half hours on the bike. The athletes look forward to cross-training, and such sessions are easy to organize with the appropriate safety precautions. Table 5.2 is a sample cross-training program.

Weather is important—I would not have a group cycle in the rain or cold. Riding in a group in the rain is potentially dangerous, and when it is cold outside athletes run the risk of illness due to the windchill factor. One of the objectives of cross-training is to add enjoyable variety to the training program, and it is much more pleasant to cycle in warm, dry conditions.

My groups train on stationary bikes to break up the monotony of ergometer sessions. It is better for the athletes to switch from the ergometer to the bike and back again during a two-hour indoor session than to do the whole two hours on the ergometer. Both activities by themselves can be extremely boring when done for long periods of time, but together they can spice up an otherwise uninteresting training session. Indoor cycling is also a good activity for injured athletes who need to maintain their aerobic base.

For any given heart rate, the athlete's lactate concentration from work on the bike is higher than in the boat. This is because rowing is a full-body activity and uses many muscles, while cycling is mainly a leg activity. For example, when Xeno Müller trains at a heart rate of 150 beats per minute in the boat he produces around 1.3 millimoles per liter. However, to reach the same lactate concentration on the bike he has to train at a heart rate of 135 beats per minute. You should test each athlete as described on page 53 in both activities. Each individual is different, but I have found the average difference in heart rate to be around 15 beats per minute, as in Müller's case. This rule applies to many activities that do not involve the whole body, such as kayaking.

Cross-Country Skiing

Cross-country skiing is an excellent aerobic alternative in the winter months. I began using cross-country skiing with the Swiss national team in the early 1990s. Cross-

TABLE 5.2   Training Program: Seville Camp Cycling and Rowing

Day	Session	Training type	Training duration	Training intensity	Stroke rate (strokes per minute)	Rest
Monday	1	Row	100 min steady-state	UT$_2$	18	
	2	Core stability				
	3	Bike	120 min			
Tuesday	1	Row	100 min steady-state	UT$_2$	18	
	2	Bike	120 min			
	3	Heavy weights				
Wednesday	1	Row	100 min steady-state Including 2 × 8' SR22/4' SR24/2' SR26/2' SR28	UT$_2$	18	
	2	Endurance weights	80 min			
	3		OFF			
Thursday	1	Row	100 min steady-state	UT$_2$	18	
	2	Core stability				
	3	Bike	180 min			
Friday	1	Row	100 min steady-state	UT$_2$	18	
	2	Heavy weights				
	3	Bike	120 min			
Saturday	1	Row	3 × 19-min pyramids (4+3+2+1+2+3+4 min)	UT$_1$ and AT	20-26-20	5 min
	2	Core stability				
	3	Bike	180 min			
Sunday	1	Row	100 min steady-state	UT$_2$	18	
	2	Core stability				
	3	Bike	180 min			

country skiing produces heart rate and lactate values similar to rowing. It is also a whole-body aerobic activity, and in most cases I have been able to set the same heart rate for training that I have used in the boat.

The limiting factor for cross-country skiing is snow. Obviously, it is far easier to find snow in central Europe, Scandinavia, and Canada than in warmer countries.

Day	Session	Training type	Training duration	Training intensity	Stroke rate (strokes per minute)	Rest
Monday	1	Row	100 min steady-state	UT$_2$	18	
	2	Heavy weights				
	3	Bike	120 min			
Tuesday	1	Row	1 × 2000 m (1000+500+500) 1 × 2000 m (1000+500+500) 1 × 2000 m (1000+500+500)	AT	24-26-28 26-28-30 26-28-30	2000 m 2000 m
	2	Endurance weights	80 min			
	3		OFF			
Wednesday	1	Row	100 min steady-state	UT$_2$	18	
	2	Core stability				
	3	Bike	180 min			
Thursday	1	Row	100 min steady-state	UT$_2$	18	
	2	Heavy weights				
	3	Bike	120 min			
Friday	1	Row	1 × 2000 m (1000+500+500) 1 × 2000 m (1000+500+500) 1 × 2000 m (1000+500+500)	AT	24-26-28 26-28-30 26-28-30	2000 m 2000 m
	2	Core stability				
	3	Bike	180 min			

Each January the Swiss team participated in a two- to three-week skiing camp. We took one or two ergometers with us, but most athletes preferred to stay on the skis. On a typical day the Swiss team did two to three hours of skiing in the morning and two hours in the afternoon. This huge volume of steady-state work was a key part of the training program each winter and helped contribute to the team's success at the Olympic Games. See table 5.3 for a sample program.

Since moving to Britain, I have begun to take the British team to Switzerland each year for a two-week rowing and skiing camp. Although none of them had ever skied before, it has worked well. Rather than the all-skiing camp I used with the Swiss, we tried another approach, rowing in the morning and skiing in the afternoon. The combination of activities has yielded excellent results on the step test.

We always have a cross-country ski coach at these camps, as technique is important for getting the best training effect. Although both skiing techniques, classic and skating, have the same aerobic benefit, skating is faster. Skating also doesn't require track preparation, allowing you to skate on roads or tracks covered with snow. The British athletes were able to learn the skating technique in a short time, and most now choose to skate.

Since technique for cross-country skiing needs to be learned properly, you should organize technique sessions with a qualified ski coach. These sessions can include exercises and drills to accomplish excellent aerobic training at the same time. During a training camp, I schedule the technique session in the morning and a regular training session in the afternoon. It took the British athletes only two training camps to become proficient enough to reap the full benefits from skiing.

Many German and Swiss rowing clubs hold ski camps during the winter break. These training camps are often held in Switzerland, home to some of the best tracks in the world.

As with cycling, cross-country skiing takes place on a changing surface, so bear this in mind when setting training heart rates. The constantly changing terrain means that athletes need to work toward an average heart rate during the session as the heart rate climbs above steady-state going uphill and falls far below going downhill. This natural interval training is an important component of the overall training program, providing a change from steady-state training in the boat.

TABLE 5.3 Training Program: Sarnen Rowing and Cross-Country Ski Camp

Day	Session	Training type	Training duration	Training category	Stroke rate	Rest
Monday	1	Row	100 min steady-state	UT_2	18	
	2	Row	90 min steady-state	UT_2	18	
Tuesday	1	Ski	90 min steady-state (day trip)	UT_2		
	2	Ski	140 min steady-state	UT_2		
Wednesday	1	Row	100 min steady-state	UT_2	18	
	2	Endurance weights	60 min			
Thursday	1	Row	100 min steady-state	UT_2	18	
	2	Row	100 min steady-state	UT_2	18	
Friday	1	Ski	90 min steady-state (day trip)	UT_2		
	2	Ski	140 min steady-state	UT_2		
Saturday	1	Row	100 min steady-state	UT_2	18	
	2	Endurance weights	60 min			
	3		OFF			

Day	Session	Training type	Training duration	Training category	Stroke rate	Rest
Sunday	1	Ski	90 min steady-state (day trip)	UT_2		
	2	Ski	140 min steady-state	UT_2		
Monday	1	Row	3 × 19 min pyramids (4+3+2+1+2+3+4 min)	UT_1 and AT	20-26-20	5 min
	2	Ski	140 min steady-state	UT_2		
Tuesday	1	Ski	90 min steady-state (day trip)	UT_2		
	2	Ski	140 min steady-state	UT_2		
Wednesday	1	Row	100 min steady-state	UT_2	18	
	2	Endurance weights	70 min			
Thursday	1	Row	100 min steady-state	UT_2	18	
	2	Ski	140 min steady-state	UT_2		
Friday	1	Ergometer, weights	45 min ergometer and 45 min weights			
Saturday	1	Ski	90 min steady-state (day trip)	UT_2		
	2	Ski	140 min steady-state	UT_2		
Sunday	1	Row	100 min steady-state	UT_2	18	

Running

I do not often use running as a cross-training method. I use cross-training to increase the volume of aerobic work, and it is extremely difficult to row and then run for two hours in a single day. An average running session is about an hour. More than this can easily lead to overuse injuries of the joints, particularly the hip, knee, and ankle. I have occasionally found it useful for larger athletes to get used to an activity that doesn't support their weight, and as most heavyweights are not good runners, small doses of running can be beneficial. Xeno Müller uses a treadmill and varies the incline angle. He also uses it for power-walking up a steep incline. He feels it is important to be able to run at a reasonable speed, so it was an integral part of his training for the Sydney Olympics.

In-Line Skating

In-line skating is a relatively new cross-training activity but has similar aerobic benefits to cross-country skiing. The leg action is the same as for ice skating, and it is very similar to the skating technique in skiing, especially if you use ski poles. The only problem with in-line skating is finding a suitable place to do it. Most 2000-meter courses have roads alongside that are ideal for in-line skating. I have not tested the lactate levels in this activity but I would assume they are similar to cross-country skiing. Correct safety equipment should be worn to minimize injuries. Athletes who are used to ice-skating may find in-line skating easier to learn than athletes with no ice-skating experience.

Kayaking

Rowers rarely use kayaking as a cross-training activity despite the fact that many kayak clubs train on the same water as we do. In 1996 and 1998, Xeno Müller occasionally used kayaking as an alternative training method, which significantly improved his balance in the rowing boat. A K1 kayak is ideal for developing balance because it is extremely difficult for a beginner to paddle a K1. When learning to kayak, beginners can remove the seat, thereby lowering their center of gravity.

Kayaking is excellent for developing upper-body strength, it gives the athletes a change from rowing, and it includes water and balance elements. If you are competent in the K1 or K2, you can usually train no matter how rough the water is. Kayaking is a useful alternative to the ergometer when the water is too rough for rowing. You could easily alternate kayaking with cycling, as one works the upper body and the other works the legs.

Photo by Marty Aitken

The Gier brothers, 1996 Olympic champions in the lightweight double sculls.

Windsurfing

When I coached in Australia during the 1980s we had Sundays off from training. We usually organized an optional bike ride down the bay from Melbourne to Frankston, a 50-mile round trip. During the summer we watched windsurfers as we rode around the bay. It looked so fun that we soon started to go windsurfing on Sundays. Everyone had their own equipment, and if the wind was strong enough we could stay on the water for hours at a time. After a few years, many of the rowers also became good windsurfers, in particular Jimmy Tompkins and Mike McKay, members of the Australian 1992 and 1996 Olympic-champion four. The main point of windsurfing was to do something together on our day off, but at the same time it built upper-body strength and was another water-based balance activity. It didn't contribute a great deal to the aerobic base, but it was a great activity on a day off.

Ball Sports

Rowers are notoriously poor ball handlers, so most coaches stay away from ball sports for cross-training. I have used various field or ball sports to vary the program, particularly in camps. Soccer is always popular with the English, although you need to be careful—at one camp 10 years ago Tim Foster, from the 2000 Olympic gold-medal four, twisted his ankle and was unable to train for several weeks.

Five-a-side Frisbee football, or ultimate Frisbee, is a good aerobic activity. It involves a lot of running and you can play it on a field of any size. European handball is another demanding ball sport, and it can be played indoors. I only use basketball occasionally, as the rowers tend to foul each other too often and get minor injuries. However, if correctly refereed, basketball can be an excellent break in a training camp.

Cross-training has helped a lot of athletes stay longer in the sport because it makes the whole training experience much more enjoyable. I am sure that this is why the age of athletes at the top level has been increasing quite rapidly over the past 10 years. Not long ago we thought that rowers over the age of 30 were well past their prime. Then two rowers made a comeback at the 1980 Olympics. Both were 32 years old and had competed in their last international race in 1970. We all thought it was ridiculous for them to try rowing again at such an advanced age. Neither made the team but they did win the King's Cup, a prestigious eights championship race in Australia. Today we see many athletes over the age of 30 winning gold medals. The obvious example is Sir Steven Redgrave, who won his fifth gold medal at the age of 38. Varied training helps keep athletes into their 30s interested in the sport.

Conclusion

Building an aerobic base is vital to developing top speed in any of the boat classes. Coaches in other sports often think that for an event that only lasts five and a half to eight minutes, we are doing too much steady-state and not enough speed work. The simplest answer to this is to simply look at how greatly speed in rowing has increased over the years. This is not only a result of advancements in boat construction and equipment but also of continuous refinement and progression in training methodology. Steady-state work is a major part of our training and probably will remain so until a breakthrough is made that convinces the coaches that a new method is better.

chapter 6

Improving Anaerobic Threshold

Wolfgang Fritsch

Just how useful is the anaerobic threshold as a measure of an athlete's aerobic capacity? I have faced this question many times in my career as a coach. Anaerobic threshold is the point where lactate starts to accumulate in the bloodstream, and the theory is that the higher the anaerobic threshold, the better the aerobic capacity. My experiences with this concept have not always been purely successful, but although anaerobic threshold is not necessarily the best way to select and evaluate rowers, it is a powerful way to control training. Two examples from my work as a German national team coach of lightweight rowers exemplify the pros and cons of using anaerobic threshold, or lactate threshold, as a measure of aerobic capacity.

The first example comes from my work in analyzing training and performance progress as well as race results. More than 20 top athletes came from all over the country to the national camp for a limited number of weekends per year for training or regattas, and I used six to eight ergometer tests to help me plan the athletes' training.

The assessments, performed on a Gjessing ergometer throughout the year, showed me the athletes' physiological development. Each assessment consisted of two tests, the first of which was an all-out, six-minute test to determine maximal physiological capacity (performance in watts and $\dot{V}O_2$max). The second test, for assessing aerobic capacity, was a progressive incremental submaximal test with three-minute test stages of increasing wattages, with one-minute rest periods in between. The results of these two tests helped me plan and regulate the rowers' preparation for the world championships.

The second example illustrates the limitations of anaerobic threshold as a measurement of aerobic capacity. Although it was very helpful in designing and controlling training, I had to make adjustments when using it for selecting athletes. In 1989, I had to choose from five apparently equally skilled scullers for a quadruple scull to represent Germany at the world championships in Bled. In contrast to selecting athletes for the eight, where physiological capacity was the only determining factor because all were technically excellent rowers, I intuitively decided to use additional criteria in choosing the quadruple scull, even though the physiological test indicated a clear ranking of the rowers regarding their physical capacities.

I selected the first three rowers based on the physiological data from ergometer tests. For the fourth rower, however, I chose the athlete who produced 15 watts less in his maximum test and 3 percent less in his anaerobic threshold test than the other rower. It was my belief that this rower fit better with the crew because even though his numbers were lower, he was able to start the race faster and more explosively than the other rower. In the end, I made the decision as a coach rather than a physiologist. My guess was right, because the quadruple scull won the world championships. This experience shows that especially when evaluating a specific rower or even race strategy, coaches should not rely completely on physiology. Although anaerobic threshold is clearly important, its usefulness depends on the coach's experience.

Anaerobic Threshold As a Control Mechanism

It is hard to imagine modern training without physiological monitoring. Training control is becoming increasingly important:

- Especially in crew rowing, it is necessary to monitor the effects of training on the individual athlete in order to avoid over- or underloading when athletes train often in large boats and the training load is the same for all rowers. **Individualization** of the training process means that coaches should be able to predict and recognize improvements in individual rowers.

- The purposeful organization of training and periodization demands a deliberate integration of **midterm goals**. Determine these goals from continuous performance checks.

- The assessment of applied training methods serves as useful evaluation of the **effectiveness of the training process** as a whole.

- Training control supports the **optimal coordination** and combination of single training sessions, certain competitions, and season planning.

Anaerobic threshold is an important parameter for regulating the endurance training and aerobic capacity development of world-class, fitness-class, and club rowers. It is also useful for evaluation and diagnostics.

The theory is that aerobic capacity prevents lactate accumulation up to the point of the anaerobic threshold. If an athlete crosses the anaerobic threshold, the body creates more lactate than it can remove from the bloodstream, eventually resulting in a drastic reduction in speed. Lactate accumulation can even make it necessary to stop the physical activity altogether. The anaerobic threshold therefore indicates how much work an athlete can do—or in other words, how fast an athlete can row or run—before the aerobic metabolism can no longer meet the body's energy demand (Bueno 1999). In other words, the higher the anaerobic threshold, the greater the aerobic capacity. The greater the aerobic capacity, the higher the average speed an athlete can maintain consistently over a longer period of time.

Measuring Anaerobic Threshold

Measuring anaerobic threshold involves a sequence of tests with progressively increasing work loads. The lactate concentration is measured at the end of each workload. There are then two methods for calculating the anaerobic threshold from this data:

1. Using a blood lactate concentration of 4 millimoles per liter as a fixed number to identify the anaerobic threshold (Mader et al. 1976).

2. Calculating the so-called *individual anaerobic threshold* using a formula that incorporates the buildup and removal of lactate in the first minutes after the performance (Stegemann and Kindermann 1982).

The term *anaerobic threshold*—and all concepts that refer to lactate measurement through aerobic and anaerobic threshold as the only parameter—are controversial because they reduce the complex regulatory mechanisms of lactate production to a single aspect, anaerobic threshold. Moreover, a precise assessment of anaerobic threshold is impossible, because the existing definitions are based on discipline-specific methodological and theoretical focal points.

Maximal Oxygen Consumption As a Reference Point

Maximal oxygen consumption ($\dot{V}O_2$max), not anaerobic threshold, is the most common, reliable measurement of maximal aerobic capacity (Zintl 1988). Maximal oxygen consumption depends on oxygen diffusion in the lungs, oxygen transport in the blood, oxygen consumption in the working muscles, and the individual's natural capacity for oxygen uptake. Athletes reach $\dot{V}O_2$max when their oxygen consumption stops increasing even though the physical work is still increasing. To reach $\dot{V}O_2$max, the body has to produce at least approximately 10 millimoles of lactate per liter of blood, and it has to reach a respiratory quotient (RQ = CO_2 output/O_2 consumption) above 1.1.

A $\dot{V}O_2$max test primarily indicates the endurance potential of an athlete. For example, an athlete may have a $\dot{V}O_2$max of 6 liters, but the anaerobic threshold is the measure that shows how high the actual, utilizable aerobic capacity of this athlete is. The possibility of increasing $\dot{V}O_2$max through training is relatively low. A healthy person will probably only be able to increase $\dot{V}O_2$max by 20 to 25 percent. If an athlete aged 18 years and weighing 85 kilograms has a maximal $\dot{V}O_2$ of 4.8 liters per minute at the beginning of intensive endurance training, at the end of training he will at best achieve a $\dot{V}O_2$max of 6.0 liters per minute. This explains why aerobically fit rowers show almost no fluctuation in their $\dot{V}O_2$max over the course of a training year. Anaerobic threshold, on the other hand, is far more directly affected by the intensity, frequency, and duration of the training.

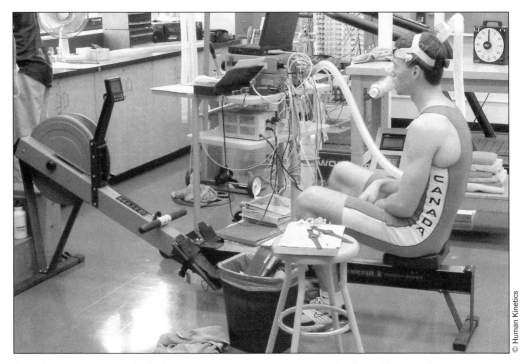

A rowing ergometer test is the best way to measure a rower's maximal aerobic capacity.

Maximal values for top rowers are 6000 to 6600 milliliters per minute $\dot{V}O_2$ (maximal oxygen consumption), or 68 to 72 milliliters per kilogram of body weight per minute (relative oxygen consumption). In rowing, the boat carries the body, so unlike in other sports such as running, relative oxygen consumption is not the most important criteria. A top lightweight rower might have a higher relative oxygen consumption than a top heavyweight rower, but her absolute aerobic capacity ($\dot{V}O_2$max)—and thus her rowing performance over 2000 meters—is not as good as that of the heavier rower.

Even well-trained endurance athletes can withstand a load at $\dot{V}O_2$max for only a few minutes (see figure 6.1). Endurance activities of longer durations are less dependent on $\dot{V}O_2$max than on aerobic endurance, the percentage of $\dot{V}O_2$max that the athlete can sustain during long periods of work (see figure 6.2).

Until the 1970s, maximal oxygen consumption ($\dot{V}O_2$max) was Germany's primary physiological criteria for evaluating a rower's aerobic capacity (Adam et al. 1977). It was not until the work of Mader and Hollman (1977) that anaerobic threshold became

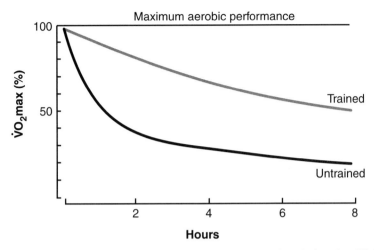

FIGURE 6.1   Oxygen consumption as a result of aerobic capacity and work duration (Weineck 2000; Åstrand and Rodahl 1977).

Reprinted, by permission, from J. Weineck, 2003, *Optimales training (Optimal training)* (Balingen, Germany: Spitta Verlag GmbH & Co. KG).

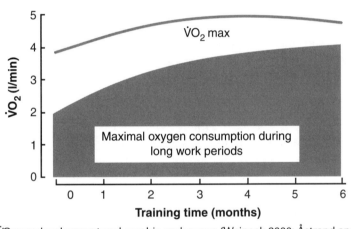

FIGURE 6.2 $\dot{V}O_2$max development and aerobic endurance (Weineck 2000; Åstrand and Rodahl 1977).

Reprinted, by permission, from Åstrand, Rodahl, Dahl, and Stromme, 2003, *Textbook of work physiology: physiological bases of exercise,* 4th ed. (Champaign, IL: Human Kinetics), 315.

significant. Although it is essential for rowers to have a high $\dot{V}O_2$max, it is also necessary to be able to endure a high percentage of $\dot{V}O_2$max for a long time.

At its peak, highly trained rowers' oxygen consumption at the anaerobic threshold is almost 90 percent of $\dot{V}O_2$max, while less trained athletes reach 55 to 60 percent. This emphasizes the importance of aerobic utilization—athletes must be able to use the oxygen they take in. To properly evaluate an elite rower's capacity, it is as important to measure aerobic utilization as it is to measure anaerobic threshold.

Despite the criticism of the methods for determining anaerobic threshold, the anaerobic threshold is an important orientation point for controlling endurance training and its intensity. To sidestep the anaerobic threshold's weaknesses, use the whole aerobic-anaerobic transition area, rather than a particular measurement point, to control training (see figure 6.3).

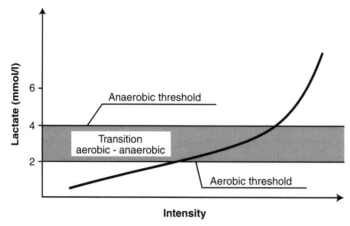

FIGURE 6.3 Lactate performance curve with lactate threshold (Zintl 1998).

Source: F. Zintl, 1988 *Ausdauertraining (Endurance training)* (Munich, Germany: BLV Verlagsgesellschaft), 65.

Why Rowers Need to Increase Anaerobic Threshold

A rower's goal is to improve endurance in order to increase boat speed without leaving the aerobic metabolism. To reach this goal, the body must make several adaptations under extreme conditions such as longer training periods or training under hypoxia (lack of oxygen to the tissues). In addition to increasing oxygen capacity, rowers must improve their aerobic fat metabolism. Aerobic metabolism has two possible sources of energy: fat and carbohydrate. During training at low intensities, the energy is mainly provided by fat (for example, until an RQ of 0.85 and 1.8 to 2.0 mmol/l). The transition to mainly carbohydrate metabolism (RQ 0.85 to 0.95 and ca. 2.5 to 4.5 mmol/l blood lactate) and more intensive training means that the duration of loading must be shorter (about 30 to 60 minutes of intensive training). Beyond this level of training, anaerobic metabolism is mainly required.

Once lactate concentration reaches approximately 7 millimoles per liter (Neumann et al. 2000), fat metabolism stops supplying energy. Moreover, the muscles' effectiveness decreases as lactate concentration increases, because lactate negatively affects the mitochondria, the energy powerhouses of the cells.

In contrast to training at maximal oxygen consumption or anaerobic threshold, training for longer periods of time at the level of aerobic fat metabolism is an effective way to stabilize the aerobic energy systems:

- If their aerobic capacity is not developed enough, rowers will be incapable of training for a longer period of time at the anaerobic threshold. They cannot tolerate more intensive workloads and need more time to recuperate.

- During longer training sessions that keep the body at the fat metabolism stage, the onset of fatigue leads to new muscle fibers being continually integrated in the movement (Neumann 1994).

Lactate concentration depends on the available energy source; fat metabolism occurs at low intensities (basic endurance; 2 to 3 millimoles per liter). A rowing race requires a physical exertion that leads to a lactate concentration of 12 to 16 millimoles per liter, an intensity that rowers can only sustain for a few minutes and is dominated by glycolysis and oxidation, not fat metabolism.

Many coaches take this into consideration and use only race-specific intensities (loads of at least 8 millimoles per liter) and intensities at the fat metabolism stage. They believe they need training that helps their rowers race the 2000 meters fast, challenging them with high stroke rates and high power efforts over several minutes or through intervals. The intensity demand should be equal to the physiological and technical race conditions of rowing. Training at fat metabolism, on the other hand, works the aerobic base for recuperation and is good for technique training as well. They believe they can leave out the intensities in between aerobic and anaerobic carbohydrate metabolism.

From my experience, however, these coaches are wrong. Training to improve the anaerobic threshold is necessary in performance rowing for several reasons:

- It improves **endurance capacity** (measured in $\dot{V}O_2max$). The most effective training intensity is around 64 to 85 percent of $\dot{V}O_2max$.

- It improves **neuromuscular control and motor variability**. The rower's power output and stroke rate during this kind of training must be above the aerobic long-distance cadence and closer to the higher race-stroke rates.

- It develops **aerobic performance capacity.** The main way to improve aerobic capacity is high training volume (approximately 60 to 120 minutes), which can only be attained if at least 50 percent of the energy comes from fat metabolism.

- Training loads around the anaerobic threshold test the **actual aerobic performance capacity** of a rower. Test races over a fixed period of time (20 to 30 minutes on a rowing ergometer) or over a particular distance (5- to 8-kilometer races) can help coaches get an exact idea of an athlete's aerobic capacity.

The Limits of Anaerobic Threshold Training

By now, the importance of the anaerobic threshold should be obvious. At the same time, it is easy to overestimate its effectiveness. Coaches must learn and respect its limits.

The following tips come from my experiences as a rowing coach as well as from theoretical studies (Mader and Hollmann 1977; Mader 1994; Neumann 1994; Fritsch 1990, 2000). They are only guidelines, not hard and fast rules. As a coach I became more and more cautious, reducing the number of sessions as well as the intensity of training at the anaerobic threshold. However, it is safe to use these training intensities throughout the year, and I had many positive experiences emphasizing these loads in specifically focused training periods.

- **Load intensity.** Intensities that demand 50 percent or more energy from carbohydrates (carbohydrate threshold) should account for no more than 10 to 15 percent of the overall training volume. These include intensities of approximately 65 percent of $\dot{V}O_2max$ or 80 to 83 percent of the anaerobic threshold.

The larger the share of carbohydrate metabolism, the shorter the session must be. This applies for the duration of each training session as well as for the overall training process.

- **Number of training sessions.** Limit intensive training methods for improving anaerobic threshold to a maximum of two times a week during the preparation period and once a week between regattas. These methods always require a warm-up and a cool-down at an intensity using fat metabolism. Don't combine these training intensities with serious strength-endurance training or race-specific training.

- **Training variability.** Vary training, not just for the rowers' psyche but also for efficiency. Vary stroke rate, power output, and duration of training sessions.

- **Overloading.** Training the anaerobic threshold also holds some dangers: A great deal of training at the anaerobic threshold develops the aforementioned benefits rather quickly, but then performance often stagnates and can even negatively affect aerobic capacity. Overloading this training intensity, which uses both carbohydrates and fat for energy, prevents the body from developing the aerobic base. Rowers can even fall so far behind that they have to start developing the aerobic base from the beginning. It can take weeks or even months to correct such overloading.

Demands of Anaerobic Threshold Training

Training methods that improve anaerobic threshold can be very unpopular with competitive rowers. I remember how taxing such training can be. As a member of the lightweight four, we trained in pairs every Saturday morning, where we raced against each other in constantly changing pairs. Our coach made us row next to each other twice for 20 minutes. At random time intervals, the coach gave us tasks such as rowing at certain stroke rates or changing power output. Sometimes we even had tactical assignments like catching up with the other boat.

One especially mischievous game involved keeping up with the motorboat while maintaining a consistent, low stroke rate. While we were rowing, the coach shifted the accelerator of the motorboat with his knee, barely increasing the velocity. This meant the pairs had to continuously increase power output, because we had to keep the stroke rate constant. It was not only the side-by-side competitive rowing in pairs but also the unforeseeable tasks that made us associate these training intensities with the sense of being tortured. We were always happy when we survived another Saturday morning.

The training sessions that improve the anaerobic threshold are hard, they really hurt, and they take time. Many rowers prefer to train at race pace rather than at such intensive endurance loads. However, experiments that reduced anaerobic threshold training have shown performance stagnation on all levels.

The anaerobic threshold is a theoretically well-defined point, a reference point for clarifying training goals. To reach the goal of improving anaerobic threshold, training needs to be at the intensity where the energy supply transitions from aerobic to anaerobic. Training needs to force an adequate change in the use of the fat and carbohydrate metabolisms. Specific goals depend on the performance level of the athletes, the boat class, the training period, the methodical objectives, and so on.

Training for Improved Anaerobic Threshold

Training sessions won't improve the anaerobic threshold unless the rower meets at least one of the following conditions:

1. The rower has a lactate performance curve based on a progressive incremental submaximal field or laboratory test. The curve must cover all performance levels from aerobic compensation to $\dot{V}O_2$max. The duration of each test stage should not be less than five minutes.
2. The rower has a very good sense of physical loads, possibly from many years of training. This enables the rower to determine the appropriate training load around the aerobic-anaerobic threshold. Nevertheless, the rower needs an objective source of information (lactate tests) to help develop this feeling.

For top athletes, the improvement of aerobic capacity at the anaerobic threshold is best measured in their sport discipline, which for a rower means in a boat or on a rowing ergometer. It is not very useful to transfer training goals to supporting endurance sports, as these sports do not have the neuromuscular adjustment and motor variability specific to rowing. Due to the danger of overloading, endurance training in additional sports should consist of large-volume training sessions that mainly use fat metabolism (> 70 percent). Some years ago we did lactate testing on our rowers when cross-country skiing at a high altitude (1800 meters above sea level). The rowers couldn't identify the intensity of their work the same way they could in the boat, and lack of technique training at a high altitude distorted their perception. For this reason all training sessions in supporting sports should be at a low or medium intensity.

Even though developing performance capacity in endurance sports could be managed with only two regulatory intensity zones (aerobic stabilization and intensity of competition) or at most three (aerobic stabilization, intensity of competition, and developing the aerobic base) (Neumann 1994), five or six regulation zones, or training categories, have been established based on methodical considerations. Figure 6.4 is one example of such intensity categories (Fritsch 1981, 1990, 1999).

These training intensities are developed specifically for training in rowing races over 2000 meters and are divided into six categories according to their function in rowing training. The intensity categories are described by their components: duration; intensity; density; relation to the race performance (best race time = 100 percent); and aerobic as well as anaerobic threshold. Obviously, these components have to be adjusted according to the fitness level of the rower.

Rowers should be aware of the zones of increased load. Increased activity in categories IV, V, and VI requires mainly aerobic performance and load. A frequent load over 4 mmol/l causes more intensive and mainly anaerobic load up to a 2000-meter best time. The time correlated to the different categories means the total training time (divided in several pieces) in these categories. In category III, for example, 6 to 10 minutes means 3 × 3 minutes (= 9 minutes) or 1 × 10 minutes at this intensity.

This system offers both rowers and coaches a useful base for planning training and systematization. It is my experience that rowers develop a better understanding of training load and effort requirements while working with these categories. This leads

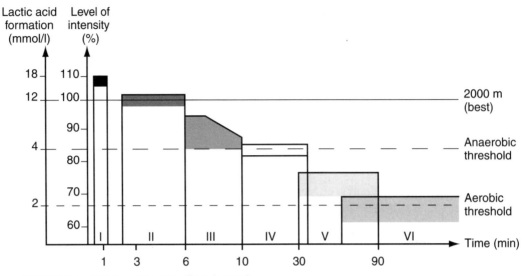

FIGURE 6.4   Training intensities (Fritsch 1981).

Source: W. Fritsch and V. Nolte 1981, *Beiheft zu leistungssport* (Berlin, Germany: Bartels and Wernitz), 4-32.

to a better identification of training loads for each rower, active thinking on the part of the athletes, and self-control.

If the categories are applied to a fictional lactate performance curve (see figure 6.5), it becomes obvious that in order to improve aerobic capacity and thus anaerobic threshold, only two or three training zones (categories III-V) are necessary.

This figure also shows the fictional points of a carbohydrate threshold and an intensity of about 85 percent of $\dot{V}O_2$max as training loads to improve the anaerobic threshold. These points vary among rowers depending on their physical fitness.

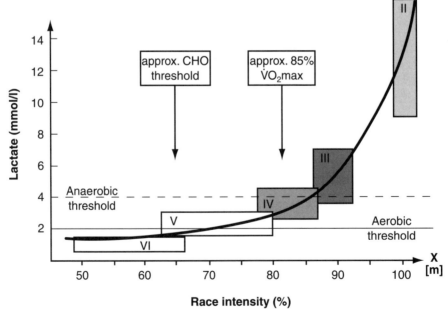

FIGURE 6.5   Lactate concentration and training intensity.

Rowing-specific training can take place in different ways (Fritsch 1990):

a. **Continuous endurance training:** Constant stroke rate and constant speed.

b. **Progressive endurance training**: Speed and stroke rate increase in small increments, such as every 2000 meters or every 3 minutes.

c. **Endurance training with sprints using anaerobic alactic energy supply**: Stroke rate and speed are constant; every 5 to 10 minutes, rowers make 5 to 12 strokes either at a high stroke rate or high power output.

d. **Systematic or arbitrary stroke rate changes in the aerobic zone:** Speed varies with change in stroke rate or power output.

e. **Systematic or arbitrary change (complex forms such as Fartlek training):** Speed varies with stroke rate or power output in sprints using anaerobic alactic energy.

f. **Test and control methods:** How fast can a certain distance be rowed? How far can you row in a certain time? In addition, you can fix the stroke rate.

Table 6.1 illustrates these training programs. It includes each program's maximal oxygen consumption, anaerobic threshold, maximal race speed, and lactate accumulation, along with approximate heart rates. The intensity categories are rowing-specific but nevertheless could apply to all endurance sports. The shaded area highlights what seem to be the most effective forms, but every method has its benefits.

As intensity decreases, the energy supplied by fat metabolism rises. Use less intensive training (lactate concentration below 3 millimoles per liter) more frequently than more intensive workouts, and don't schedule these workouts more than once or twice a week. During the competition period, schedule this sort of exertion very carefully, but do not eliminate it entirely from training.

Threshold Testing

The purpose of assessing anaerobic threshold is not only to diagnose fitness, it is for establishing training intensities as well. Rowers should train at their individual optimal heart rate or boat velocity, which are based on their lactate performance curve.

Some studies (Heck and Rosskopf 1993; Mader 1994; Neumann 1994; Neumann, Pfützner, and Berbalk 1999) assert that assessing optimum training intensity through lactate measurement and heart rate evaluation is extremely problematic, because using only blood lactate as a controlling parameter is not exact enough and could lead to incorrect assessment. As this applies also to the concept of individual anaerobic threshold, Heck and Rosskopf recommend getting rid of the threshold concepts altogether. Although this position has yet to be fully proven, it is possible to adapt training intensities to certain metabolic situations based on a lactate and a $\dot{V}O_2$ test, independent of a threshold concept. It is best to combine these testing methods and develop the perceived exertion and subjective feeling for the training zones.

On the Rowing Ergometer

On the rowing ergometer the load increases progressively depending on the performance level of the athlete, the starting stage, the time for each test stage, and the

TABLE 6.1　Rowing Programs for Increasing Anaerobic Threshold

Training program	Category	Percentage of $\dot{V}O_2$max	Percentage of anaerobic threshold	Percentage of race speed	Lactate	Heart rate
Long-distance races over 6-8 km Type a, f	III-IV	80-92	90-105	85-90	4.0-7.0	Approaching maximum
3 × 3000 m (rest 15 min), stroke rate: race rate minus 4-8 beats Type a, f	III-IV	80-92	90-105	85-90	3.0-7.0	Approaching maximum
2 × 12 min (rest 5-8 min), increasing stroke rate every min (18-20-22- ...-32) Type b, d	IV	60-90	75-100	75-88	3.0-5.0	210 – age
4 × 7 min or 3 × 10 min (rest 3-4 min), stroke rate: race rate minus 6-10 beats Type a	IV	65-85	85-100	80-85	3.0-5.0	210 – age
Change stroke rate: one minute 20 beats, one minute 28 beats per minute for 20-30 minutes Type d, e	IV	70-80	85-95	75-80	3.0-4.0	200 – age
60 min, with 3 × 20 min, increasing stroke rate (18 to 21 to 23 or 21 to 24 to 27 consistent for 20 min) included Type a, b, f	V-IV	65-75	75-85	70-80	2.5-4.0	200 – age
90 min steady state, stroke rate 18-23 with 8-10 strokes race pace (alactic) every 5 (or 2 or 10) min Type c, e	V	55-70	70-80	70-75	2.5-3.5	190 – age
120 min steady state, stroke rate 19-21 Type a	V	50-65	65-70	65-70	2.0-2.5	180 – age

For training types a through f, see page 73.

number of increments. During the test the ergometer measures heart rate, lactate levels, and oxygen consumption. The increase in lactate (lactate performance curve) provides information about aerobic and anaerobic performance capacity. A lactate concentration of 2 millimoles per liter or less is aerobic metabolism, and the aerobic-anaerobic transition occurs at a concentration of 2 to 4 millimoles per liter. As I mentioned earlier, the exact specification of a threshold and the discussion surrounding it are academic in nature and barely influence the training load in each specific intensity zone. It is impossible to adjust the training load through the measurement of the metabolic output for one specific point; however, it is possible to identify a certain area of intensity (Neumann 1998).

In the Boat

Testing in the boat takes more time, but it gives a more precise assessment. Often, only three levels of increasing speed in the aerobic-anaerobic transition provide enough results to help create the training plan. The test stages have to be longer (6 to 10 minutes) and are measured by increased power output and stroke rate. A major advantage of this procedure is the training of a rower's sense of the different intensities. The individual can connect subjective feeling with objective data like heart rate, stroke rate, lactate, and boat velocity. This helps the rower recognize different training intensities.

Disadvantages derive from external factors (weather, wind, current) and measurement limitations. $\dot{V}O_2$max, for example, is extremely difficult to measure in a boat, although there are new testing methods such as the measuring bag that help. In addition, it is also not easy to test a team of four at once.

Simple Procedures

Elite rowers and fitness rowers alike can use the following simple test on the rowing ergometer. The test is simply rowing 20 minutes on the rowing ergometer, which provides enough information to analyze aerobic performance capacity at the anaerobic threshold, including average work, total distance, 500-meter splits, heart rate, and stroke rate. Repeat the same test every four to six weeks to observe the development of these parameters.

Athletes can conduct this test even without reaching total exertion. The athlete performs at 90 percent of the intensity of the last maximal test of the same duration (20 minutes) and records the heart rate. Anaerobic threshold improvement occurs when the heart rate decreases over a period of time.

The rowing ergometer can help standardize test conditions, and there are no limits but imagination to developing appropriate test procedures. These test procedures are for planning the training process and evaluating rowing capacity. They are not as valid for the selection of rowers. Moreover, coaches need information about an athlete's training and nutrition in order to evaluate the results. Glycogen depletion, for example, leads to a right-shift of the lactate performance curve. This may be the result of incomplete recovery after repeated, intensive training, or it could be due to inadequate carbohydrate consumption in the days before the test. A test under such circumstances will show a falsely higher aerobic capacity (right-shift), as well as a lower power capacity (low lactate levels at exertion).

Conclusion

Assessing anaerobic threshold is a way to recognize changes in performance capacity. It helps optimize performance only in conjunction with efficient analysis of training and competition results. Intensive endurance training, or training at the anaerobic threshold, is absolutely necessary for developing aerobic endurance as well as neuro-muscular adaptations, and it is an important part of the training process for rowers of all levels.

Carefully plan all anaerobic threshold training. Overloading as a result of intensive endurance training leads to a stagnation in aerobic performance.

Coaches must not only use high-intensity training very carefully but must also evaluate all physiological data with a critical eye even when the data originate from extensive metabolic tests. Test scores are important, but performance in the actual race is more important. The coach's job is to select the right rowers and prepare them for their race. In the end, coaches need knowledge as well as experience to properly apply anaerobic threshold training.

chapter 7

Sprinting and Speed Work

Declan A.J. Connolly

In January of 2002, a 50-year-old athlete with more than 30 years of rowing experience came to the University of Vermont Human Performance Laboratory for a battery of physical fitness tests. His $\dot{V}O_2$max was 48.5 milliliters per kilogram per minute and his peak anaerobic power output was 713 watts (7.8 watts per kilogram). He reached anaerobic threshold at a heart rate of 150 beats per minute and had a steady-state work rate of 500 meters every 2:00 minutes on the rowing ergometer. He wanted to improve race performance and complained about stagnancy in his training program.

Based on his fitness scores we advised him to increase interval training and limit long, slow workouts to two per week. In addition, we suggested a resistance training program to improve power output. When the subject returned later that year, his $\dot{V}O_2$max had actually decreased to 47 milliliters per kilogram per minute. However, anaerobic threshold had increased to 157 beats per minute, peak anaerobic power had increased to 762 watts (8.6 watts per kilogram), and steady-state work rate had decreased approximately 5 seconds per 500 meters, improving his race time by 20 seconds.

My goal is to help you, like the rower who came into our lab, race faster. The first step is gaining an understanding of the body's energy systems. Rowing competitions are unique in that they demand exceptional development of multiple metabolic systems.

There are three interacting metabolic, or energy, systems. The first and most powerful system is the short-term ATP–PC (adenosine triphosphate–phosphocreatine) system. This system is the main energy source in events of high intensity and short duration lasting up to a maximum of 20 seconds, such as 100-meter sprints and throwing events. In these events the body produces large amounts of energy, or force, very rapidly over a short period of time. For example, powerlifters lift weight for less than one second but generate power in excess of 2000 watts. In contrast, in rowing large power outputs are typically only seen at the start of the race, when rowers need to accelerate the boat, and do not exceed 1000 watts (heavyweight men). Usually power output at the start of a race is around 600 watts, as 1000 watts is a true maximal effort that would render the athlete useless after about 30 seconds.

Next is the anaerobic system, also known as the lactic acid or glycolytic system. It is the main energy source in events of a lesser intensity and slightly longer duration, from 20 seconds up to 90 seconds. The third system is the aerobic system, which is the main energy source in events lasting from four minutes up to several hours.

These systems always act together, but one system often predominates in a particular competitive event. Understanding the demands of a sport allows athletes to develop a training program to target the necessary energy system. All energy systems contribute at all times, but intensity is the primary factor that determines the amount of energy that comes from a particular system. Exercise duration is a secondary factor, regulated by intensity. Figure 7.1 shows how the usage of carbohydrates and fats in the energy supply depends on intensity. The rower's challenge is to develop all energy systems to allow maximal contribution by the primary energy system for the start of the race, the middle of the race, and the end of the race. The energy requirements for elite rowing are about 70 percent aerobic. The remainder comes from the other two energy systems, mainly at the start and end of the race.

Identifying the primary energy systems for competitive rowing is challenging because athletes vary in physiological profile and dependency upon energy systems. As mentioned, the aerobic system contributes about 70 percent of total energy for

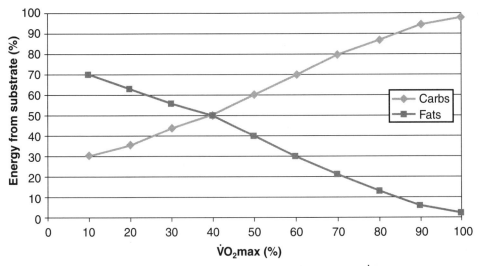

FIGURE 7.1   Fat and carbohydrate usage as a function of intensity (percent $\dot{V}O_2$max).

elite athletes. Elite athletes are well trained and efficient, so as we move to lower levels of competition the percent contribution of energy systems varies. In spite of this, we can analyze energy needs based on duration, intensity, and previous analysis in rowing and other sports.

We can also look at the physiological profiles of successful rowers, a practical approach that is often overlooked. In general, the longer the event, the lower the intensity of work. Short events such as the 100-meter sprint in track are very intense, while a 10K run is less intense. In both events the athlete puts forth maximal effort, but the speed of movement relative to the athlete's maximal speed is lower in the 10K because of the greater distance. Work by Hagerman et al. (1996) using simulated rowing and competitive oarsmen concluded that approximately 70 percent of energy released was aerobic and that anaerobic energy dominated the early stages of work. Because a rowing competition over 2000 meters lies in the middle of multiple energy systems, preparation is a challenge.

Demands of the Sport

Successful athletes often have similar physiological characteristics, and summary data have established some minimum requirements for successful endurance performance. These requirements hold true for most endurance sports, including running, rowing, cycling, and cross-country skiing (Hawley et al. 1997). The requirements include the following:

- Maximal oxygen consumption ($\dot{V}O_2$max) > 70 milliliters per kilogram per minute
- Ability to perform at a high percentage of $\dot{V}O_2$max for duration of event
- High power output or speed at the anaerobic threshold
- Good technique
- Ability to utilize fat as a fuel source during exercise of longer duration at high work rates

These characteristics seem straightforward. However, we must first establish if in fact rowers are endurance athletes. There is some controversy about the true classification of rowers. Elite rowers compete for six minutes, which would not generally be considered pure endurance, but it is also outside the limits of the anaerobic system. According to Hagerman et al. (1996), elite male rowers' $\dot{V}O_2$max scores are about 75 milliliters per kilogram per minute, while females' scores are around 65. These are world-class numbers for endurance athletes in any sport and certainly exceed aerobic values needed by elite anaerobic athletes, which are rarely higher than 60. From a physiological point of view, rowers are endurance athletes.

However, rowers also require a high degree of anaerobic capability. Some argue that an athlete does not need a high $\dot{V}O_2$max to row fast for six minutes since this is a relatively short time. While this is true, I would argue that in order to train properly to race for six minutes athletes do need a high $\dot{V}O_2$max and a high anaerobic threshold. Six minutes at maximal effort is a long time, and only the aerobic system is capable of providing sufficient energy over this time period. In addition, recovery is always aerobic, regardless of whether an individual exercises aerobically or anaerobically. Ability to recover during work sessions of short-term, high-intensity exercise depends on aerobic fitness.

Rowing uses both the aerobic and anaerobic systems, but at some point the predominant energy system develops a higher capability. In rowing, this appears to be the aerobic system. Thus, rowing fast requires a high $\dot{V}O_2$max with a great deal of anaerobic power. Rowers need a carefully designed training program that incorporates both power and endurance to stimulate the necessary anaerobic and aerobic adaptation. In general, aerobic conditioning should precede anaerobic conditioning, as quality anaerobic work requires a minimum aerobic fitness.

Once athletes reach a certain $\dot{V}O_2$max (55 milliliters per kilogram per minute for women and 60 for men), they must perform not only more aerobic work but also a high degree of anaerobic work to increase $\dot{V}O_2$. For example, one January a 39-year-old rower reported to our lab for testing and produced a $\dot{V}O_2$max of 50 milliliters per kilogram per minute. She achieved these results from a training program of predominantly steady-state endurance work with little or no interval or resistance training. We advised her to include resistance exercises and interval training designed to increase power output, not mass. The following January her lab scores showed a $\dot{V}O_2$max of 59 milliliters per kilogram per minute and a substantial improvement in performance in spite of a 60 percent decrease in aerobic work.

A further point to consider is that when athletes are aerobically well conditioned, they can maintain their aerobic fitness even when high-intensity (anaerobic) work is the sole mode of training for four to eight weeks. This provides the basis for many successful tapering approaches (Mujika 1998).

Training Techniques

Rowers face multiple training challenges. They have to develop a high $\dot{V}O_2$max, a high anaerobic threshold, and a high degree of speed or power production. These challenges require varied training methods that include fast and slow work on the water or ergometer and time in the weight room to help develop power. Figure 7.2, a modified version of a model proposed by Hawley in 1993, shows a training progression that increases in intensity and decreases in volume as competition approaches. It also shows a transitional approach to aerobic work, threshold work, and power and speed work.

Most athletes understand that the training protocol for improving $\dot{V}O_2$max and establishing an aerobic base is distance work that progresses in intensity. Distance work is naturally subject to the law of diminishing returns. This means an athlete can continue endurance training for long periods of time and see only marginal increases in $\dot{V}O_2$max that may or may not lead to better performance. Therefore, anaerobic training may be the best way to further improve aerobic performance.

The transition to higher intensity work is crucial to race performance. The objectives are to improve endurance, anaerobic performance, and fatigue resistance. There are several training methods for accomplishing this goal, including continuous distance work for aerobic base development, pace or tempo training as a means of transitioning, and then interval and speed work to improve race speed and anaerobic threshold. Studies have repeatedly shown that the optimal intensity for improving $\dot{V}O_2$max lies

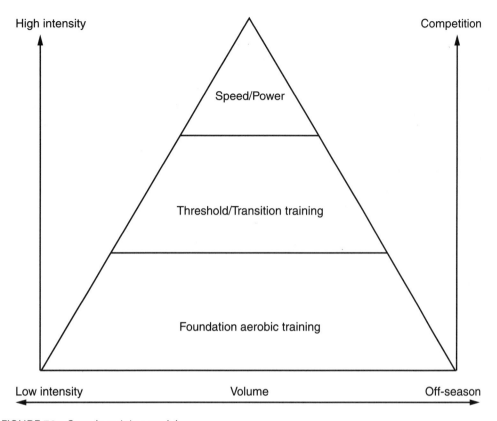

FIGURE 7.2 Sample training model.

between 90 to 100 percent $\dot{V}O_2$max, and both interval and high-intensity continuous exercise achieve just that.

While rowers have practiced these methods for 30 or 40 years, there is limited scientific data from training studies on rowers. Researchers have, however, widely investigated these training methods in cyclists, swimmers, and runners. Work by Lindsay and colleagues (1996) on elite cyclists found significant improvement in power output after only four weeks when cyclists replaced 15 percent of aerobic-base work with six high-intensity training sessions over a 28-day period. The subjects performed these sessions at 80 percent of peak power (86 percent $\dot{V}O_2$max) for five minutes with one minute of recovery.

Additional work by Stepto and colleagues (1999) found similar results. Their study used a variety of interval training protocols in addition to aerobic training over a three-week period. This study suggests that a long period of high-intensity training may not be necessary. The athletes performed intervals ranging from 30 seconds to 8 minutes at power levels ranging from 80 to 175 percent of peak power (measured as power at $\dot{V}O_2$max). The subjects significantly increased their peak power and their $\dot{V}O_2$ peak. In performance they saw an increase in time-trial speeds. As in Lindsay's study, subjects had not participated in interval training during the previous four months.

One rower's experience with interval training led to a collegiate lightweight world record at the C.R.A.S.H.-B. Sprints World Indoor Rowing Championships. This improvement occurred over a three-week period (from http://home.hia.no/ ~ stephens/woodslet.htm).

The training was ergometer-specific and comprised one hour a day, 6 days a week. Most days the athlete performed at a steady stroke rate of 16 to 18 (vent setting 3 on a Concept2, type C ergometer). The athlete maintained a heart rate above 144 beats per minute. The athlete then pulled hard until reaching a heart rate of 160 (90 percent max), held it for 30 to 45 seconds, and then paddled light until the heart rate returned to 144.

Twice a week the athlete performed a demanding series comprised of 10 × 1 (1 minute on, 1 minute off) with an open rating of 36. In the end, the rower's CRASH B time dropped 15 seconds. This story suggests that the key ingredients for fast endurance performance appear to be both a high $\dot{V}O_2$max and a high anaerobic threshold, both of which require high-intensity training. However, even when $\dot{V}O_2$max is lower, rowers can improve race performances with a higher anaerobic threshold, suggesting that anaerobic threshold may be more important than aerobic capacity. Speed work, or work done above anaerobic threshold, is often overlooked by endurance athletes, but it is necessary to increase the anaerobic threshold.

The Quest for Speed

Acquiring speed involves both nature and science, and it requires elevation of the anaerobic threshold and increased speed of movement. Speed training can take various forms. The following are the most straightforward approaches:

1. High-intensity continuous exercise (often called pace rowing)
2. Interval training
3. A combination of both

An athlete must be well conditioned before embarking on higher intensity workouts. A simple guideline is to time your best effort over 5000 or 6000 meters. Pay attention to your 1000-meter splits. If your last 1000-meter split is the same as your first, you're probably ready for higher intensity work. If it is not, you need more steady-state endurance training.

Both interval training and high-intensity continuous exercise require athletes to spend certain periods of time above their anaerobic threshold. It takes trial and error to determine the correct intensity for this. Athletes need to ensure that they develop their intensity levels using sound information. Heart rate is a common measure, and rowers can also use speed as a measure. In fact, for interval training this is sometimes wiser. Intervals tend to take place at or above race pace, so heart rate is maximal for many levels of intervals and often does not accurately determine intensity.

In high-intensity continuous exercise (HICE), the athlete works for 20 or more minutes at an intensity level above the anaerobic threshold, as determined on a continuum of 10 to 100 percent $\dot{V}O_2$max. The length of the exercise session determines intensity, which should be at a level that allows the athlete to complete the session just before exhaustion. New technologies on most boats and nearly all ergometers that measure speed, distance, and stroke rate make this training fairly straightforward for rowers. High-intensity continuous rowing simulates racing conditions, except intensity is maximal only toward the end and for a shorter period of time.

With interval training, athletes do shorter but much more intense intervals above the anaerobic threshold. In fact, interval speed is often higher than race pace since it lasts a shorter time and includes recovery. The ratio of work to rest varies depending on the number of intervals in a session. I recommend a minimum of 4 intervals per session and a maximum of 10. Intervals do not need to be the same length or intensity within a session. A session should usually include shorter distances in the middle or end of the session.

Intervals are also valuable for training athletes to row fast. Some argue that this can compromise technique. However, athletes should be able to focus on proper technique since the periods are shorter. If an athlete's technique falls apart, then the coach has identified that the athlete cannot maintain good form at higher work rates. Swimmers have successfully trained this way for many years, and I believe that intervals of varying length are more productive because they help athletes gauge effort and practice mental focus in different situations.

Remember, training must include intervals that require athletes to perform faster than race pace. This is central to the interval approach, and because the time spent at speeds faster than race pace is shorter than in an actual race, athletes can handle it. When first starting higher intensity training, schedule only one session per week for three weeks. This allows rowers to adapt to the new speed. Then schedule two sessions per week at least three days apart. Two sessions per week are generally enough; training can progress in the form of a shorter rest period or a faster interval.

Table 7.1 gives some examples of both types of threshold training based on a profile generated from laboratory tests. This is real data! Anyone can apply the same principles of organization even though this data is from an older male athlete.

In this example, the athlete's anaerobic threshold occurs at a heart rate of 158 beats per minute or an ergometer time of 1:50 minutes per 500 meters. (Making your crews converse is a simple guideline for anaerobic threshold when you cannot scientifically measure it. When the rowers have trouble conversing or they become quiet, they're at the anaerobic threshold.) Using these numbers, we can now create threshold workouts.

TABLE 7.1 Physiological Profile of a Male Rower

Age	47
Mass	76 kg
Height	170 cm
Max heart rate (MHR) (220 – age)	173 bpm
True MHR	175 bpm
% max anaerobic threshold	80%
$\dot{V}O_2$max	56 ml $\times$ kg^{-1} $\times$ min^{-1}
HR at anaerobic threshold	158 bpm
$\dot{V}O_2$ at anaerobic threshold	44 ml $\times$ kg^{-1} $\times$ min^{-1}
500m split max	1:37 min
500m pace at anaerobic threshold	1:50 min
2000m best	6:40 min

For a HICE session, the athlete should be able to sustain a heart rate of 158 to 163 for up to 60 minutes. As heart rate increases, session time decreases. Alternatively, the rower could row at a heart rate of 156 to 157 per 500 meters indefinitely. Regardless, effective speed and threshold work must occur at more than 158 beats per minute and at a split less than 1:50 minutes per 500 meters.

As an additional note, in a HICE session heart rate creeps up over the duration of the workout even though the speed remains the same. This phenomenon is called cardiovascular drift and in most cases is due to increasing body temperature. Rowers can offset it with regular fluid replenishment. However, athletes may have to slightly decrease workout intensity to compensate for cardiovascular drift. For sessions of shorter duration, intensity must correspondingly increase. For example, if the session is only 20 minutes, then the athlete might elect to start at a heart rate of 160 to 167 beats per minute. In HICE sessions the athlete should approach maximal effort at the end of the session.

In interval training we know that an athlete who can row 6:40 minutes for 2000 meters should be capable of a 1:40-minute pace for 500 meters, which produces maximal heart rate at the end of the 2000 meters. Therefore, rowers can do intervals of varying distances using 500-meter splits less than 1:40 minutes and 500 meters at 1:40 to 1:55 minutes. Speeds slower than 1:50 minutes per 500 meters constitute a recovery phase. Interval sessions can vary in speed or stay the same throughout. Table 7.2 shows an easy interval session using a 1:1 ratio for the rower profiled in table 7.1.

Table 7.2 is only one example, but it shows how to plan work and recovery phases. Also pay attention to stroke rate during intervals. Athletes may choose to set guidelines for stroke rates during slower intervals as this can help power and tempo. The basic goal of interval or high-intensity training is to complete a given volume of work (e.g., 10 × 500 meters) at a faster pace than the pace of your best 1 × 5000 meter piece. This does not include recovery time.

Here's another example that a New England high school championship team actually used a few years ago.

Days on the water: 5 (3 technical, steady-state days; 2 interval days)

Intervals are different on each day.

Day One

Supramaximal intensity 500-meter pieces

30-minute warm-up, including start sequences

Two sets of 3 × 500 meters: The first uses a start, the second begins off the paddle at race pace, and the third is on the fly with a sprint finish

Allow 90 seconds rest between each of the three intervals in a set and 4 to 5 minutes of recovery between sets

Cool-down

Day Two

Long intervals ranging from 4 to 8 minutes at 85 to 90 percent race pace with 3 to 5 minutes of recovery

TABLE 7.2 Sample Interval Training Workout

Time (min)	Session	500m split
0:00-5:00	Warm-up	2:30
5:00-8:00	Recovery speed	2:10
8:00-11:00	Interval 1	1:50
11:00-14:00	Recovery speed	2:10
14:00-16:30	Interval 2	1:45
16:30-19:00	Recovery speed	2:15
19:00-21:00	Interval 3	1:40
21:00-23:00	Recovery speed	2:15
23:00-24:30	Interval 4	1:35
24:30-26:00	Recovery speed	2:15
26:00-27:00	Interval 5	1:30
27:00-28:00	Recovery speed	2:15
28:00-29:00	Interval 6	1:30
29:00-30:00	Recovery speed	2:15
30:00-35:00	Cool-down	2:30

The competitive athlete will want to do more intervals faster than race pace than will the recreational athlete. The competitive athlete should also design intervals with progressively decreasing recovery periods. As mentioned, intervals progress by first increasing the time of the interval, second by decreasing recovery, and third by increasing speed. The savvy coach and athlete will monitor heart rate, stroke rate, and ability to sustain intervals, which will help assess adaptation and guide progression. Preparing periodization tables for the athletes is a necessary first step. Implement intervals and speed work shortly before the competitive season and in the off-season after athletes have performed endurance, strength, and power work.

The amount of recovery time between training sessions depends on the intensity of the session, whether more than one session was performed in one day, and perhaps most important, the athlete's diet. Arguably the most important time for an athlete to eat is immediately after exercise, especially high-intensity exercise, which is glycogen-dependent. The quality of this food intake is crucial to glycogen replenishment. Quality foods are foods high in carbohydrate and protein concentration. Glycogen replenishment takes about 24 hours, so avoid consecutive days of hard intervals and allow two days between sessions for adequate recovery.

When to Start Interval or HICE Training

If we refer back to our pyramid model in figure 7.2 (page 81), we can see that these types of workouts require a solid aerobic foundation. Rowers typically develop the aerobic foundation in the off-season or winter season. Since higher intensity training is more demanding, it requires a decrease in training volume, not unlike a tapering program. In fact, numerous studies have documented the effectiveness of tapering programs that use only high-intensity, low-volume training. High intensity sessions should begin 8 to 10 weeks before competition.

Another goal of intervals or HICE is to simulate race intensity and psyche, so schedule these sessions just before the competitive season. Table 7.3 shows some examples, adapted from Bompa (1999), of the year-long preparation for endurance sports.

TABLE 7.3 Sample Long-Term Training Plan

Phases	Year-long periodization plan					
Subphases	Preparation phase		Competition		Recuperation	Transition
Macrocycle	Volume	Intensity	Maintain	Maintain	Fun and cross-training	Aerobic and skill development
Microcycle						

Adapted, by permission, from T.O. Bompa, 1999, *Periodization: Theory and methodology of training*, 4th ed. (Champaign, IL: Human Kinetics), 195.

Conclusion

There isn't any other way to prepare for competition than with high-intensity workouts. Be sure to plan properly and base sessions on individual data. Finally, think about and plan the recovery time for intervals very carefully. Recovery times are just as important, for they regulate the quality of work. With too little rest, fatigue comes too quickly; too much rest and there is less stimulus for adaptation.

The bottom line is this: *You need to row fast in order to row faster.* Rowing fast requires physiological, psychological, and biomechanical effort. It is also uncomfortable and for many athletes this is the greatest challenge. At higher work intensities breathing discomfort, heaviness in the legs and arms, and burning in the chest are real, racelike symptoms. Spending time rowing fast, above the anaerobic threshold and at or near maximal heart rate, prepares athletes for the race environment.

chapter 8

Building Strength

Ed McNeely

Over the past 40 years strength training has become a critical part of a rower's preparation. Strength training for rowing has evolved from strength-endurance circuits using homemade equipment and body-weight exercises into a science that incorporates training methods originally developed in weightlifting, powerlifting, and track and field. Rowing presents unique challenges in designing a strength program: No other sport requires such high levels of both strength and aerobic fitness for a championship performance. As boat speed increases and race duration decreases, generic strength-training programs from the pages of your favorite fitness magazine won't be enough to take your performance to the next level. A rowing-specific strength program is the only answer.

Strength Demands of Rowing

There are several ways to determine the strength demands of a sport. One method is biomechanical analysis of the forces generated on the footstretchers, oar lock, or at the blade, which reveals how much force a rower develops with each stroke. Elite rowers generate their highest forces on the first stroke of a race. These forces have been found to reach 1352 Newtons or 135 kilograms for men and 1019 Newtons or 102 kilograms for women (Hartmann et al. 1993). In 1975, research on the East German national team indicated that rowers need to be able to generate forces of at least 133 kilograms for international competition (Secher 1975). With increases in boat speed and changes in oar technology since then, today's rowers undoubtedly must be able to generate even higher forces.

A second method for determining strength demands is examining elite competitors. Rowers who win medals at the Olympics or world championships are usually the strongest athletes in the sport. This isn't always true because technical efficiency and aerobic fitness also play a large role, but it is a good starting point. In order to study maximal force generation at various points in the rowing stroke, Secher (1975) developed an isometric apparatus that could be adjusted to individual rowing positions. A study using Dutch Olympic, national, and club rowers found that on average international rowers generated 204 kilograms of force, national rowers generated 183 kilograms of force, and club rowers generated 162 kilograms of force. The study also included general strength tests, such as isometric arm pull, back extension, trunk flexion, and leg extension. It found that regardless of the test, the higher the competition level of the rower, the greater the strength.

Strength and Body Weight

Strength is either absolute or relative. Absolute strength is the maximum weight that a person can lift in one repetition. Because they carry more muscle mass, larger individuals tend to have higher absolute strength than smaller individuals. Relative strength, on the other hand, is the maximum amount of weight that a person can lift relative to body weight. Relative strength is more important to a rower than absolute strength because the amount of weight in a boat affects the drag through water. An increase in absolute strength is of no benefit if the weight gain offsets the strength gain by increasing resistance through water. When rowers increase relative strength, on the other hand, they find it easier to accelerate the boat because they've increased strength without increasing drag. Because relative strength is more important to rowers than absolute strength, the strength goals in this chapter are expressed as percentages of body weight.

Strength Goals

The goals in table 8.1 come from consultation with athletes of all levels, from high school rowers to Olympic champions, as well as from an examination of past force and strength research. Because the goals are multiples of body weight, they apply to both heavyweight and lightweight rowers.

To use the table, take your body weight and multiply it by the listed factor. For instance, if you are a 91-kilogram male club rower you should be able to bench pull 95 kilograms at one time (91 kilograms body weight × 1.05 = 95 kilograms).

If you meet these goals, you can focus on other areas in your training. If you can't meet these goals, strength may be holding your rowing back.

Strength Testing

There are two ways to estimate maximum strength. Maximal strength testing, often called 1RM, measures the maximum amount of weight that an individual can lift one time. Submaximal repetition testing uses lighter weight, more repetitions, and a formula.

TABLE 8.1 Relative Strength Goals

MEN					
	High school	**U 23**	**Club**	**National**	**Olympic**
Squat	1.0	1.3	1.4	1.7	1.9
Deadlift	1.0	1.3	1.4	1.7	1.9
Bench pull	0.7	0.9	1.05	1.2	1.3
WOMEN					
	High school	**U 23**	**Club**	**National**	**Olympic**
Squat	0.8	1.0	1.25	1.4	1.6
Deadlift	0.8	1.0	1.25	1.4	1.6
Bench pull	0.6	0.8	0.95	1.1	1.2

MASTERS: MEN								
	35-39	**40-44**	**45-49**	**50-54**	**55-59**	**60-64**	**65-69**	**70+**
Squat	1.37	1.30	1.2	1.15	1.03	0.95	0.82	0.60
Deadlift	1.37	1.3	1.2	1.15	1.03	0.95	0.82	0.60
Bench pull	1.02	0.98	0.94	0.88	0.78	0.71	0.62	0.45
MASTERS: WOMEN								
	35-39	**40-44**	**45-49**	**50-54**	**55-59**	**60-64**	**65-69**	**70+**
Squat	1.22	1.16	1.08	1.00	0.91	0.80	0.72	0.50
Deadlift	1.22	1.16	1.08	1.00	0.91	0.80	0.72	0.50
Bench pull	0.93	0.88	0.82	0.76	0.69	0.60	0.55	0.38

1RM Tests

Maximum strength testing (1RM testing) can be time consuming, taking anywhere from 20 to 40 minutes per exercise. The procedure is as follows:

1. Warm up using a light weight that you can easily handle for 5 to 10 repetitions.
2. Rest 2 minutes.
3. Increase the weight by 10 to 20 percent and do a second warm-up of 3 to 5 repetitions
4. Rest 2 minutes.
5. Increase the weight by another 10 to 20 percent and perform a final warm-up of 2 to 3 repetitions.

6. Rest 3 to 4 minutes.

7. Increase the load by 5 to 10 percent and try one repetition.

8. Rest 3 to 4 minutes.

9. If the last attempt was successful, increase the weight by 5 percent and try another repetition. If it was not successful, decrease the weight by 2.5 to 5 percent and try again.

10. Repeat this process until you can perform only one repetition with proper technique. Always rest 3 to 4 minutes between attempts.

Ideally you will find your 1RM within five sets of finishing the warm-up. If the test takes more than five sets, fatigue may affect accuracy. This test is accurate to within 5 percent of your true 1RM.

Predicted Tests

Estimated tests are a time-efficient alternative to 1RM tests. These tests use formulas to predict maximum strength, and in most cases they are as accurate as the 1RM test. They are less accurate in athletes who train very close to their maximum strength for long periods. The procedure is as follows:

1. Warm up using a light weight that you can easily handle for 5 to 10 repetitions.

2. Rest 2 minutes.

3. Increase the weight by 10 to 20 percent and do as many repetitions as possible. You should reach failure between 2 and 10 repetitions.

4. To calculate your max, use the formula

$$[(0.033 \times reps) \times weight] + weight = 1RM$$

where reps are the number of times you lift the weight, and weight refers to the amount of weight lifted. For instance, if you lifted 100 kilograms five times you would get

$$[(0.033 \times 5) \times 100] + 100$$
which gives you $[(0.165) \times 100] + 100$
which equals $16.5 + 100$
giving you a 1RM of 116.5.

If you do more than 10 reps, take a 10-minute rest, increase the weight by another 10 to 20 percent, and try again.

Test Exercises

The three test exercises are the squat, deadlift, and bench pull. They use all the muscles rowing uses, require minimal equipment, and are easy to standardize.

Squat

Place the bar across your back. Your hands should be as close together as possible, your elbows should point toward the floor, and your feet should be slightly wider than shoulder-width. Take one step out of the rack, take a deep breath, and, contracting your abdominals to stabilize your trunk, descend slowly into a squat. Once you reach a full squat, drive with your legs and return to a standing position.

Keep squat depth consistent from test to test; otherwise you won't know if you are improving. At the proper depth your hamstrings should touch your calves. Many athletes believe that squatting deeper than 90 degrees causes knee problems, but there is no research to back this contention. Strength improvements are specific to range of motion, and as a rower it is vital to achieve knee angles in the squat that are similar to those that you achieve in the boat. If you don't squat deep enough, you won't increase your strength at the catch. (See figure 8.1.)

FIGURE 8.1   Squat.

Bench Pull

Lie facedown on a high bench. When you grasp the bar, your arms should be straight and your hands shoulder-width apart. Keeping your head, upper body, and legs flat on the bench, pull the weight up until it touches the bottom of the bench. If you don't have a high bench, you can place a flat bench onto a couple of aerobics steps. If you do this, make sure the bench is stable and balanced. Try to use the same bench each time you test, as the thickness of the bench affects how far you have to pull. (See figure 8.2.)

FIGURE 8.2   Bench pull.

Deadlift

Stand in front of a bar with your feet shoulder-width apart. Squat down and grasp the bar with an overhand grip (palms toward you). Keeping your back flat, take a deep breath, tighten your abdominals, and stand up, using your legs to start the movement. It is important to feel your legs working. Be careful—if you straighten your legs too soon in a movement similar to shooting your slide, it becomes a back lift and can cause injury. (See figure 8.3.)

FIGURE 8.3   Deadlift.

If you are unfamiliar with these lifts, take a few weeks to practice technique before attempting any sort of test.

Regular testing is part of any good training program. It helps you establish goals and provides concrete evidence about the program's effectiveness. You should repeat strength tests every training cycle or every four to six weeks.

Designing a Rowing-Specific Program

A year-long strength program has four phases: symmetry and hypertrophy, maximum strength, power, and power endurance. Each phase builds on the physical abilities developed in the previous phase, so be sure to do them in order.

Symmetry and Hypertrophy Phase

Strength training during the first part of the year corrects muscle imbalances that develop as a result of training and racing. Athletes that only row one side can develop strength imbalances between the right and left sides of the body in the low back and legs, which can lead to chronic back pain. While scullers don't have this worry, they are still susceptible to strength differences between the quadriceps and hamstrings, which can lead to chronic back pain and acute low-back injuries.

Hypertrophy is an increase in muscle size, necessary for increasing maximum strength and power. Hypertrophy training comes early in the year when the volume of aerobic training is still relatively low, because when aerobic volume increases beyond four to six hours per week it becomes impossible for the rower to gain muscle mass.

Many lightweights worry that they will increase in size and have trouble making weight later in the year. However, the high volume of aerobic training prevents rowers from developing much muscle. The amount of muscle mass a rower gains through a short cycle of hypertrophy training is usually no more than one or two kilograms. If rowers don't slightly increase muscle mass, they will find it very difficult to maximize power later in the year.

Duration   The symmetry and hypertrophy phase lasts 8 to 12 weeks and consists of two or three training cycles of 4 to 6 weeks. Younger athletes and masters returning to rowing after several years off should use three cycles of 4 weeks. Seasoned athletes who have been strength training regularly for at least two years can cut this phase to two 4-week cycles. A cycle consists of 3 weeks of increasingly harder work followed by a recovery week of reduced training volume and intensity.

Intensity   Intensity refers to the percentage of maximum weight that you use during the training session. You can calculate the intensity for each exercise using the procedure on page 90. Throughout the training phase and across each training cycle intensity gradually increases.

You will find strength differences between the right and left side of the body in some of the exercises in this phase. To correct strength imbalance use the same weight on both sides. This means using a lower percentage of max on the strong side, but it is the only way the weaker side can catch up.

The first cycle, which emphasizes symmetry, uses low intensities, 60 to 70 percent 1RM. In the subsequent cycles, where hypertrophy is the goal, intensity varies from 70 to 80 percent 1RM.

Volume   Volume refers to the total number of repetitions for each muscle group or exercise. You calculate volume by multiplying the number of repetitions by the number of sets. For instance, if the program calls for three sets of 10 repetitions the volume is 3×10, or 30 repetitions. During this phase volume varies from 30 to 40 repetitions per muscle group. If you do 4×10 squat repetitions, you perform a total of 40 repetitions for the quadriceps muscles and do not need to do leg extensions, leg presses, or any other exercise for the quadriceps. Doing more exercises and increasing volume do not increase strength, they only increase recovery time and risk of overtraining.

Exercises   A core group of exercises are part of the rowing program year-round. Phase-specific exercises supplement the core exercises. Table 8.2 lists the core and supplemental lifts for the symmetry and hypertrophy phase. These exercises will be familiar to most rowers, but if you need a refresher on proper technique please see the books *Explosive Lifting for Sports* by Harvey Newton (Human Kinetics) and *Strength Training for Young Athletes, Second Edition,* by Kraemer and Fleck (Human Kinetics) for detailed instruction.

You'll do the same core exercises each week but you can change the supplemental exercises from week to week. During the symmetry cycle emphasize dumbbell work and exercises that work the legs independently, like step-ups and split squats.

TABLE 8.2 Core and Supplemental Exercises

Core exercises	Supplemental exercises
Squat, front squat	Step-up, split squat, one-leg squat
Leg press	Dumbbell bench, incline press
Bench pull	Straight-leg deadlift, leg curl
Deadlift	Triceps exercises
Power clean, power snatch	Rotator cuff series
Seated row	Back extension
Arm curl	Pull-up, pull-down, pullover, dumbbell row

TABLE 8.3 Symmetry and Hypertrophy Phase Sample Program

Day 1	Day 2	Day 3	Day 4
Squat	Step-up	Front squat	Split squat
Power clean	Deadlift	Power snatch	Dumbbell incline press
Bench pull	Dumbbell bench press	Dumbbell row	Rotator cuff series
Single-leg curl	Pullover	Dumbbell arm curl	Triceps
Dumbbell arm curl	Seated row	Straight-leg deadlift	Back extension
Abdominals		Abdominals	

Week	Sets × reps	Volume (total reps)	Intensity (% 1RM)	Speed (reps per min)
1	4 × 10	40	60	18
2	4 × 8	32	65	20
3	5 × 6	30	70	22
4	3 × 8	24	50	18
5	5 × 8	40	70	18
6	5 × 7	35	75	20
7	5 × 6	30	80	22
8	3 × 8	24	50	18
9	5 × 8	40	70	22
10	5 × 7	35	75	20
11	5 × 6	30	80	18
12	3 × 8	24	50	18

Rest three to four minutes between each set. Lift and lower weights at the same speed. Retest 1RM following weeks 4, 8, and 12.

Speed   Speed of movement is one of the most important yet neglected variables in strength programs for rowing. Rowers must train for both force and velocity in order to optimize power performance. Strength adaptations are specific to training speed; in other words, training at high velocities increases strength at high velocities and training at low velocities increases strength at low velocities. Rowers need a combination of high- and low-velocity strength.

Rowers possess large percentages of slow twitch fibers that must be trained to produce as much force as possible. Training at a lower velocity allows slow twitch fibers to work, so training velocity during the symmetry and hypertrophy phase is low, 18 to 22 repetitions per minute.

Table 8.3 presents a sample program for the symmetry and hypertrophy phase.

Maximum Strength Phase

Maximum strength is critical at the start of a race, when the boat's momentum is low and the forces required to accelerate the shell are very high. Additionally, increasing maximum strength increases strength endurance. Stronger athletes can work at a lower percentage of their maximum and accomplish the same amount of work as weaker athletes. If an athlete needs to pull with 60 kilograms of force on every stroke during a race and his 1RM in the squat is 100 kilograms, he is working at 60 percent of his maximum strength, which is difficult to maintain for 210 strokes. An athlete whose 1RM in the squat is 150 kilograms only works at 40 percent of his 1RM when he rows with a force of 60 kilograms per stroke, which is much easier to do for 210 strokes. If the stronger athlete rows at 60 percent of his 1RM, he produces 75 kilograms of force on each stroke, making the boat go that much faster.

Duration   The duration of the maximum-strength phase depends on your strength level. If you are close to or exceed the strength goals on page 89, the phase will last 4 to 6 weeks. If you still have a lot of work to do to reach the strength goals, this phase will last 8 to 12 weeks. You need to be close to the strength goals because developing power and power endurance at championship levels depends on a solid base of maximum strength. Even if you are at the strength goal for your level of performance, you may want to spend 8 to 12 weeks working toward the strength goals for the next performance or age group.

Intensity   Intensity is high during this phase. Maximum strength relies not only on the muscular system but also on the nervous system, which activates the muscles. Training with very heavy weights teaches the brain to activate more muscle fibers, allowing you to increase strength without increasing muscle size.

Rowers with at least four years of strength training can use 90 to 95 percent 1RM. Train for two weeks using 90 percent 1RM, then take a one week recovery at 60 percent 1RM. Follow this up with two weeks at 95 percent and then another recovery week. Retest your strength and repeat the process.

Less experienced rowers should follow a pattern similar to that in the symmetry and hypertrophy phase. Start with 80 percent 1RM and increase intensity each week in 2.5 to 5 percent increments until you reach 90 percent 1RM. Make every fourth week a recovery week.

Volume   Because the intensity is quite high, training volume is low. Volume ranges from 3 to 15 repetitions per body part. This does not result in shorter workouts, however, because rest time between sets increases so that you can safely handle heavy weights. Rest periods between sets should be at least 3 to 4 minutes, and should last as long as 7 to 10 minutes if you are using more than 90 percent 1RM.

Exercises   This phase uses the same exercises as the last. Do the rotator cuff series only at 70 to 80 percent 1RM. Higher intensity training could injure this relatively fragile group of muscles.

Speed   Make the movements as explosive as possible in order to stimulate the nervous system. Actual movement speed will not be very fast because the weight is heavy, so the intent to move as fast as possible is crucial.

Table 8.4 gives a sample program for the maximum strength phase.

TABLE 8.4   Maximum Strength Phase Sample Program

Day 1	Day 2	Day 3	Day 4
Squat	Step-up	Front squat	Split squat
Power clean	Deadlift	Power snatch	Dumbbell incline press
Bench pull	Dumbbell bench press	Dumbbell row	Rotator cuff series
Single-leg curl	Pullover	Dumbbell arm curl	Triceps
Dumbbell arm curl	Seated row	Straight-leg deadlift	Back extension
Abdominals		Abdominals	

Week	Sets × reps	Volume (total reps)	Intensity (% 1RM)	Speed (reps per min)
1	3 × 3	9	90	18
2	3 × 2	6	95	20
3	3 × 6	18	70	22
4	4 × 3	12	90	18
5	4 × 2	8	95	18
6	3 × 8	24	70	20

Rest three to four minutes between each set.
Lift and lower weights at the same speed.
Retest 1RM following weeks 3 and 6.

Power Phase

The power phase lasts six to eight weeks and develops rowing-specific power through weight-room and on-water training. The goals of the power phase are to transfer your newly developed weight-room strength to on-water performance and to create a more dynamic leg drive.

Intensity   It is very difficult to measure intensity during on-water strength pieces. If you have a speed coach boat, you can use speed as a rough measure of how hard you are working. The can's size or number of bungee also allow you to compare one training session to the next, but they don't provide hard data on your progress.

Rowers generate different levels of power throughout a race. For this reason, in this phase exercise intensity is periodized, or broken into separate blocks with specific goals. During the first four weeks the rower develops power at high loads, as during the start spurt. Then in the final two to four weeks the rower trains for higher speed, power, and sprinting.

Start on-water power training after you've been on the water for about three weeks. Begin with one session per week and over six weeks gradually increase to a maximum of three sessions. On-water power work is still resistance training, so it should be set up with sets and repetitions. When the emphasis is strength, the sets should be short, 5 to 10 strokes at a very low rate of 8 to 12 strokes per minute for a maximum of 60 strokes. Even though the rate is low you have to be dynamic during the drive, accelerating as fast as possible up the slide to achieve rates of 30 strokes or more. Watch posture and body position when doing on-water power training; it is as much about skill as it is pulling hard.

Dryland training has two purposes during this phase: improving power and maintaining strength. To improve power you will use lighter weights, 40 to 50 percent 1RM lifted explosively. Plyometric exercises with a light medicine ball or body weight can replace squats and deadlifts. Do strength maintenance once a week at an intensity of 80 percent 1RM.

Exercises Resisted rowing is the primary exercise during the power phase. Add resistance to the boat by wrapping bungees around the shell or by tying a can or small bucket to the rigger. Plyometric movements like double-leg long jumps and squat jumps can help create a more dynamic leg drive, but only include jumps if you are close to the strength goals for your performance level. Do the core exercises listed in table 8.2 one to two times per week for strength maintenance.

Speed Power is the combination of strength and speed. The first four weeks develop strength while the last two to four weeks develop speed. During this phase speed of movement approaches or slightly exceeds the stroke rate in racing. The emphasis is on creating explosiveness at the beginning of each movement, which will help develop power early in the stroke cycle. Again, this keeps the strength and power demands of training similar to the demands of racing.

See table 8.5 for a sample program for the power phase.

TABLE 8.5 Power Phase Sample Program

Day 1	Day 2	Day 3
Bungee row	Front squat 4 × 6 at 80% 1RM	Bungee row
6 × 10 at 10 strokes per min	Power clean 4 × 6 at 80% 1RM	6 × 10 at 10 strokes per min
4 × 8 at 8 strokes per min	Bench pull 4 × 6 at 80% 1RM	4 × 250 m starts
	Arm curl 4 × 6 at 80% 1RM	

Rest two to three minutes between sets.
Be as dynamic and explosive as possible during low-rate rowing. A speed coach should keep track of splits.

Power-Endurance Phase

Power endurance is the ability to continue to work at a high power output and depends not only on strength but also on anaerobic fitness and aerobic base. Power-endurance training comes at the end of the precompetitive phase and lasts six weeks into the competitive season (see chapter 9). Power-endurance work trains the energy systems. Some coaches use lower intensity, high-repetition circuits earlier in the year to improve anaerobic threshold or $\dot{V}O_2$max. This type of endurance circuit is appropriate for elite rowers but may detract from the long-term development of rowers who have not yet achieved the appropriate strength goals. For the purposes of this chapter we will focus on the anaerobic energy systems.

Anaerobic training consists of all-out sprints that last anywhere from 10 seconds to 2 minutes. Energy for the initial 20 seconds of the race comes from the anaerobic alactic energy system, which uses the energy (ATP-CP) that is stored in the muscles. You can improve this system either through training or a creatine supplement. While taking a creatine supplement is a fast way to improve the anaerobic alactic system, it often results in water retention and weight gain, which can offset any performance improvement the supplement may provide.

Anaerobic alactic training involves short sprints of 5 to 20 seconds that are done from a stop or while the boat is moving. Add one to two sprint sessions per week about six weeks before major competition begins. You can occasionally practice sprints during winter training, but not more than once a month.

The anaerobic lactic energy system (anaerobic glycolysis) supports the final sprint across the last 300 to 500 meters of the race. Training the anaerobic lactic energy system improves its rate of energy production and increases the body's ability to tolerate lactic acid. Like alactic sprints, anaerobic lactic training begins six to eight weeks before major competition and is done no more than once a week. Keep at least one day between anaerobic training sessions. Table 8.6 outlines training guidelines for both alactic and lactic training.

TABLE 8.6 Anaerobic Training Guidelines

Component	Anaerobic alactic	Anaerobic lactic
Work	5-20 s	20-120 s
Rest	4-6 × work time	5-7 × work time
Pause	5 min	5-10 min
Volume per set	60 s work	120 s work
Total volume	5 sets	3-5 sets

Work refers to the duration of each sprint.

Calculate rest time by multiplying work time by the appropriate number. For example, a 10-second sprint requires 40 to 60 seconds of rest (10 s work × 4-6 s rest).

A pause is a period of active rest following each set.

Each set is 60 or 120 seconds of work. For example, a 10-second sprint requires six repetitions per set (60 s per set, 10 s per sprint).

Strength training has become a crucial part of a rower's training program. Follow this chapter's guidelines for year round strength work and you'll be on your way to decreased risk of injury, improved health, and increased boat speed.

chapter 9

Designing Your Training Plan

Ed McNeely

Being a successful rower is more than just pulling hard. You need to develop many different physiological systems and abilities, including aerobic base, anaerobic threshold, $\dot{V}O_2$max, strength, power, and speed. Some, like strength and $\dot{V}O_2$max, are difficult to improve simultaneously. Trying to improve them both at once can be very frustrating—it keeps both systems from properly developing and it compromises performance.

Carefully planning the year's training ensures optimal progress, and periodization is the best way to accomplish this. Periodization involves breaking the year into blocks that have specific training goals. Each block complements the previous block and prepares you for the next. The main elements of periodization are volume and intensity, which vary in order to provide adequate training stimulus and recovery time.

Determining Training Volume

Training volume refers to the amount of work rowers perform. Many coaches and rowers use meters or kilometers rowed to measure training volume. While this is an acceptable measure it does not always give the full picture. For example, if rower A does a 20-kilometer workout in 90 minutes and rower B covers the same 20 kilometers in 60 minutes, they are not doing the same workout. They won't get the same training effect even though the distance is the same. Time is a better measure of volume because it allows comparison of rowers of different abilities.

Annual training volume directly affects performance (Steinacker et al. 1998). Work, school, and family influence many rowers' training volume, limiting them to four or five hours of training per week. As in almost every sport, you get out of rowing what you put in. Your training goals and time commitment need to match—expecting to win an Olympic medal by rowing six hours per week is as unrealistic as winning a national championship by rowing three hours per week. Table 9.1 shows the training volume that each competitive level demands. To improve within your competition level or move to a higher level you must increase training volume from year to year. Even at the elite level total training volume has steadily increased over the past 30 years, rising from an average of 924 hours per year in the 1970s to 1128 hours per year in the late 1990s, a 20 percent increase (Fiskerstrand and Seiler 2004).

TABLE 9.1 Training Volume by Competitive Level

Competitive level	Training volume (hours per year)
International	800-1200
National	600-800
College or provincial	500-600
Club or high school	300-500
Recreational	200-300

You must increase training volume gradually because rapid increases in volume can lead to overtraining and injuries. This often happens when an athlete makes the jump from one competitive level to another without having trained for the transition the previous year. For example, high school students who move to college programs may double their training volume. College students who move to a national team often find themselves in the same situation, particularly if they make the jump in an Olympic year when training volume is at its highest. As a rule, annual increases in training volume should not exceed 10 percent of the previous year's volume. If you are a high school rower who eventually wants to row at the national level, it will take you at least five years of progressive volume increases to get there. Table 9.2 shows a five-year loading pattern to move from high school to national training volumes.

TABLE 9.2 Annual Increases in Training Volume

Year	Training volume (hours per year)
1	500
2	550
3	605
4	665
5	732

Distributing Training Volume

Selecting the appropriate training volume is the first step in designing your yearly training program. The next step is allocating that time to training types and intensities. There are many ways to determine training intensity. Most methods involve an incremental lactate test and are built around the same physiological points: aerobic threshold, anaerobic threshold, $\dot{V}O_2$max, and peak power. In this chapter aerobic threshold refers to any training at or below 2 millimoles of lactate, typically long-duration, low-intensity work that you can maintain for several hours. Anaerobic threshold refers to training at 2 to 4 millimoles of lactate, an intensity that you can maintain for 40 to 90 minutes. $\dot{V}O_2$max refers to interval training that includes work intervals of 2 to 8 minutes. Peak power refers to strength training and anaerobic sprints for on-water speed development.

The distribution of training volume across these intensities depends on the type of races in which you will compete. 1000-meter racers slightly emphasize high-intensity training, while head racers slightly emphasize low-intensity work. If you race in multiple disciplines it is best to train year-round as a 2000-meter racer.

Intensity distribution has changed substantially over the past 30 or 40 years. There is a much greater emphasis on low-volume endurance work and less emphasis on high-intensity interval training. Aerobic threshold training for elite rowers has increased from 30 to 50 hours per month while $\dot{V}O_2$max interval training has decreased from 23 to 7 hours per month (Fiskerstrand and Seiler 2004). This change allows rowers to better recover between training sessions while maintaining the high volume of work needed to perfect stroke technique. Table 9.3 shows the typical breakdown of training volume by intensity.

TABLE 9.3   Training Volume Distribution by Intensity

Training intensity	Percentage of yearly training volume: 2000-meter racing	Percentage of yearly training volume: 1000-meter racing	Percentage of yearly training volume: head racing
Aerobic threshold	50-55%	30-35%	55-60%
Anaerobic threshold	15-20%	15-20%	25-30%
$\dot{V}O_2$max	5-10%	15-20%	3-5%
Peak power	10-15%	20-25%	5-8%

If you are training 500 hours per year for a 2000-meter race you will spend approximately 275 hours on low-intensity aerobic threshold training, 100 hours on anaerobic threshold training, 50 hours on high-intensity $\dot{V}O_2$max intervals, and 75 hours on strength and anaerobic sprint training.

Setting Up the Year

The year can be broken into logical training periods, including the preparatory phase, the precompetitive phase, the competitive phase, and the transition phase. Table 9.4 shows the breakdown of training by phase and intensity for the athlete who is training 500 hours per year. Percentages of training volume are in parentheses so that you can make calculations based on your own training volume. Note that training volume builds throughout the year, peaking during the precompetitive phase. At the same time training intensity continues to increase. This pattern has started to emerge across many sports over the past decade and is slowly replacing the traditional pattern

TABLE 9.4 **Training Distribution of 500 Hours of Training**

Phase	Phase duration (weeks)	Aerobic threshold	Anaerobic threshold	$\dot{V}O_2$max	Peak power	Hours per week
General preparation	12	70 (25%)	20 (20%)	0	25 (33%)	8.75
Specific preparation	12	75 (27%)	35 (35%)	5 (10%)	20 (27%)	11.25
Precompetition	12	95 (35%)	25 (25%)	15 (30%)	20 (27%)	13.0
Competition	8	35 (13%)	20 (20%)	30 (60%)	10 (13%)	11.9
Transition	8	0	0	0	0	0

of volume decreasing while intensity increases. This change is at least partly due to better nutrition and recovery practices.

Preparatory Phase

The preparatory phase falls at the beginning of the training year. This phase consists of the general preparation and specific preparation periods. General preparation is the first and longest of the two, lasting anywhere from 12 to 16 weeks. The goals of the general preparation period are to improve weaknesses and to build a base for the more intense specific preparation. This phase emphasizes strength training, flexibility, and aerobic conditioning. A long, productive general preparation period allows the athlete to peak in major competitions.

Training volume tends to be slightly lower during the general preparation period. Rowers do about 60 percent of aerobic training at or below the aerobic threshold in the form of long, steady-state workouts of 60 minutes or more. Rowers can use cross-training during the general preparation period to alleviate boredom and prevent overuse injuries. Cross-training can make up 50 percent of aerobic threshold training.

The specific preparation period lasts 8 to 16 weeks and takes advantage of the base the rowers developed during the general preparation period. Their newly acquired fitness is put to work in rowing-specific situations. This period emphasizes rowing-specific aerobic, anaerobic, and power work. During this period training volume increases, rowers do more work near the anaerobic threshold, and cross-training volume decreases to 10 percent of training. This period includes strength maintenance sessions one or two times per week.

The preparation phase is the ideal time to work on skill. Since work volume is high but intensity is low, the athletes should not experience the high levels of fatigue that negatively affect skill development. The general preparation period is an excellent time to work on individual parts of a skill, such as body position during the leg drive or feathering the blade, while the specific preparation period is a good time to work on the overall skill.

Precompetitive Phase

The precompetitive phase, or preseason, lasts four to eight weeks. Training volume peaks during the precompetitive phase and intensity continues to build. Low-intensity

The general preparation phase is the best time to work on specific parts of skills.

aerobic threshold training continues to account for about 60 percent of training time but it includes intervals done just above and just below anaerobic threshold, with about 1 1/4 hours per week dedicated to race-pace intervals. Strength training in the weight room features full-body maintenance sessions, but in general strength training focuses more on water work and anaerobic sprint training.

Competitive Phase

Design the competitive phase of the training plan first; the lengths of all other phases depend upon this one. Choose three or four main competitions for the year and then one or two minor competitions for practicing race plans. When the competitive season is very long because of the scheduling of the main competitions, you can break it into early and late competitive periods. The early competitive period is an extension of the precompetitive phase, focusing on physical preparation. The main competition of the year normally falls at the end of the competitive phase.

The goal of training during the competitive phase is to develop boat speed and rowing-specific power. The volume of low-intensity work drops to about 35 percent of total training hours. About 31 percent of training volume is dedicated to race-pace intervals, some of which are done in minor races.

One of the characteristics of the competitive phase is the taper, a period of decreased training volume and increased intensity that allows you to fully recover and adapt to the year's training. A well-designed taper can increase performance anywhere from 3 to 11 percent (Houmard et al. 1994; Johns et al. 1992; Zarkadas, Carter, and Banister 1994).

Not every athlete benefits from tapering. Before you start planning, consider your need for a taper. Novices with limited training experience won't see much improvement from a taper. Most novices haven't mastered the technical skills to the point that they will be limited by their fitness. Instead they'll benefit from a high volume of skill and tactical training with one or two days off just before the race.

Athletes training less than six hours per week also won't benefit much from a true taper. These athletes can take a day or two off right before a race and recover sufficiently to race at their best. If you are in this category, you may want to plan a short sprint session on the last training day before the competition, focusing on starts and sprints of up to 500 meters. This training session is the last of the week before two days of rest right before the race.

Choosing your races for the year is the first step in designing your taper. You can use tapers before most competitions or tests that are part of team selection, but use only one major taper and no more than three or four minor tapers per year. Tapering more frequently decreases yearly training volume to the point that performance suffers.

If you are racing in more than eight competitions per year, think of the extra races as hard training sessions. Focus on a specific technical or tactical aspect of the race rather than just wins and losses. For instance, you may want to work on your start or your ability to make a move in the final 500. These minor races will help you refine your training program and create a better race plan for major competitions.

Minor Taper   Use the minor taper before tests and less important races like club events that aren't qualifiers. The length of the minor taper depends on normal training volume. Athletes training 6 to 10 hours per week take one day completely off before the test or race, those training 10 to 15 hours per week use a three-day taper, and those training more than 15 hours per week use a five-day taper. Table 9.5 shows a typical minor taper.

TABLE 9.5   Minor Taper

Taper	Day 1	Day 2	Day 3	Day 4	Day 5
One-day	OFF				
Three-day	OFF	5 × 150 m, 20 min paddle	3 × 250 m, 20 min paddle		
Five-day	3 × 1500 m just below race pace	45 min steady-state paddle	5 × 10 stroke starts, 3 × 500 m, 1 × 1500 m, 20 min paddle	4 × 500 m, 30 min paddle	4 × 250 m, 30 min paddle

Major taper   Use the major taper before the year's main competition. Because of its duration only use the major taper once a year.

Duration   Rowers who are training more than six hours per week and are not novices need to plan their major taper according to work volume. Table 9.6 gives some guidelines for the duration of a major taper.

During a taper, training volume progressively decreases by about 70 percent. If you train 10 hours per week and are doing a seven-day taper, you will only train about 3 hours that week. The decrease in volume is not accomplished in one cut; it is progressive. If you are doing a longer taper you may want to consider the progression in table 9.7.

TABLE 9.6   Major Taper Duration

Training hours per week	Major taper
6-10	7 days
10-15	14 days
15+	21-30 days

TABLE 9.7   Taper Percentage Decreases in Volume

Training hours per week	Training hours first taper week	Training hours second taper week	Training hours third taper week
6-10	Decrease by 70%	-----	-----
10-15	Decrease by 45%	Decrease by 70%	-----
15+	Decrease by 30%	Decrease by 50%	Decrease by 70%

Frequency   The number of workouts per week does not decrease during a major taper; the duration of each workout decreases. The goal of tapering is recovery and regeneration, and it is easier to recover from a short workout because it does not fully deplete energy stores. Longer, less frequent sessions do not allow the athletes to fully recover or adapt to the training, particularly since intensity increases during the taper. Less frequent training negatively affects technical performance because athletes start to lose the "feel" for rowing.

Intensity   Intensity increases as training volume decreases. Steady-state work is gradually replaced by higher intensity intervals, short sprints, and starts. By the final week almost all training is at or above the anaerobic threshold. The final week of a taper might look something like table 9.8.

The effects of the sprint work in the last two days are more psychological than physiological. Sprints give the athletes a feeling of speed, power, and confidence that they can take with them into race day. This means it is important for the final training

TABLE 9.8   Major Taper: The Final Week

Monday	Tuesday	Wednesday	Thursday	Friday	Saturday	Sunday
40 min easy steady-state	4 × 5 min above anaerobic threshold, 10 min rest between	5 × 2 min, 30 min easy steady-state	OFF	4-6 × 250 m sprints, 10 min easy between	4 × 2 min at race pace, 5 min easy between	RACE

session to leave the athletes feeling energized, not fatigued. Ideally this final training session takes place on the race course so that the crew can familiarize themselves with the course.

Special Considerations   You should practice tapering at least once before the major competition of the year. It is not necessary to practice a full 21-day taper, but you must do the final week at least once, before a less important competition. This gives you an opportunity to adjust the taper to your individual needs and experiment with different combinations of intervals and sprints.

The taper can be a time of high psychological stress for both the coach and athletes. Coaches tend to worry about the season's overall training, the duration of the taper, and many other concerns that arise before a major competition. It is important for the coach to project confidence both in the season's training and in the taper. If the coach is openly worried about the athletes' preparation or starts making changes to a planned taper, the athletes may begin to question their preparedness and ability to win.

Athletes handle decreased training volume differently. Many athletes enjoy the feelings of speed, power, and renewed energy. Others worry about detraining and don't know how to cope with the extra time they have on their hands as a result of the decreased volume. Coaches need to be aware of each athlete's response and be prepared to deal with the worriers.

Transition Phase

The transition phase is the time between the last race of the season and the beginning of serious training for the next season. It lasts four to eight weeks depending on the length of the racing schedule and the rower's level. Some international competitors take four or five months off following the Olympic Games because of the huge volume of training the Games require. Regardless of your competitive level, if you want to improve you need to have a transition plan.

There are four components to a successful transition: rest, rehabilitation, prehabilitation, and cross-training.

Rest   A period of rest immediately following the season provides both a physical and psychological break from the rigors of training and competition. To avoid losing your hard-earned fitness, the rest period should not exceed two weeks. During this time you don't do any form of training. This is the time to catch up with family and friends, do some light yard work, and put your boat away for the winter.

Rehabilitation   Aches, pains, and injuries are an accepted fact of sport. Some are acute and you know exactly when they happen, while others creep up over time as a result of overuse. Immediately following the rest period you should seek medical attention for these aches and pains. Medical attention should be sought for acute injuries immediately following the season; the soreness that normally develops from a hard racing season may make it difficult to diagnose underlying problems. While rest may relieve many of the symptoms, it doesn't correct the problem. A therapist can help you overcome chronic muscle spasm and relieve recurring pain.

Prehabilitation   Prehabilitation means taking care of injuries before they happen. Strength and flexibility imbalances are a leading cause of injury, and rowers have to correct imbalances by strengthening weak muscles or working the weaker side of the body a little more. Sweep rowers are particularly vulnerable to bilateral asymmetries, or strength differences between the right and left side of the body. Studies have reported significant strength differences between oarside and non-oarside legs as well as between the right and left erector spinae, the large muscles running parallel to the spine. If uncorrected, these imbalances can result in chronic back pain or injury. The strength ratio between the quadriceps and hamstrings can be a problem for both sweep rowers and scullers. Rowers tend to have relatively weak hamstrings, which can change the mechanics of the pelvis during the stroke and cause back pain. The hamstrings should be at least 70 percent as strong as the quadriceps.

These are the most common imbalances in rowers, but most people have unique imbalances. An athletic therapist or physiotherapist can help you identify and correct your particular pattern of imbalance.

Cross-Training As soon as you begin the prehabilitation period you can also start cross-training. Training volume for cross-training should be 50 to 70 percent of training volume during the rowing months. If you train six hours a week during the year you need to do three to four hours of cross-training per week during the transition phase. This allows you to maintain aerobic fitness and still recover from the previous season. Any cross-training activity is fine, but swimming is particularly good for maintaining upper-body endurance.

Keep the intensity low during the transition. You should not feel fatigued after cross-training. If you can carry on a normal conversation while training, you are at the right intensity.

One last piece of advice: Good record keeping is a must when designing your program, and a training log is a must during the season. Planning your year will take some time, but it is the only way to ensure that you are training the appropriate systems at the appropriate times. I think you'll find the effort well worth the rewards.

part II

Technique

chapter 10

Rowing Biomechanics

Margaret McBride

The rower's primary goal is to achieve maximal average boat velocity for the duration of the race. This goal is simple, yet it is difficult to achieve. The rowing stroke is a complex, dynamic interaction between athletes, oars, boat, and water. The challenge of rowing is working around the factors that affect boat velocity.

In the past, rowers improved technique with the help of skilled coaches who visually assessed the athletes and experimented with changes in technique and equipment. Knowledge of mechanical principles, judicious use of stopwatch and video, and trial and error produced significant improvements in rowing performance. However, this process was limited by the inability to precisely quantify specific aspects of individual and crew technique while measuring instantaneous boat velocity. This prevented coaches from establishing definite links between technique and boat speed.

The science of rowing biomechanics is devoted to giving coaches the data they need to analyze technique and boat speed. It deals with the precise measurement of forces and the resulting motion of the athlete, oars, and boat. It develops theoretical models to explain and optimize the complex interactions between athletes and equipment. Recent advances in technology allow scientists to simultaneously monitor oar force, oar position, footstretcher force, and motion of the sliding seat for each rower. Today's technology correlates these variables with instantaneous boat velocity and immediately displays the information on a computer in the motorboat, allowing coaches to associate the rower's actions with fluctuations in boat velocity.

Scientists have spent years creating instruments for obtaining immediate results while rowing on the water. The next step was working with rowing coaches to identify performance indexes, present them in a meaningful fashion, and then use the results to evaluate and optimize rowing technique.

Coaches with access to biomechanics technology are now able to identify factors that limit rowing performance, reinforce positive technique modifications, and abandon unsuccessful ones. Biomechanical feedback can help coaches develop innovative models of efficient technique. It can also improve efficiency by allowing coaches to adapt equipment design, gearing, crew selection, and race strategy.

The Rowing Stroke

Many factors affect the final time in a rowing race, but successful performance ultimately depends on average boat velocity over the 2000-meter race distance. The average velocity of the boat during each stroke depends on stroke rate and distance traveled during the stroke cycle (figure 10.1).

Rowers can influence distance in the pull phase of the stroke by altering the force they apply to the oar, the arc traveled by the oar, and the duration of the pull. Equipment can affect pull distance through blade design; aerodynamic drag on the oars, boat, and athletes; and hydrodynamic drag on the submerged portion of the shell (Dal Monte and Komor 1989).

During the recovery phase of the stroke, the athlete cannot apply propulsive force to the oar. However, the crew's mass and the velocity of each rower's center of gravity as they approach the catch position can dramatically alter recovery distance (the distance traveled by the boat during this period). Inertial forces, recovery duration, and air and water resistance also influence recovery distance (Schneider and Hauser 1981; Spinks 1996). In addressing the hierarchy of variables that may limit rowing performance, researchers have focused on factors associated with the drive phase while analysis of the recovery phase has been largely overlooked. A typical analysis may include multi-oar evaluation of peak force, stroke length, work per stroke, boat velocity, and a variety of temporal characteristics such as the time taken to reach maximum oar force (Asami et al. 1978; Ishiko, Katamoto, and Maeshima 1983; Gerber et al. 1987; Dal Monte and Komor 1989; Hartmann et al. 1993).

Biomechanical Assessment of Rowing

A multitude of interrelated parameters affect final race time, and biomechanists have developed methods to measure many of these factors. However, scientists attempting to obtain this on-water rowing data have to overcome a series of challenges. The instrumentation must not alter the orientation or height of the oar or the rower's position in the boat. The sensors must be lightweight, waterproof, portable, sturdy, and battery powered. Finally, results must be immediately available to the coach and biomechanist so that they can establish relationships between measured variables and visual cues that the coach detects. Real-time visual feedback can accelerate the

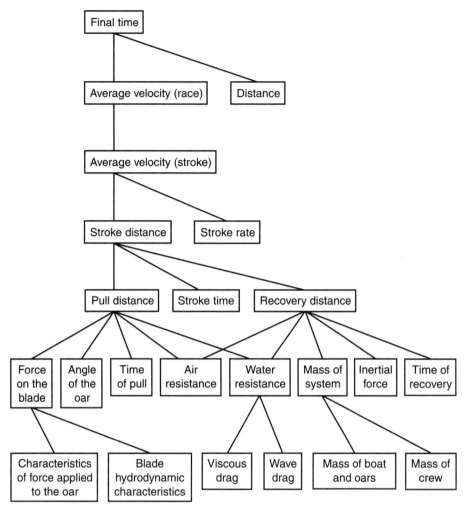

FIGURE 10.1 Basic factors that influence rowing performance (Dal Monte and Komor 1989; adapted from Schneider and Hauser 1981).

Adapted, by permission, from E. Schneider and M. Hauser, 1981, *Biomechanical analysis of performance in rowing*, edited by A. Morecki, K. Kedzior, and A. Wit (Baltimore, MD: University Park Press), 430-435.

learning process by immediately reinforcing technique changes that are linked to improved boat velocity (Smith and Loschner 2000).

Biomechanical analysis of on-water rowing dates back to 1860 with kinematic descriptions of the typical rowing pattern (Bachev, Tsvetkov, and Boichev 1989). Research soon turned to the measurement of oar force as the main factor in propulsion (Bompa, Hebbelinck, and Van Gheluwe 1985; Dal Monte and Komor 1989; Smith and Spinks 1995). Atkinson in 1898 and Lefeuvre and Pailliotte in 1904 developed early methods of measuring oarlock forces (Nolte 1984; Dal Monte and Komor 1989; Affeld, Schichl, and Ziemann 1993). Although these variables are still relevant today, the methods used to obtain, store, and analyze data from the rowing shell have evolved considerably in the past hundred years.

Baird and Soroka (1951) modified riggers in an eight-oared racing shell to measure propulsive forces on the oarlocks using strain gauges. They put the heavy equipment for recording and storing data in a trailing motorboat and had an umbilical cable connected to the rowing shell. This created an artificial environment that may have influenced boat movement and the rowers' technique.

In 1971, Ishiko used an FM transmitter to send data to a land-based recorder where the data could be stored for later analysis. This breakthrough eliminated the hard wire connection to the boat, making it possible to measure rowing performance with minimal disruption to the athlete's environment. However, data were not immediately available, limiting the ability to utilize biomechanical details to modify technique during the training session.

Schneider, Angst, and Brandt (1978a) further advanced biomechanical analysis by combining strain-gauge measurements of oar force with oar angle and boat acceleration. This information was transmitted to a motorboat where the coach could see immediate results on an eight-channel oscilloscope.

Today, the most advanced telemetry systems take measurements more than 100 times a second from over 20 variables with a transmission range over 2 kilometers (Gerber et al. 1987; Smith, Spinks, and Moncrieff 1988; Kleshnev 2000; McBride, Sanderson, and Elliott 2001).

Researchers have also used linear proximity sensors mounted to the inboard portion of the oar to determine oar force by the bend in the oar under load (Gerber et al. 1987; Smith, Spinks, and Moncrieff 1988). Shortcomings of this method include the time required to instrument and calibrate each oar and the inability to change the oars or alter the equipment during the test session. Researchers have used rubber band electrogoniometry to measure oar angular displacement, and turbines and impellers to measure boat velocity (Schneider, Angst, and Brandt 1978a; Smith, Spinks, and Moncrieff 1988; Duchesnes et al. 1989).

Although oar force during the drive phase of the stroke is critical, individual and combined crew technique during the recovery phase has a significant impact on range of velocity fluctuations within a stroke. Variables that can affect boat velocity during the recovery phase include reactive force at the footplate (Körndle and Lippens 1988; Smith and Loschner 2000) as well as instantaneous position and velocity of each sliding seat (McBride 1998; Loschner, Smith, and Galloway 2000).

Several researchers have met the challenge of measuring forces on the footplate. Nolte (1991) provided graphs from German research illustrating the horizontal and vertical forces on the footplates in conjunction with oarlock force measurements but gave no information regarding instrumentation methods or interpretation of results. Körndle and Lippens (1988) found that footplate force measurements help detect differences in force produced by a sweep rower's inside leg and outside leg. Researchers have also measured footplate force in order to evaluate power production (Kleshnev 2000; Smith and Loschner 2000).

Scientists have also evaluated boat motion during the drive and recovery phases using accelerometers mounted to the hull of the boat. This method allows researchers to quantify rapid changes in velocity at the catch that adversely affect average boat velocity (Nolte 1984; Pelham et al. 1993; Kleshnev 2000).

Loschner, Smith, and Galloway (2000) used tri-axial gyroscopes to describe the boat orientation in three dimensions. They found that yaw, pitch, and roll depend on athlete mass, skill, and weather conditions. Wagner, Bartmus, and de Marees (1993) have provided rolling and yawing data in conjunction with the force differential between the left and right oar of a single scull but do not relate these measurements to instantaneous boat velocity.

Over the years, researchers have devoted a great deal of effort to developing instrumentation systems that precisely measure rowing performance. However, this technology is meaningless without the ability to interpret the results and apply them to the practical task of improving boat velocity.

Oar Motion

The oar is a lever used to increase the rower's mechanical advantage when propelling the boat. Gearing, oar length, blade area, and blade shape determine the oar's effectiveness.

When the oar moves through the air during the recovery phase, it travels in an arc about a fulcrum created by the oarlock pin. When the oar is underwater during the pull phase of the stroke, many rowers visualize their oar locking into a pocket of water that becomes the fulcrum about which the oar and boat move. This visualization is incorrect; water is a fluid medium and therefore can't act as a fixed fulcrum. In fact, the pulling force on the submerged oar sets the water in motion, causing both the oarlock pin and the tip of the oar to translate. Oar manufacturers strive to maximize translation of the oarlock pin and minimize blade movement. However, boat propulsion is not possible without movement of the blade both laterally (away from the boat) and in a direction parallel to the boat's motion.

Kinematical analysis allows researchers to trace the path of the blade tip (figure 10.2). In the analyzed stroke of a single at race pace, the tip of the blade slices through

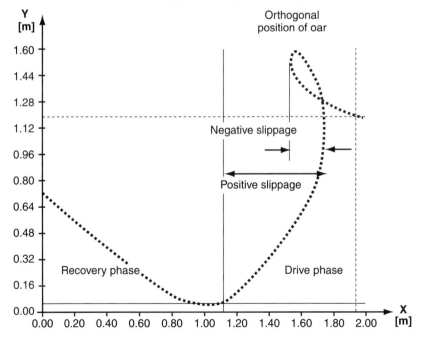

FIGURE 10.2   The tip of the blade's path in the water during the stroke cycle as the boat moves from left to right. Following the catch (vertical line), the submerged oar demonstrates simultaneous x and y translation (adapted from Nolte 1984).

Adapted, by permission, from V. Nolte, 1984, *Die Effektivitat des ruderschlages (the efficiency of the rowing stroke)* (Berlin, Germany: Bartels and Wernitz).

the water in the same direction as the boat (X-direction) for the first 42.3 percent of the pull phase (Nolte 1993). At the same time, the blade must move laterally until it reaches the orthogonal position (maximum displacement in the y-axis direction). Movement of the oar in the same direction as the boat is called positive slip (Nolte 1993).

For the next 42.3 percent of the pull phase, the blade moves in the direction opposite that of the boat, called negative slip. The magnitude of the negative slip is estimated to be 30 to 35 centimeters per stroke for a men's eight rowing at 38 strokes per minute (Lueneburger 1995). This negative slip has been associated with a decrease in the rower's power to propel the boat (Affeld, Schichl, and Ziemann 1993). Once the oar passes through the orthogonal position, the blade moves laterally (toward the boat) until it comes out of the water. During the final 15.4 percent of the pull phase, the rower pulls the oar through the water in the same direction as the boat's movement (Nolte 1993).

This pattern of oar motion is evident in all rowers and scullers. Oar manufacturers have modified the size and shape of the blade with the goal of minimizing slippage and increasing propulsive efficiency (Carter, Pelham, and Holt 1993; Nolte 1993). However, some researchers believe that positive slippage during the first phase of the stroke actually facilitates boat motion by generating propulsive lift force on the blade (Nolte 1984; Affeld, Schichl, and Ziemann 1993; Nolte 1993).

Blade Forces

Regardless of the object moving through a fluid, hydrodynamic resistance consists of two perpendicular components: drag force and lift force. The drag force vector is always parallel to the flow of fluid over the object and acts to oppose motion. In contrast, lift force is perpendicular to the flow of fluid and may assist movement of the object in some circumstances.

Drag Force

The negative effect of drag force on the hull of the boat is most evident when the boat slows down when the athletes cease rowing. However, drag force also offers essential resistance to the submerged oar that the rower can lever against to propel the boat. An increase in the amount of blade surface area exposed to the flow of water will increase the amount of drag force. Therefore, drag force is at its maximum when the oar is at a right angle to the water flow (when the oar is perpendicular to the boat). In addition, relative velocity, or the difference between the velocity of the blade and the velocity of the water flowing past the blade, dramatically affects drag force on the blade. Drag force increases in proportion to the square of the relative velocity. The influence of relative velocity is evident in the difference in perceived load when rowing with or against a strong current.

Many researchers have identified drag force as the dominant propulsive force in rowing, prompting coaches to predict that pulling force on the oar is most effective when the oar is perpendicular to the boat (Herberger 1989; Affeld, Schichl, and Ziemann 1993). However, if the blade translates in the positive x-axis direction for the first 42.3 percent of the pull phase, drag force cannot fully account for boat propulsion (Nolte 1993). Further, if only drag force propelled the boat, technique would evolve to shorter strokes with a reduced arc on either side of the orthogonal position.

Lift Force

The asymmetrical, hydrofoil shape of the blade; the high relative velocity of the water over the blade; and the angle of attack have caused some researchers to speculate that hydrodynamic lift forces may significantly contribute to boat velocity (Nolte 1984; Affeld, Schichl, and Ziemann 1993; Nolte 1993). The angle formed between the blade and the direction of water flow, called the angle of attack, causes a difference in the velocity of the water flowing over each side of the oar as it passes through the water. The different velocities result in lower pressure on the back side of the blade, which creates a hydrodynamic lift force that pulls on the posterior surface of the blade (Nolte 1993) (figure 10.3). According to this theory, lift force reaches maximum values at the catch and finish of the stroke (Kleshnev 2001).

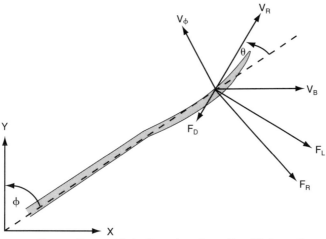

FIGURE 10.3 Forces acting on the oar blade (F_D = drag force; F_L = lift force; F_R = resultant blade force; θ = angle of attack; ϕ = oar angle; V_ϕ = linear velocity of the blade as a result of oar rotation; V_B = linear velocity of the boat).

Although there is a solid rationale for lift forces on the rowing blade, the dynamic and challenging environment of rowing makes it difficult to scientifically confirm their existence. However, attempts to determine blade forces indirectly through boat velocity, oar velocity, and athlete moment of force calculations indicate that lift force is acting on the blade surface (Affeld, Schichl, and Ziemann 1993; Kleshnev 1999). Supporters of this theory claim that lift force substantially contributes to boat propulsion when the blade is at certain oar angles (figure 10.4). In addition, successful elite scullers frequently use extremely large catch angles. Perhaps these athletes are using lift force on the blade to optimize the magnitude and direction of the resultant force vector on the blade.

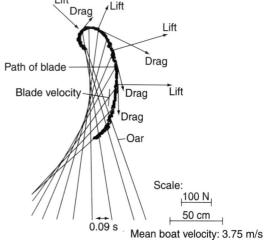

FIGURE 10.4 The blade's path during the propulsive phase and the resultant lift and drag forces (Affeld, Schichl, and Ziemann 1993).

International Journal Sports Med: from K. Affled, K. Schichl, and A. Zieman. *Assessment of rowing efficiency,* 1993: 14:S39-S41. Reprinted by permission.

Resultant Force

Resultant blade force (F_R) is the summation of all forces acting on the blade, and this is what rowers feel when they "lock on" to the water. Resultant blade force is assumed to be at right angles to the blade surface, acting as the center of the blade. As the oar travels through the water, the angle of attack and the relative velocity between the blade and water are constantly changing. As a result, the ratio of drag and lift forces on the blade force will vary throughout the stroke. The relative contributions of all forces acting on the blade at any time will determine the orientation of the resultant force vector (figure 10.5).

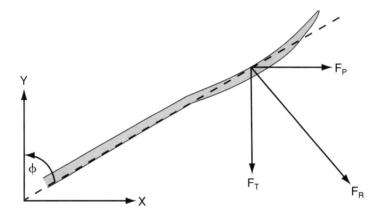

FIGURE 10.5   Resultant oar forces acting on the oar blade (F_R = resultant blade force; θ = angle of attack; F_P = propulsive force; F_T = transverse force).

Lift force likely dominates the resultant blade force at the beginning and end of the stroke (when the angle of attack is low) and drag force dominates at the middle of the stroke (when the angle of attack is large). The existence of lift force may cause the resultant force vector to be more optimally aligned, resulting in a more effective propulsive blade force and improved boat velocity during the stroke. Further research on these forces would prove beneficial to both oar manufacturers and rowing coaches.

A rower can achieve a firmer lock on the water by improving drag force (increasing blade surface area), enhancing lift force (increasing catch angle), and increasing relative velocity between the blade and the water (optimizing catch timing).

Propulsive and Transverse Oar Force

During each stroke, the oar travels through an elliptical path so that at any time, only a portion of the resultant blade force will act parallel to the longitudinal axis of the boat and therefore contribute to boat propulsion (propulsive force in figure 10.5). A second portion of the resultant blade force acts in a direction that is perpendicular to boat motion and introduces a rotational (turning) component that is not involved in boat propulsion. Vector resolution allows us to calculate the relative contributions of the propulsive (F_P) and transverse (F_T) components of the blade resultant force.

It is not possible to completely eliminate the nonpropulsive component of the resultant force on the oar, but optimizing the relationship between the two components of the resultant blade force during the drive phase may improve average boat velocity. Manipulation of the net ratio between the lift and drag components of water resistance could influence the proportion of the resultant blade force that serves to propel the boat.

Oar Force

Over the past decade, researchers have evaluated rowing technique by analyzing the shape and characteristics of individual force-angle graphs (Dal Monte and Komor 1989; Roth et al. 1993; Spinks 1996). This allows researchers to superimpose several consecutive cycles of data on the same graph (figure 10.6). In a standard graph of oar angle, zero degrees occurs when the oar is perpendicular to the longitudinal axis of the boat. Negative oar angles occur early in the stroke as the oar moves from the catch to the orthogonal position (in front of the pin), and positive oar angles occur as the oar moves toward the finish position (behind the pin).

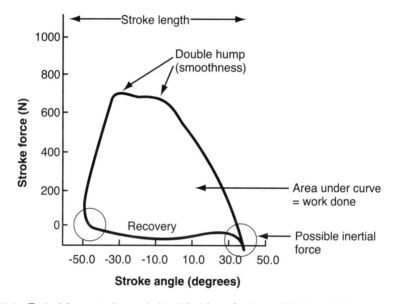

FIGURE 10.6 Typical force-angle graph (modified from Smith and Spinks 1989).

Reprinted, by permission, from R. Smith and W. Spinks, 1989, "Matching technology to coaching needs: on water rowing analysis." In *Proceedings of the VIIth international symposium of the society of biomechanics in sports,* edited by W.E. Morrison, (Melbourne, Australia: Footscray Institute of Technology), 277-287.

By plotting oar force against oar angle, the area under the curve represents the stroke's work output. The strength and coordination of the leg, back, and arm motions influence the size and shape of the force-angle profile, or total work output. An explosive leg drive at the catch may produce a steep slope in the force-angle profile that may be advantageous to power development (Schwanitz 1991). Any technique changes are reflected in the shape, size, and smoothness of the force-angle profile. In 1987, Millward questioned whether it would be possible to train a rower to achieve a specific force-curve shape that would improve boat speed. With recent advances in rowing biomechanics and the ability to provide immediate visual feedback to the athlete, this level of intervention may be possible.

The majority of published research comments on the significance of various force curves and the ideal pattern of force application but still focuses on objective description of rowing technique (Gerber et al. 1987; Dal Monte and Komor 1989). Most researchers do not correlate results to intrastroke fluctuations in boat velocity, and although theoretical models exist, most overlook the complex interaction between individual or crew technique and the impact on instantaneous boat velocity.

Researchers have assumed that optimal boat propulsion results from a uniform pattern of force application from all crew members (Asami et al. 1978; Wing and Woodburn 1995). It has been expected that similar force-time profiles would minimize turning moments on the boat that result from unequal forces (Wing and Woodburn 1995). Schneider, Morell, and Sidler (1978b) describe the selection of crew members based on similarities in force-time profiles. However, biomechanical analysis of on-water trials has revealed considerable force-time variations even within an elite crew (Ishiko 1971; Mason, Shakespear, and Doherty 1988; Smith et al. 1994).

Other researchers believe that effective boat propulsion in a two-oared sweep boat requires each rower's force-time profile to be different in shape, power, and timing (Roth 1991; Zatsiorsky and Yakunin 1991; Hill 2002). Each seat requires its own specific technique. To reduce intracycle deviations off course, the rower in the stern of the boat must emphasize the early and mid-drive period and reach a greater peak force than the bow-seat rower (Schneider, Angst, and Brandt 1978a; Zatsiorsky and Yakunin 1991; Roth et al. 1993). Most experienced pair rowers recognize the turning advantage of the bow-seat rower. This is primarily due to the position of the oarlocks relative to the fin and the moving mass of the crew during the stroke (Schneider, Angst, and Brandt 1978a). Figure 10.7 shows the theoretical force-angle curves for each position in a coxless pair.

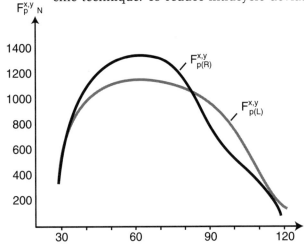

FIGURE 10.7 The theoretical force-angle curve for stroke-seat rowers ($F^{x,y}_{p\,(R)}$) and bow–seat rowers ($F^{x,y}_{p\,(L)}$) in a coxless pair (modified from Zatsiorsky and Yakunin 1991).

Adapted, by permission, from V.M. Zatsiorsky and N. Yakunin, 1991, "Mechanics and biomechanics of rowing: a review," Int J Sport Biomech 7:229-281.

Roth et al. (1993) theorize that the highly specialized force-time curves result in unique physiological demands for each seat position. Their results indicate that stroke-seat rowers have higher metabolic rates (blood lactic acid, oxygen consumption, heart rate) than bow-seat rowers, and each position has specific muscle morphology (Roth et al. 1993).

McBride, Sanderson, and Elliott (2001) supported this theory with a multistage biomechanical analysis of 10 national men's pairs. The fastest crew demonstrated the classic seat-specific technique, but not all successful crews displayed this pattern. To further test the theory, they created a new crew of two rowers who demonstrated the ideal seat-specific technique. After five training sessions, their boat velocity was 14.25 seconds faster over 2,000 meters compared to four unaltered crews. In contrast, a crew of two rowers with similar technique produced an estimated race time that was 6.1 seconds slower than the control group.

Boat Velocity

The modern rowing shell has footplates and riggers fixed to the hull and a sliding, wheeled seat on tracks. These features allow rowers to use the strong extensor muscles of the legs and trunk to generate propulsive force while increasing the arc of the oar through the water. Unfortunately, the movement of the rowers and oars combined with intermittent force on the oar and drag on the boat create significant oscillations in instantaneous boat velocity during each stroke cycle (Celentano et al. 1974; Martin and Bernfield 1980; Zatsiorsky and Yakunin 1991).

Hydrodynamic drag increases proportionally to boat velocity raised to the second power, so the ideal technique eliminates oscillations in boat velocity and maintains constant boat velocity during each stroke. This is impossible to achieve, however, so efforts must be made to reduce the difference between maximum and minimum boat velocity. Amplitude of boat velocity fluctuations is one of the most important factors in rowing performance (Dal Monte and Komor 1989).

Although it is obvious that boat velocity varies during each rowing stroke, it is incorrect to assume that velocity does not increase during the propulsive phase (when the oars are in the water) and decrease during the recovery phase. Biomechanical analysis shows that movement of the rowers and oars with or against the direction of the hull dramatically affects the motion of the shell. This is evident to spectators watching the bows cross the finish line in a close race. The crew that approaches the line during the early recovery phase (when the oars are out of the water) will experience an obvious surge in boat velocity and will cross the line before opponents in the drive phase.

Biomechanical analysis can explain this apparent anomaly. Each component of the rower–boat–oar system moves at a different velocity and has its own center of gravity that moves relative to the other components during the stroke cycle. The horizontal momentum of each component is the product of its mass and horizontal velocity. Because the total mass of the rowers may be four to seven times greater than the mass of the hull (Pannell 1979; Martin and Bernfield 1980), and because this mass can experience rapid changes in horizontal velocity (especially at the catch), the rowers' momentum can significantly affect boat velocity. For this reason, rowers strive to minimize horizontal displacement and acceleration of their center of gravity during the drive and recovery phases (Nolte 1993). Figure 10.8 summarizes the velocity oscillations for a single scull, but a similar pattern exists for all boat categories.

Maximum boat velocity occurs during the recovery phase of the stroke cycle (Pope 1973; Martin and Bernfield 1980; Affeld, Schichl, and Ziemann 1993). It is during this phase that the oars are out of the water and the rowers' bodies are moving in a direction opposite that of the boat. Although the boat is accelerating relative to the water during the early recovery phase, the total system is decelerating. A significant forward reaction force acts on the relatively light rowing shell as the combined mass of up to eight rowers starts to move toward the stern of the boat. This force momentarily exceeds the persistent hydrodynamic drag on the shell and the boat accelerates. Eventually, the rowers' forward velocity declines as they approach the front of the slide and their combined horizontal momentum decreases. As a result, drag forces once again exceed the forward reactive force of the rowers and boat velocity rapidly decreases (Martin and Bernfield 1980).

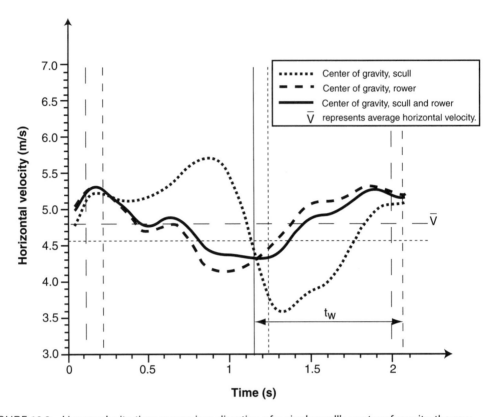

FIGURE 10.8 Linear velocity-time course in x-direction of a single scull's center of gravity, the rower's center of gravity, and the rower and boat together when t_w represents the drive (Nolte 1984).

Adapted, by permission, from V. Nolte, 1984, *Die Effektivitat des ruderschlages (the efficiency of the rowing stroke)* (Berlin, Germany: Bartels and Wernitz).

The rowing shell velocity continues to decrease after the oars enter the water, reaching a minimum velocity approximately 17 percent into the drive phase. Martin and Bernfield (1980) concluded that several factors contributed to this phenomenon. First, they disregarded the possibility of lift force and claimed that the oars are in an inefficient position at the beginning of the stroke. They felt that a large proportion of the oar force is oriented away from the boat in the early drive phase and is therefore nonpropulsive. Second, the force generated on the footplate must accelerate the mass of the rowers toward the bow of the boat, causing the boat to move toward the stern. When the explosive push on the footplate occurs before oar submersion, the negative effect on boat velocity is obvious.

If rowers could modify technique to extend the periods at which boat velocity is above the mean value, they could improve overall boat velocity. In a study of eight men's coxless pairs, McBride (1998) found that boat velocity exceeded the mean value for 62.6 ± 2.1 percent of the stroke cycle, and the duration for which instantaneous boat velocity exceeded the mean value significantly correlated (r = .80) with average boat velocity. Some rowing coaches attempt to minimize fluctuations in boat velocity by encouraging their athletes to move out of the bow at the finish of the stroke in a smooth, sequential manner. After extracting the oar from the water, rowers can move the arms and hands without adversely affecting boat velocity if they restrict the movement of the heavier body segments. They follow with controlled trunk motion by pivoting about the hip joint without knee flexion. Finally, they maintain trunk angle and gradually flex their knees to get into the catch position.

Conclusion

The complex system of rowers, oars, and boat are in continual dynamic oscillation, which is a challenge to coaches and rowing biomechanists. However, rowers can optimize average boat velocity by maximizing the propulsive contribution of each rower while manipulating crew dynamics to reduce the amplitude of velocity fluctuations and decrease the period of negative boat acceleration. This elusive goal is even more difficult to achieve when stroke rate increases and crew members must translate their mass along the length of the boat in a shorter period of time. They must manage the resulting increase in the rowers' momentum as much as possible to minimize the deleterious effect on boat velocity.

chapter 11

Rigging

Volker Nolte

Rowers and coaches often ask me about rigging. They ask, "I'm coaching lightweights, which measurements should I use?" Or, "In the last race, my crew was leading to the thousand but couldn't hold onto their lead. Should I consider changing the load?" Sometimes they ask, "We're planning to buy a new boat—what specification should we give the boatbuilder?"

Rigging is one aspect of rowing that is surrounded by myths. It seems so basic that any child could do it, yet it also seems to take hours of meticulous work with special tools. Sometimes rowers are not supposed to make a fuss about small misalignments on their boat, and sometimes they are.

Considering the time that rowers and coaches actually spend rigging boats in boathouses around the world, it must be an important enough task. The reason for all this effort is the desire to provide crews with a boat that allows them to put all their power into propulsion. Rowers and coaches have to thoroughly check the boats before the first row of the season and recheck them again every so often. They have to set the fitting load for the specific crew. They have to choose the most appropriate gearing for the weather conditions. In addition, they have to stay on top of the constant development of rowing equipment. Having said all this, many people still declare that rowers and coaches spend too much time rigging and that good rowers can row with any kind of equipment.

You will find support for each of these views, but this chapter is not meant to be a rigging manual. There are already several good rigging manuals that answer many if not all rigging questions (Davenport 1992; Piesik 2000). The point of this chapter is to introduce proper rigging and discuss a few specific rigging concerns.

I believe the following principles:

- Basic rigging is simple and every coach should be able to prepare a boat.
- A coach or rower needs to understand the biomechanical basics to know what to do.
- Rigging requires proper equipment.
- Rigging has to be done with accuracy and care.
- Experience will help improve rigging and the identification of possible problems.
- Many technical problems, especially in beginners, are due to improper rigging.
- Every rower will have better technique, enjoy rowing more, and row faster with a properly rigged boat.
- Proper rigging helps prevent injuries.
- Fine-tuning a racing shell requires biomechanical understanding, a great deal of thought, and sophisticated equipment.

In this chapter, *rigging* refers to setting up and adjusting rowing equipment so that rowers can effectively apply their physical power to propel the boat. Rigging must follow certain guidelines, but it must also account for individual body types and abilities.

The main goal is to prepare the boat so that the rowers can do the following:

- Safely control the boat
- Learn and execute proper technique
- Avoid injuries
- Propel the boat effectively
- Work together as a team

If a boat is not rigged correctly, rowers will certainly experience problems in one or more of these areas. Figures 11.1 through 11.6 explain the boat measurements used in rigging.

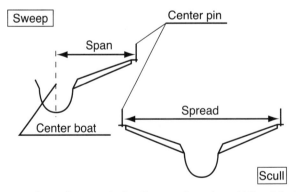

FIGURE 11.1   In a sweep boat, the span is the distance from the middle of the boat to the center of the pin. In sculling, the spread is the distance from the center of the starboard pin to the center of the port pin. Always measure at the bottom of the pin. If you measure at the top, any pitch of the pin will give an incorrect reading of the spread.

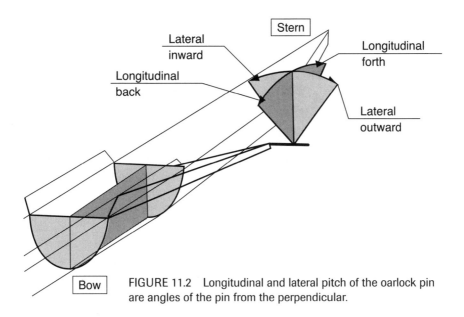

FIGURE 11.2 Longitudinal and lateral pitch of the oarlock pin are angles of the pin from the perpendicular.

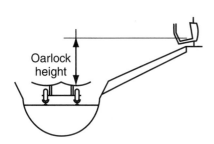

FIGURE 11.3 Oarlock height is the distance from the bottom of the oarlock to the lowest part of the seat when in the farthest stern position.

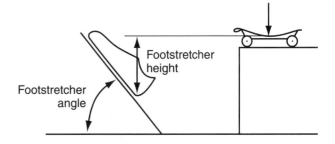

FIGURE 11.4 Footstretcher height is the distance from the bottom of the heel to the lowest point on the seat. Angle refers to the angle of the footstretcher relative to the horizontal of the boat.

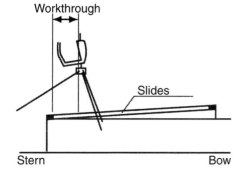

FIGURE 11.5 Workthrough is the distance from the face of the oarlock to the stern end of the usable slide.

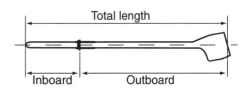

FIGURE 11.6 The total length, inboard, and outboard of an oar are measured along the center of the oar shaft.

The Importance of Rigging

Although often considered menial work, rigging is the single most important basic work of a coach to help a crew to successfully learn technique, train, and race. The technique that rowers learn as beginners is difficult to alter later on. Coaches spend tremendous time and effort teaching the basic movement patterns, but they are unable to prevent all movement errors. However, most of these technical errors are actually due to poor rigging. For example, in sweep boats beginners often lean away from their riggers when drawing the outside shoulder down in the finish (see figure 11.7). Leaning is a natural reaction in a boat with low-rigged oarlocks or underpitched blades. The coach spends countless hours correcting this error later in the rowers' development when she could easily have prevented the problem in the first place through proper rigging.

Researchers provided beginners with either intensive coaching and feedback or with specifically rigged boats and feedback only in response to the athletes' questions. The rowers with the well-rigged boats showed better progress in their learning. This suggests that a properly rigged boat is more important to the learning process than coaching. These results are from a preliminary test for a larger study that was never carried out, however, so we are left only with a suggestion of the importance of rigging.

It seems obvious that if the equipment allows the rower to move naturally, it aids the learning process. If the oar falls in the oarlock in the proper position so that it does not dig or wash out, the rower won't have to compensate and will receive accurate tactile feedback. If the footstretcher position is correct, the beginner can apply forces efficiently. If the oar length is appropriate, the rower will find the lock more easily.

FIGURE 11.7 Rowers leaning away from their riggers because the oarlocks are too low.

A properly rigged boat is not important only for beginners. World-class rowers also need a boat that allows them to row as fast as possible. It is simply impossible to row fast without a properly rigged boat. Of course, a world-class rower can compensate for a rigging mistake better than a beginner, but such mistakes still prevent optimal performance. For example, Melch Bürgin (world champion 1966 and 1967 in the 2x) mismatched his Macon sculls in one heat of an international single scull race, using port scull on starboard and vice versa. European sculls traditionally had inbuilt pitch, so Bürgin rowed with heavily underpitched blades. He managed to survive the heat, but he made sure to put his sculls in the proper oarlocks for the final!

Even if you argue that a small rigging error won't affect the experienced athlete's boat speed, it can still result in injury. The chance of injury increases greatly because the rower must compensate for the misaligned boat.

The good news is that with experience the rowers learn to actually feel the connection between their rowing technique and rigging imperfections. However, it can be difficult to measure and quantify the rigging changes the rowers suggest. Normal rigging tools can't accurately measure 0.5-degree pitch, 2-millimeter oarlock height, or 5-millimeter footstretcher height. These numbers are examples of rigging irregularities that experienced athletes can feel but are impossible to measure with certainty.

© Joel W. Rogers

In addition to preventing accidents and injury, proper rigging allows maximum speed and performance.

We aren't certain that such minor changes affect a crew's speed. Nonetheless, a slightly underpitched scull may cause rowers to adjust the pitch by tightly gripping the handle or leaning away from the underpitched blade. These technique alterations can cause tendonitis or back spasms if done for thousands of strokes.

These examples show both the importance of rigging and its limitations. Now let's examine the principles of rigging. Although the definition of rigging is the adjustment of the boat to an individual rower in a specific situation, there are still some basic principles that should be the foundation of any rigging.

Principle 1: Know Your Numbers

The first principle is use basic measurement values. A measurement is a comparison, and you need to know the correct values for the different rigging measurements. At the beginning of a rigging session, always identify a *basic measurement* for the boat part you are going to work on (span, length of inboard, footstretcher angle, and so on). Then adjust this number according to the individual athlete's size and ability and the specific equipment (boat, blade, and so on). This number becomes the athlete's *normal measurement* for that specific equipment. It is also the base number for making adjustments for race and weather conditions, called *specific measurements*.

Table 11.1 is an overview of all the rigging numbers you need to prepare a boat. It is difficult to provide concrete numbers since many factors influence the final measurement. An athlete's anthropometrics and conditioning affect the number, as do equipment from different manufacturers and even different types of equipment from the same manufacturer. However, table 11.1 tries to provide the widest range of measurements. The following examples will give you an idea of how to use the table.

Example 1:

You need to rig a boat for a lightweight women's 2x. The following are the basic measurements for this crew:

Spread = 1.60 m	
Oar length = 2.88 m	Inboard length = 88 cm
Oarlock height = 18 cm (starboard)	17.5 cm (port)
Pitch on pin: Longitudinal = 0 degrees	Lateral = 0 degrees
Pitch on oarlock = 4 degrees	
Footstretcher: Height = 18 cm	Angle = 39 degrees

The crew is light and flexible, experienced but not very powerful. The double will use Smoothie oars. You need to adjust the basic measurements to come up with normal measurements for this crew:

Spread = 1.61 m	
Oar length = 2.87 m	Inboard length = 88.5 cm
Oarlock height = 17 cm (starboard)	16.5 cm (port)
Pitch on pin: Longitudinal = 0 degrees	Lateral = 0 degrees
Pitch on oarlock = 3 degrees	
Footstretcher: Height = 17 cm	Angle = 40 degrees

TABLE 11.1 Overview of Measurement Numbers for Rigging Rowing Boats

SPAN/SPREAD AND OAR LENGTH							
			Faster, more powerful, less skill →				
			← Slower, less powerful, more skill				
	Boat	**Span (m)**			**Oar length (m)**		
Sweep	2-	0.88	0.86	0.85	3.70	3.72	3.75
	2+	0.89	0.87	0.86	3.70	3.72	3.75
	4-	0.87	0.85	0.84	3.71	3.73	3.76
	4+	0.88	0.86	0.85	3.70	3.72	3.75
	8+	0.86	0.84	0.83	3.71	3.73	3.76
	Boat	**Spread (m)**			**Scull length (m)**		
Scull	1x	1.62	1.60	1.58	2.85	2.88	2.91
	2x	1.62	1.60	1.58	2.85	2.88	2.91
	4x	1.61	1.59	1.57	2.86	2.89	2.92

OAR INBOARD	
Inboard sweep = span + 0.30 m Inboard scull = (spread / 2) + 0.08 m	
Example: Span = 0.86	Inboard = 0.86 + 0.30 = 1.16 m
Example: Spread = 1.58	Inboard = (1.58 / 2) + 0.08 = 0.87 m

OARLOCK HEIGHT			
	← Larger, heavier, more skilled		
	Smaller, lighter, less skilled →		
Sweep		19 cm	17 cm	16 cm
Scull	Starboard	20 cm	18 cm	16 cm
	Port	19.5 cm	17.5 cm	15.5 cm

(continued)

TABLE 11.1 *(continued)*

PITCH ON PIN/OARLOCK			
Pitch on the pin	Longitudinal	Always 0	
	Lateral	Always 0	
	← More skill, Smoothie blade Less skill, conventional big blade →		
Pitch on the oarlock	3 degrees	4 degrees	5 degrees
FOOTSTRETCHER POSITIONING			
	← More flexible, shorter shins Less flexible, longer shins →		
Footstretcher height	16 cm	18 cm	20 cm
Footstretcher angle	41 degrees	39 degrees	37 degrees

The middle number in the group of three is considered to be the basic measurement to start. The arrows direct to the range of the measurement according to the indicated factor of the athlete. See text for examples.

Example 2:

You need to rig a boat for a novice men's eight. Here are the basic measurements for this crew:

Span = 84 cm
Oar length = 3.74 m   Inboard length = 1.14 m
Oarlock height = 17 cm
Pitch on pin: Longitudinal = 0 degrees   Lateral = 0 degrees
Pitch on oarlock = 4 degrees
Footstretcher: Height = 18 cm   Angle = 39 degrees

This crew is not very experienced, but it is powerful. It is also quite heavy and a bit inflexible. The crew will use older Big Blades. You adjust the basic measurements to come up with these normal measurements:

Span = 83.5 cm
Oar length = 3.76 m   Inboard length = 1.14 m
Oarlock height = 17.5 cm
Pitch on pin: Longitudinal = 0 degrees   Lateral = 0 degrees
Pitch on oarlock = 5 degrees
Footstretcher: Height = 19 cm   Angle = 39 degrees

Normal measurements are the numbers to use for a specific crew, but in certain situations you need to adjust normal measurements. In a race in headwind, for example, you need to shorten the oar. If oars start washing out, you need to reduce pitch on oarlock. These are specific measurements.

We have not discussed the longitudinal positioning of the footstretcher or the workthrough. Richardson clearly explains this measurement in the context of the proper finish (chapter 13).

Principle 2: Work in Sequence

Once you know which measurement to use, you can follow the step-by-step rigging process outlined in figure 11.8. Following these steps in sequence is the second principle of rigging.

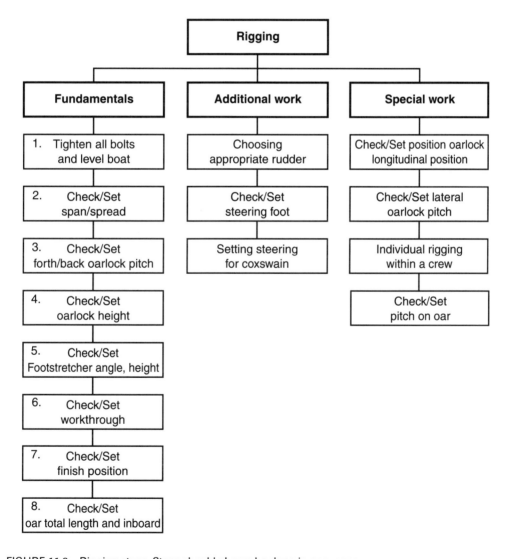

FIGURE 11.8   Rigging steps. Steps should always be done in sequence.

Always perform the rigging steps in sequence so that an adjustment does not affect others that are already done. For example, if you adjust the pin pitch before you set the span, you have to check the pitch again because the lateral movement of the pin most likely has changed it. You could, however, skip some steps if you do not plan to make certain adjustments. For example, if you only need to check oarlock height, you can do the first step and then the fourth without working on the span and the pitch. The only caveat is that you don't know what the span and the pitch are, and you're blindly trusting that the measurements have not changed from your last work on the boat.

Principle 3: Use Proper Rigging Tools

When you use the right rigging tools, you avoid damaging the boat and you can be sure you're getting accurate measurements. Although adjustable wrenches are an easy way to have the necessary size on hand for a range of bolts, they damage the bolts and eventually affect the security of the boat. Today's boat builders use two or three different sizes of bolts, so you only need a few wrenches.

If you want to get the right measurements, you need certain tools. Unfortunately, accuracy comes with a price tag: The more accuracy you demand, the more expensive the tool. However, you can reduce costs through smart buys and proper maintenance. Table 11.2 lists equipment that you need for the different rigging tasks.

TABLE 11.2 Rigging Tools

Rigging task	Necessary tools (Each bullet represents a different tool option for the task)
Span, spread	• 1 span measure (special tool, sometimes combined with height meter) • 1 tape measure
Pin pitch	• 1 pitch meter, 1 spirit level • 2 spirit levels • 1 angle meter, 1 spirit level
Oarlock pitch	• 1 pitch meter, 1 spirit level • 1 angle meter, 1 spirit level
Oarlock height	• 1 height meter, 1 tape measure (some height meters have built-in tape measures) • 1 straight bar (at least 1.50 m), 1 tape measure
Footstretcher height	• 1 tape measure, 1 spirit level • 1 tape measure, 1 straight bar (0.50 m)
Footstretcher angle	• 1 pitch meter (Be careful: Not all pitch meters work!) • 1 protractor
Workthrough	• 1 T square or tri-square, 1 tape measure • 1 rope, 1 tape measure
Oar length, inboard	• 1 tape measure

Table does not include the required wrenches and screwdrivers.

There are two types of accuracy. The first is absolute accuracy, which means that you know without doubt that your measurement of 3.5-degree pitch on the oarlock is correct. You know that you measured 3.5 degrees and not 3.0 or 3.55. Such accuracy is only possible with very expensive equipment. Most tape measures are only accurate to 1 millimeter and most pitch meters are only accurate to 1 degree (see table 11.2). However, such accuracy is not so important in practice. It is more important to always measure the same amount for the same situation with the same tools. This is called repetitive accuracy, or precision. The absolute overall oar length may be off by 1 millimeter using your tape measure, but it will always be off by the same margin. For repetitive accuracy you need tools without moving parts or play in their linkages. As long you always use the same tools, maintain them so that they won't wear out, and always use the same measurement procedure, your measurements will be precise.

Principle 4: Do It Right the First Time

Rigging takes time! Accuracy again is the focus. If you have to rig a boat, take your time and set it up the right way to get the best results.

Always put the boat on level ground in a dry, well-lit area. Get the necessary tools together and then find someone to help you control the lateral level of the boat, stabilize the boat when making adjustments, hold one end of the tape measure, and so on. Make your measurements and adjustments as accurate as possible. Finally, check that all screws and bolts are in place and tighten all bolts. Do your job to the best of your abilities, and you will save time and get the best possible results in training and racing.

Principle 5: Test Things Out

You won't know which measurements are better for your crew unless you try them out. Who can tell you if an oarlock height of 17 centimeters is better than 18 centimeters? And no one can tell without trying it out if your crew is faster with a 3-degree or 3.5-degree pitch on the oarlock.

You may have theories on why one measurement is better than the other, but when the numbers are close, only testing will give you the answers. However, even testing has its limits. For example, if you perform 500-meter pieces at maximum speed in flat water without wind to determine the best oar length, you will get results that are only correct for these particular circumstances. You can't necessarily use the results for your 2000-meter races.

Despite their limitations, I would encourage you to conduct tests. You will always learn from the process, and it is good training anyhow. You will learn from the measurements (normally times for a fixed distance), and the rowers will learn to feel differences that you can also take into consideration.

Here are a few guidelines to follow when conducting tests:

- Repeat test pieces as much as possible, and repeat the complete test on several different days. If the results are correct for one day, they should be correct on another day.

- Try to make your tests similar to race situations. If you want to know if a certain workthrough helps with the start, do starts. If you want to know more about the gearing for a 2000-meter race, do 2000-meter pieces. Doing four 1000-meter pieces will give you more feedback for a 2000-meter race than four 100-meter pieces.

- Take measurements that are as accurate as possible. Make sure you have fixed markers for your course. It is better to have a fixed post for the start and one for the finish and not know the exact distance than to have two buoys anchored exactly 500 meters apart that shift in the wind.

- Set up a timing team. Two people in fixed positions are better than taking times from a running motorboat.

- If you use video analysis, make sure that you tape the crew at the same stroke rate, in the same stage of fatigue, and from the same angle.

- Always use the same procedure. If you use a running start for your pieces, always start at the same distance in front of the starting line with the same sequence of strokes.

- If you compare rigging features, test only one change at a time. For example, if you want to see the influence of the oarlock height on the bladework, only change the oarlock height. Do not try to check the footstretcher angle and the workthrough at the same time.

Additional Work

In addition to adjustments and maintenance, you need to do some rigging work to check the boat before a race. Most boats allow you to change the rudder, which may be necessary for certain types of regattas. The larger the rudder, the easier it is to change the course of the boat. This helps crews choose their course, but it also means more drag (because of a larger wetted surface), greater influence of small rudder movements (e.g., small involuntary steering movement), and larger rolling movements that upset the balance of the boat. The disadvantage of increased drag must be balanced with the advantage of maneuverability and the ability to steer with very small rudder movements. A boat with a larger rudder can change course quickly, such as after losing course in a race after a crab, and is beneficial in most of the head races. For example, when coaching the Canadian lightweight men's eight, we always used a larger rudder at the head of the Charles. This allowed the crew to maintain rowing full strength on both sides in all turns of the Charles River.

Once one of my crews came back from a race with a loose steering foot where the bolt had come off during a race. After that I always checked the steering mechanism to make sure all screws were tight and wires intact.

Be sure to set the steering mechanism for coxswains as well as for foot-steered coxless boats. The tightness of the wires depends on the mechanism and personal preference. The tighter fit allows smaller adjustments, but it is not so easy to find the straight or neutral position. On the other hand, slack wires allow the rudder to return to the neutral position by itself, but they make it more difficult to make fine adjustments. In general the tighter fit is more appropriate for experienced athletes.

Special Measurements

All coaches should be able to perform the fundamental rigging steps I just described. If you have questions, you can always ask a colleague or even your boat builder. The important thing is to gain experience by doing it! If you want to take your rigging to the next level, consider the special work rigging adjustments in figure 11.8.

In sculling boats the two oarlocks of each rowing place should be directly across from each other so that their position to the stern or bow is the same. It is important to check this since play in the fittings of the riggers, rigger damage, or even incorrectly built riggers can mean the oarlocks are in different longitudinal positions. If the play in the fittings is not enough to correct these differences, you'll have to get help from the boat builder.

Some new boats allow you to fit the riggers at different positions on the boat, meaning you could put the oarlocks in different longitudinal locations. With a longitudinal shift of the oarlock, you have to move the footstretcher in the same direction to put the rower in the proper position. The transfer of the rower's weight in turn changes the trim of the boat, or how the boat sits in the water. If, for example, the bow rides up out of the water at race pace and does not cut the water properly, you should move the oarlock toward the bow so that the boat sits in the water as it was built to do (see figure 11.9).

a

b

c

FIGURE 11.9   Longitudinal trim: *(a)* too much bow out of the water; *(b)* proper trim; *(c)* bow too deep in the water.

You can only check the lateral pitch on the oarlock (see figure 11.2 on page 129) if the boat is leveled. Inward pitch, when the top of the pin points toward the middle of the boat, makes it extremely difficult to row. This incorrect position reduces the pitch of the blade at the catch and adds pitch in the finish of the stroke. For example, if a blade has 4 degrees at the perpendicular position, a 2-degree inward pitch causes a scull to have a 2.5-degree pitch at the catch and a 5-degree pitch at the finish. Since blades tend to go deep in the catch and shallow at the finish, these tendencies would be even worse with inward pitch. A rower normally cannot row well with inward pitch.

Outward pitch, when the top of the pin points away from the boat, can sometimes help a rower with bladework. Outward pitch on the pin increases the pitch of the blade in the catch and reduces it at the finish, keeping the blade from going too deep at the catch and too shallow in the finish. Although such rigging may help in the short run, it only patches problems that are caused by other rigging mistakes, such as improper oarlock height, or by faulty technique, such as tight handle grip.

The lateral pitch on the pin should be 0 degrees, which means that the pin should be perpendicular to the horizontal plane of the boat. This is why the boat needs to be leveled before you start rigging. A leveled boat allows you to check the pitch of the pin forward, backward, and laterally since you can test it with a simple spirit level that swivels around the pin.

If you need to adjust the lateral pitch on the pin, it is best to ask the builder how to make the correction. However, builders know that this procedure is difficult and try to construct their riggers so that customers can assume this pitch is set properly.

Similarly, rowers and coaches can usually assume that the oars are properly pitched, meaning that the angle between the blade and face of the sleeve is correct (see figure 11.10). However, the inbuilt pitch on the oar can change through wear, storage, or other influences like temperature. The pitch on the oar is very important because it helps define the angle of the blade in the water, which is the foundation for proper bladework, balance, and propulsion. You need to check oar pitch once in a while or

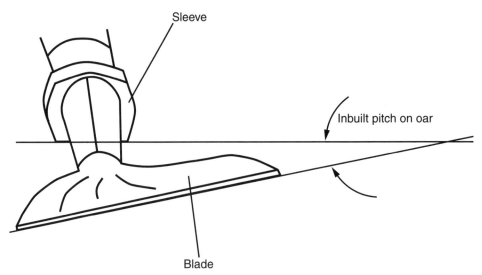

FIGURE 11.10 Inbuilt pitch on the oar is based on the angle between face of the sleeve and the face of the blade.

have it checked by manufacturers who offer such services at certain regattas. Check with the manufacturer for measurement and adjustment details, because almost every blade requires a special measurement. For some blades, the oar builders even offer special measurement jigs that allow you to easily and accurately measure the inbuilt pitch.

If possible, you should try to set all seats in a boat the same way. This guarantees that forces are in the same direction and on the same level, resulting in good balance and straight run. However, since you can adjust each individual seat, you have the opportunity to fit the boat to each rower. If possible, try to avoid individual measurements such as a shorter span for a smaller athlete, but when athletes on a crew have very different body sizes individual measurements may be necessary. The only rules are to act logically and test any changes you make.

Effects of Rigging on Boats

As mentioned in the beginning of the chapter, it is almost true that you do not need a coach for technique training if the boat is properly rigged. Athletes will perform the movement correctly, or at least better, in a well-rigged boat.

Span and inboard define the horizontal arc of the oar during a stroke. However, inboard is in large part a function of span since these two measures must complement each other (see table 11.1 on page 133). If they are not set to complement each other, the rower's work moves too far out from the middle line of the boat and becomes less effective. Narrowing the span lengthens the arc and moves the work toward the finish. Widening the span shortens the arc and moves the work toward a wider catch and creates a shorter finish angle. It also shortens the drive, which is why the load feels lighter even though the actual leverage, or force on the handle for a given force on the oar, is the same.

Oar length and inboard size directly influence leverage. A shorter oar and a longer inboard reduce the rower's perceived load. Say you need to make adjustments on race day because of wind. In tailwind, you would lengthen the oar and shorten the inboard. In headwind, you would do exactly the opposite, except that a headwind requires a greater adjustment than a tailwind of the same strength.

Oarlock height greatly affects the rowers' bladework and power. The oarlocks have to be set according to the athletes' weight, the athletes' skill level, and the boat construction. Oarlocks that are too low reduce the effectiveness of the rowers' power. When the oarlocks are too low rowers produce a large amount of vertical pulling force, putting the blades too deep in the water. Oarlocks that are too high also negatively affect technique, causing the blades to wash out and unbalance the boat.

The footstretcher position helps rowers reach a relaxed but powerful catch. Footstretchers that are too steep or too high do not allow the rower to reach for a long catch, resulting in rushing and lunging. Footstretchers that are too low or too flat result in a weak catch and can cause muscle cramps in the calf.

The workthrough must allow the rower's shins to be perpendicular at the catch without hitting the frontstops of the slides. Not enough workthrough reduces catch length and causes launching, while too much workthrough lets the shins go beyond perpendicular, putting the rower in a weak catch position and thus reducing the sharp push-off.

Conclusion

How much difference does 1 centimeter make in an oar? How much more or less can a rower pull if you alter the height of the oarlock by 0.5 centimeters? Will the crew row faster if you change the footstretcher position longitudinally? The answers are difficult and vary from crew to crew. Like many other coaches, I have had very different experiences. The lightweight men's eight that I coached in 1993 struggled to beat their U.S. counterparts at the Canadian Henley Regatta. Before the world championships they insisted on shortening their oars by 1 centimeter. The boat flew from the first day at camp in Munich, and the crew handily won the world championship. Was it the rigging change that helped them go so fast, or was it the crew's working together as a team to convince me to make the change?

In 1981 I was helping to develop the sliding rigger single. Leo Wolloner, the boat builder I was working with, produced a prototype that had only a few shortcomings. One of the problems was that the carbon-fiber wing rigger did not allow for changing the spread. After many adjustments of the slides, the oarlocks ended up off center by 1 centimeter. The span of the starboard oarlock was 78 centimeters while the span on the port side was 80 centimeters. I only discovered the misalignment after winning several races in the boat, including setting a course record in the 10K head race in Dortmund against several national team athletes.

In 1993, one small adjustment made the difference in the pursuit of championship. In 1981, the physical and psychological advantage of the new construction overcame a small rigging mistake. In both cases the overall setup was successful. Nevertheless, in races where a few hundredths of a second can make a difference, or even when rowers are just trying to learn good rowing technique, you want to provide the athletes with a boat that is prepared to the best of your rigging ability.

Rigging is logical and all the steps make sense. Add to this the time coaches and rowers spend on rigging, and you would imagine that all boats are rigged properly. Unfortunately, the opposite is true. There are still many misconceptions, maintenance problems, poor measurement tools, and so on.

In an ideal world, you would only have to rig a boat once. However, experience tells us that somehow rigging changes over time. It seems that each rower has to fiddle around with the rigging on their place, and rigging has to endure rough travels, loose bolts, and unfortunate hits. And sometimes coaches change their minds about rigging configurations. You simply have to check the adjustments and measurements on a regular basis. Use the information in this chapter to ensure that your boat is set up in the best way possible for you or your rowers.

chapter 12

Bladework

Mike Spracklen

Whether I'm coaching or observing crews the first thing I notice is the movement of the blades, since bladework reflects technical skill. Blade control is a vital skill because it is the blade that moves the boat. Most technical problems involve the blade, and blade control is seldom an athlete's strong point. Changing learned movements is not easy for mature athletes, and learning new blade skills is no exception. The best blade control I've ever seen was that of Sir Steven Redgrave when he rowed in the coxless pair with Andrew Holmes in 1987 and 1988. Andy also had strong technical skills, and the uniformity they created through bladework made them a formidable team.

Bladework can influence performance in countless ways. Here's one example: The eight was not moving smoothly and the athletes complained that the boat was not running on an even keel. Despite coaching for balance, the problem persisted. When the coach checked the rigging, he found that one swivel was 2 1/2 centimeters higher than it was supposed to be—the athlete had altered it without consulting the coach. The crew was working on blade depth and the athlete had raised his swivel thinking that it would help keep his blade from going too deep midstroke.

Unfortunately, increasing the swivel height did not change the way his hands drew the stroke. Despite a swivel that was 2 1/2 centimeters higher, the blade still went too deep. The higher swivel affected the other swivels as well. Those on the opposite side were forced higher and those on the same side lower. The athletes with lower work leaned away from their riggers to make more room to clear their blades, and when they leaned to balance the boat, others leaned the opposite way. It became a fight no one could win, keeping the boat from running level. After the coach restored the rigger to its correct height the boat ran more smoothly and the oarsmen were able to concentrate on their bladework.

Good bladework is the result of drawing the hands in a straight line. Alterations to rigging will not correct movements that deviate from that line. In this case raising the height of the swivel not only didn't keep the blade from traveling too deep, it also caused a whole new set of problems.

Bladework and Competitive Rowing

Rowing is a power-endurance activity. An athlete's level of performance depends on physical strength to produce power and endurance to maintain that power. The efficiency with which an athlete applies power relies on technical skill, particularly blade control. Bladework is perhaps the most important part of competitive rowing.

In the early years of the sport, coaches considered bladework to be paramount, but today's standards give the impression that this skill is less important. In the competitive world where standards are always rising and races are won by the narrowest margins, it is surprising that this essential skill is so overlooked. Many factors contribute to success, but bladework remains essential.

Factors Influencing Boat Speed

The three factors that determine boat speed are *rate*, the number of strokes rowed in a minute; *power*, force multiplied by the speed of the pull; and *length*, the distance the blades move the boat while they are in the water. Bladework influences all three.

The higher the stroke rate, the faster the boat will travel as long as length and power are maintained. High stroke rates maximize boat speed and can be achieved relatively quickly. However, as rates increase, blade control becomes more difficult, and as blade control deteriorates, length and power deteriorate.

The greater the athlete's power, the faster the athlete can drive the blades through the water. Power comes from the coordination of muscular strength, but the efficiency with which athletes apply their power depends on the direction in which the blade travels through the water.

The longer the stroke the farther the boat travels per stroke, provided that power remains consistent. Length depends on a long forward reach and where the blade grips and releases its grip on the water.

Oars are both first- and second-class levers. As a first-class lever the rowing pin is the fulcrum and the water is the load. As a second-class lever the submerged blade is the fulcrum and the boat or pin is the load. The stroke can be thought of as the blade moving through the water from beginning to finish or the blade remaining stationary in the water as it levers the boat past. The blade actually travels through the water a short distance, called *slip*.

Figure 12.1 shows the path of an efficient blade. The blade enters the water quickly and accelerates at a uniform depth, covered but with the loom clear of the water. The blade leaves the water cleanly at the finish, turns onto the feather, and travels forward at a constant height until the rower brings it down close to the surface, ready for the next stroke.

Figure 12.2 shows the path of an inefficient blade. The blade carries forward too close to the water, rises high to square, and misses too much length on reentering the water. The blade travels downward to the middle of the stroke and upward to the finish, reducing the effect of directional force, grip, and length. A ragged extraction takes speed off the boat.

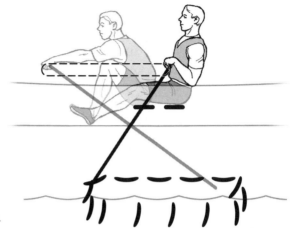

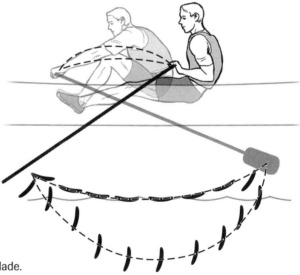

FIGURE 12.1   Path of an efficient blade.

FIGURE 12.2   Path of an inefficient blade.

Beginning of the Stroke

The stroke begins when the blade grips the water. The grip, sometimes called the catch, can be thought of as the blade locking against an imaginary wooden post, levering the boat forward. A long forward reach is necessary for a long stroke, but of equal importance is the precision with which the blade grips. Water will not compress, and the faster the blade moves into the water and into its path to drive the boat forward, the sooner and stronger it will achieve grip and the longer will be the stroke.

Rowers use their legs to quickly achieve blade grip. Pushing the feet hard against the stretcher before the blade locks in the water slows boat speed, but only the legs have the power for an efficient beginning. The rower expends some leg drive before the blades grip, but accurate timing keeps losses at a minimum, leaving sufficient leg drive to complete the stroke. Some loss of reach is inevitable, but again, good timing helps.

Two or more athletes in a boat apply greater force when they grip the water at the same time. It often appears that the blades are entering the water together, but if angles and speeds of entry differ the rowers are probably not applying power at the same time. Uniform hand and body movements are important. For all blades to grip at the same time, they must enter the water in the same way (see figure 12.3).

Photo by Mike Spracklen

FIGURE 12.3   Uniformity of all rowers beginning together.

Blade Splash

The splash a blade makes when it enters the water provides feedback on stroke efficiency. Small splashes indicate a well-timed entry, although bigger splashes are to be expected when a crew is at full load and rowing at high rates. A single splash rising from the blade face, or frontsplash, shows that the stroke is shorter. A single splash rising from the back of the blade, or backsplash, is the result of a slow entry and a shortened stroke. Both examples indicate reduced length and power.

An efficient entry creates a small splash on each side of the blade, the frontsplash a little larger than the backsplash (see figure 12.4). The more accurately the blade enters the water, the more efficient the rest of the stroke will be. Once a blade begins on a particular path in the water, the rower cannot change its direction without hurting stroke efficiency.

Photo by Mike Spracklen

FIGURE 12.4   The splash made by the blade shows efficient entry.

Middle of the Stroke

A light racing boat responds instantly to a solid beginning, and the blades must accelerate to maintain maximum driving force. The best way to achieve this is a straight path from beginning to finish, with the blade submerged and the loom clear of the water (see figure 12.5). Some force is lost if the blade moves up and down or travels deep into the water at an angle. Efficiency is also hurt when the blade goes so deep that the loom breaks through the water. Since the oar is a second-class lever with the boat as the load and the blade as the fulcrum, the water covering the loom obstructs the oar.

Some argue that rowing the blade deep means it will slip less. However, the disadvantages far outweigh any advantage. Disadvantages include extra time needed to row the stroke; deviation from its path; ragged extraction; loss of directional force; and backwatering of the loom.

Photo by Mike Spracklen

FIGURE 12.5   The middle of the stroke, showing a straight drive through the water.

Stroke Finish

The power that the blades apply at the finish of the stroke determines boat speed. While every part of the stroke is important, the boat travels only as fast as the blades push it at the end of the stroke. An accelerating blade that is covered to the last moment contributes to a long stroke and a strong thrust. The longer the blades are kept in the water the greater the force they produce, a force that is maximized when every blade pushes together.

The boat moves at its fastest just after the blades leave the water in a clean release that allows the boat to run unrestricted (see figure 12.6). When the blade is on the right path, it makes a hollow in the water that allows for a clean extraction. When the blade drags out of the water it reduces boat speed.

Two common errors are finishing short and allowing the blade to rise out of the water, or wash out, before the end of the stroke.

Photo by Mike Spracklen

FIGURE 12.6   A clean extraction from the water at the finish of the stroke.

Puddle

The blade creates turbulence as it leaves the water. This turbulence is called a puddle and is an aggressive swirling of water (see figure 12.7). The stronger the force of the blade, the more aggressive and long-lasting the puddle it creates. The size, depth, and consistency of the water forming the puddle reveal the power and accuracy of the stroke. A blade rowed too deep leaves a smaller puddle and disturbed water where the loom has broken the surface. A blade that is uncovered at the finish produces frothy water at the rear of the puddle, commonly referred to as washing out. The blade should travel into undisturbed water, and there must be no froth in front of the blade until it is extracted. A blade that drags out at the finish leaves a puddle with a trail of froth. Sometimes a crew's puddles are linked by the froth of ragged blade release.

Photo by Mike Spracklen

FIGURE 12.7   A good puddle formed after blade extraction.

Recovery

The time between strokes is called the recovery. It begins when the blades leave the water and finishes when the blades enter the water for the next stroke. During the recovery the rowers feather the blades to reduce wind resistance and use the blades to balance the boat. The rowers keep the blades at a uniform height at which they can square the blades without lifting them higher off the water. In preparation for the next stroke the rowers square the blades and bring them close to the water so that the blades can be covered quickly.

A common mistake is restricting the natural rolling motion of the boat by carrying the blades too close to the water. Athletes do not move exactly alike, and crews must accommodate differences. When the blades scrape the water the rowers have less freedom to move, which creates tension. In addition, a blade that is too close has to rise off the water to be squared when it should be coming down for the next stroke. A blade that is rising just before entering the water is difficult to control, missing too much of the stroke and upsetting the boat's balance.

Body Position and Movement

Boat speed depends on physical strength for producing power and endurance for maintaining that power. To maximize performance, athletes adopt good posture with a firm, straight back and relaxed arms and shoulders and row rhythmically, allowing the body some recovery. A stroke has two phases: the power phase in which the blade drives through the water and the recovery phase in which the athlete has a chance to recover.

Power Phase

The power phase begins with the legs driving the blade into the water. The body holds firm and the arms are straight as the legs apply force by pushing against the stretcher. The body follows the legs by levering open from the hips, and the arms finish the stroke by drawing the oar handle to the chest. Rowers achieve maximum power by using proper posture to connect the legs and blade; using the trunk as a lever; keeping movements as horizontal as possible; and working the strongest muscles first.

Single Oar

The rower holds the oar with the hands 10 to 15 inches apart. One hand is at the end of the handle where it has the most leverage (see figure 12.8). Both hands pull the blade through the stroke, but the main function of the outside hand is to draw the blade through the water, and the main function of the inside hand is to control the blade's path. The outside hand holds the oar in the fingers and the inside hand holds it closer to the palm, rolling it into the fingers for feathering the blade.

FIGURE 12.8   Hand position in the sweep.

Sculling

The sculler's movements are similar to the single-oar athlete's. The difference is the sculler has to control two blades, one in each hand, at the same time. The hands have to cross during both the power phase and the recovery phase. To keep the boat level, one hand moves ahead of the other. The lower hand fits beneath the upper hand to keep the handles on a level plane. In the same way the single-oar rower's inside hand holds an oar, the sculls are close to the palm of the hand during the stroke and then they roll into the fingers during the recovery.

A common error is dropping the wrists to feather the blades. This leaves less room for the blades to clear the water and can create tension in the arms and shoulders.

Recovery Phase

The recovery begins from a position of good posture with a firm, straight back and relaxed arms and shoulders at backstops. The hands move down and around the turn, feathering the blade as soon as it clears the water. The trunk pivots forward from the hips, and when at full reach the seat leaves backstops and moves to frontstops. During the transition to frontstops, the athletes relax to allow their bodies some recovery and to prepare themselves for the next stroke. This rest, though small, helps the athletes maintain full power for the entire race.

Stroke Length

Length depends on blade control and full extension of the body. The distance the body reaches from backstops determines forward length. This reach begins with hinging from the hips after the hands have moved away. When the body is at full reach it moves to frontstops without changing position. In the forward position the shins are vertical, the head is high above the knees, the back is straight, the arms are straight, and the chest is between the knees. The athlete is relaxed and poised, like a cat ready to spring on its prey.

The hands guide the blade into the water as the legs drive against the stretcher. The body stays in this position until the blades grip, and then it levers open ahead of the arms, drawing to the finish.

A common mistake is reaching forward for more length after the seat has left backstops. It is particularly detrimental to stretch for more length when the seat is at frontstops. Athletes must be ready before beginning a stroke, as any undesirable movement at frontstops will detract from the stroke's precision.

Keeping the back straight increases stroke length and provides good leverage. A firm back also makes a solid connection between the legs and blade and guards the athlete against injury.

Equipment measurements affect stroke length. To increase stroke length, decrease the span (the distance from the pin to the center of the boat) and increase the outboard oar measurement. To reduce stroke length, increase the span and decrease the outboard. Changes to the span affect load about two and a half times more than changes to the outboard. Increasing length by altering span and outboard puts a greater load on the athletes; therefore a compromise between oar length and span is necessary. Changes to the inboard oar measurement can affect length, but alterations should not deviate far from 30 centimeters overlap for single-oar rowing and 19 to 21 centimeters for sculling.

The athlete's position in the boat affects the stroke arc and to some extent stroke length. The blade is most efficient when it goes from 45 degrees at the beginning to 135 degrees at the finish. The stroke becomes less efficient when the blade moves beyond 45 degrees and when the body prevents the oar from drawing past 130 degrees at the finish. These two factors control stroke length. Most crews are unable to row effectively beyond these angles, so a good target length is from 45 degrees at the beginning to 130 degrees at the finish. Some movement of the blade is necessary to achieve grip, and it is necessary for the athletes to reach beyond 45 degrees to achieve catch at this point (45 degrees).

For complete unity in a crew, the angle of each member's oar should be the same throughout the stroke. Body position at the finish governs the length to which the oar can be drawn, so the athletes are set in the same position at backstops. The crew achieves this by setting the seats at backstops the same distance from the line of work. The recommended measurement from line of work to center of seat at backstops is 58 centimeters. The athletes adjust foot position to accommodate leg length.

Blade Shape

The main advantage of the modern hatchet is that the center of the blade, the point where it has the most grip, is closer to the water for a quick entry. The shape also permits the blade to be covered while keeping the oar loom above the water. Be wary of claims by oar manufacturers that a particular blade design has reduced slip. Essentially, reduced slip means more load. Load must be based on athletes' strength, technical coordination, and ability to strike an efficient rhythm. The correct load is a compromise between span, oar length, and blade design.

Pitch

The blade's path through the water is influenced by its angle to the perpendicular, referred to as pitch. In theory, the blade is more effective with zero pitch, but in practice zero pitch makes it more difficult to balance the boat. Pitch on the blades helps stabilize the boat and allows the athletes to concentrate on other skills.

Pitch can be on the oar, the swivel, or the rowing pin, but rowers can control the blade more easily when it is set on the swivel with the rowing pin vertical. If the pin leans forward or has lateral pitch, it gives more pitch to the blade at the beginning of the stroke and less pitch at the finish. A pin that leans back or inward has the reverse effect.

As the boat rolls from side to side and the bow rises and falls, the pitch on the pins constantly changes. When a boat rolls down to the port side, for example, the port pins lean out and the starboard pins lean in. The opposite happens when the boat rolls down to the starboard side. As long as pitch on the blade stays positive these movements will have little effect on performance. However, if the pitch becomes negative the athlete will have trouble controlling the blade. Four degrees on the blade is the minimum to keep pitch positive throughout these changes. The pin should be vertical with pitch plugs of 4 degrees in the swivels. The blade is locked more securely when pitch is on the swivels than on the oars. Beginners benefit from the greater stability of 6 degrees of pitch.

Work Height

Blade control is in the hands of the operator, but height can make a difference. The rowing swivels should be at a height that allows a strong draw to the finish and clean blade extraction. Rigging that is too high makes it more difficult to keep blades covered, and when it is too low it makes it difficult to extract the blade cleanly. As a guide, a college crew averaging 86 kilograms would be set between 16 and 18 centimeters from seat to swivel. When the blade is just covered at backstops, the outside forearm should be parallel to the boat and the hand should be at the lower ribs.

Bladework Exercises

Rowers can perform certain exercises to improve bladework. This section describes the best of these exercises.

ANGLE OF ENTRY 1

Sit in the forward position with good posture, shins vertical and chest between the knees. The blade should be square and covered. Lower and raise the hands repeatedly to uncover and cover the blade, keeping the arms straight and pivoting at the shoulders. Repeat the movement several times, beginning slowly and gradually increasing until you're performing the movement as fast as you can without losing control. This exercise teaches hand movement for achieving good blade entry.

ANGLE OF ENTRY 2

Building on exercise one, note the height of your hands when the blade is covered. Row 10 strokes with your hands passing through that position. The first few strokes will feel heavy as a result of the increase in stroke length achieved. As the boat gathers speed the heavier feeling will gradually cease as the blades begin to revert to missing some of the forward reach. The object is to hold good entry for 10 strokes, using the heavy feeling as a gauge of the extra length achieved and noting the number of heavier strokes rowed before the strokes get lighter as the blade begins to miss length forward.

ANGLE AND SPEED OF ENTRY

To maximize length, the blade must enter the water as close as possible to the vertical. It must move quickly to achieve grip and take a direct path to maximize force. This exercise helps you realize these movements.

Adopt the forward position described in Angle of Entry 1 and row the first half-meter of the stroke several times, keeping the blade square. Keep your arms straight and pivot at the shoulder to cover the blade and set it on its path into the stroke. The trunk stays set as the legs kick the blade into the water.

QUICK ENTRY 1

This exercise demonstrates the value of a quick entry. As the athletes row, they should drive the blade from a position higher off the water. The blade gathers speed through the air, resulting in a quicker beginning and higher boat velocity. Perform this exercise at different pressures and stroke rates. Mature athletes will have trouble changing movements for very many strokes and blade height will gradually diminish, but they will still gain quicker entry.

QUICK ENTRY 2

Quickness and accuracy of blade entry are skills that short slide exercises help improve. The blade scribes an arc as it travels through the water. When a full stroke is rowed, the blade begins on an arc across the line of travel from which it is relatively easier to achieve grip on the water. As the blade continues on its path it reaches a point at 90 degrees when it is applying force directly opposite to the direction in which the boat is traveling. This is the part of the stroke when the blade is moving faster relative to the speed of the boat. When strokes are rowed short forward the blades enter the water at this faster part of the stroke and have to enter quickly in order to achieve grip. Reducing stroke length by reducing slide length forces the legs to move quickly so that the blades can grip the water.

Begin by sitting at the finish position with good posture, the body leaning approximately 15 degrees toward the bow. Row with only the arms, focusing on covering the blade at the beginning of the stroke and drawing on a horizontal plane to the finish. Maintain rhythm, with a longer recovery than stroke. This stage demonstrates the weakness of the arms.

In the next stage the body swings, hinging from the hips to add length and power to the stroke. Keep the arms straight as the blades grip the water and then accelerate to the finish. You will feel the power of the body as a lever as it hinges open from the hips.

In the last stage, introduce one-quarter of the slide to bring in leg drive. The legs can move quickly from this position and add liveliness to the stroke. The body position holds steady to transfer leg drive to the blade and then opens to support the draw to the finish. Increase to half slide, three-quarter slide, and then full slide.

MAINTAINING UNIFORM DEPTH

An efficient blade travels on a straight path through the water at a uniform depth. When a blade goes deep it loses directional force and the looms create resistance.

In this exercise the rowers cover the blades at the correct depth at the beginning, middle, and finish while the boat is stationary. Next they row with the blades at the correct depth until pressure gradually increases and causes the rowers to lose control of blade depth. Repeat the exercise frequently until it is possible after a period of time to row at full pressure and rate with a controlled blade.

STRENGTHENING THE FINISH

The blades' speed at the finish determines the boat's speed. A good way to create blade acceleration is to build the stroke in stages from the finish.

Row with light pressure. At 10-stroke intervals increase the speed of the hands for the last 15 cm of the stroke, the last 30 cm, the last 60 cm, the last 120 cm, and so on until you reach full length.

BALANCING THE BOAT

During the recovery the blades balance the boat. One way to work on balance is to pause at different positions in the recovery at the command of the coxswain or coach. Begin by pausing with the blades at 90 degrees, sitting at backstops, and then at three-quarter slide position. When you master balance in these positions, pause at other places in the recovery.

RHYTHM AND BALANCE

The stroke involves fast and slow movements, and rhythm emphasizes the difference between them. Coaches have different opinions on rhythm, but most agree that there must be a difference in the time the blade spends in the water and out of the water.

A good exercise is to row with a difference of three parts to one. The crew counts aloud and rows with one part in the stroke and three parts in the recovery. Count aloud "In, out, three, four" or "One, two, three, four." "One, two" equals one part and "two, three, four" equals three parts. This rhythm can be described as five fence posts and four panels. For example, the time between "one and two" (blade in and blade out) may be one second. The time between "two and three" is then one second, the time between "three and four" is one second, and the time between "four and one" is one second. One second is in the water and three seconds are out of the water. The rhythm is based on a one-to-three ratio. The goal is to hold the three-to-one rhythm at the highest possible rate by beginning low and gradually increasing until losing the ratio.

To improve timing and balance, increase the recovery time. Increase the numbers to one to four, one to five, and more as the skill level rises. As recovery time increases the athletes need to keep the wheels of their seats moving.

BEGINNINGS, FINISHES, AND BALANCE

Square-blade paddling helps athletes control the blade. When they carry the blade forward on the feather, it must be at a height that allows them to square it without dropping the hands. Keeping the blade on the square shows the athletes the height from where the blade can enter the water quickly without losing too much forward reach. Square-blade rowing also teaches the athletes to draw at the correct height, allowing the hands to move down and around the turn to clear the blades.

Communication

As I mentioned before, mature athletes have difficulty changing movements they have "grooved in" over years, to the frustration of both coaches and athletes. Sometimes it is a question of communication—it may be necessary for the coach to explore different ways of explaining the need for a change.

Changes that improve boat speed motivate athletes, but sometimes changes are necessary for other reasons. During winter I coached my athletes to balance their boats and keep the blades clear of the water during the recovery. One athlete was slow to respond and her blades hit the water almost every stroke. I tried many different ways to help the athlete but without success. I feared that when she sculled in a crew boat her poor blade control would prevent good balance, upsetting the other athletes in the boat.

The day before I was to form new crew combinations I was still concerned about the problem. As a last resort, I tried something different. I informed her that for 2000 meters I was going to count the number of strokes she sculled without the blade touching the water at light pressure in a double. I followed on a bicycle and with the aid of an electric megaphone counted aloud each stroke she cleared the water. At the end of the 2000 meters she had managed to clear only 10 strokes.

That evening at dinner I noticed that she was upset, and I made a point of sitting opposite her at the table. "You humiliated me," she said, red-faced and quite distraught. Once again I explained the importance of keeping blades off the water, but she was clearly upset and did not respond. She remained unfriendly to me for a long time after. But, from that outing onward she kept her blade clear and I didn't have to tell her about it again! She went on to achieve a high level of rowing skill.

Conclusion

One hundred years ago bladework was considered an important part of rowing. Beginners learned blade control in the rowing tank or in wide, stable boats before they rowed in a racing shell. Only when they acquired a reasonable level of blade control were they allowed to advance to racing boats. Today, beginners step straight into racing boats that are light, sensitive, and difficult to balance, giving them little chance to learn blade control.

It is not that modern coaches have less interest in blade work, but that beginners are not taught correct blade skills. Undesirable movements become habitual and difficult for even the best coach to change later on, so correct bladework must be taught from the beginning.

chapter 13

The Catch

Brian Richardson

I first realized the importance of the catch when I left high school and started rowing in a senior club crew at Adelaide University. The coach emphasized correct application of the catch, which led me to look at my previous career. All through high school I was in crews that trained hard but had no success. When looking at photographs of those crews I noticed a common fault—our hands were always low in the boat at the catch, putting the blades high off the water. This of course led to a poor catch and short stroke length. At Adelaide, on the other hand, our crew went on to an undefeated season and state championship because we worked on improving the catch.

Power and Recovery

This chapter deals with the part of the stroke known as the catch. The stroke cycle has two phases, the power phase and the recovery phase. The power phase is when the blade is in the water and the rower is applying power. The recovery phase is when the blade is out of the water and the athlete is recovering from applying power. The catch is the blade's entry into the water, the link from the recovery phase to the power phase.

The catch occurs from the moment the blade enters the water until the blade is completely covered, or locked, into the water. The stroke cycle should be continuous, so the catch should be a smooth transition from relaxed recovery to absolute power. Other chapters in this book deal with the two phases of the stroke cycle in more detail. However, because it is important for rowers to properly prepare for the catch, it is necessary to discuss the recovery sequence.

The catch is possibly the most challenging part of the stroke cycle. It is difficult to apply power correctly and efficiently at the catch while in a compressed position. Staying balanced and dynamic while in a compressed position on a moving platform requires excellent balance and coordination. It greatly helps to eliminate any unnecessary movements when approaching the catch; this is why the correct sequence of movements from the finish to the catch is important. A solid catch can only occur if the recovery is done correctly.

Preparation

Because the catch is the most difficult part of the stroke cycle, coaches must do two things. First, they must rig the boat correctly. Second, they must coach the athletes to eliminate as many faults as possible before getting to the catch position. By learning the correct sequence through the recovery phase the athletes will be in the proper posture for the catch, making the catch less complicated. For example, if rowers get length by swinging the body late in the recovery phase, or if the hands are low on the recovery, a good catch will be hard to achieve. In general, unnecessary movements right at the catch make a good catch more difficult. Teach athletes the correct technique before faults become ingrained in the athletes' muscle memory.

Effective Stroke Length

For many years top international crews have demonstrated that longer strokes generate faster boat speeds. Effective stroke length is very important, as the athlete has to repeat the stroke over and over again. A typical 2000-meter race takes more than 220 strokes, and these strokes are rowed at an average of 38 to 40 strokes per minute. For good length at the catch, rowers have to reach out using arm length, body swing, and slide compression. They must also be careful not to reach too far, as excessive reaching puts the body in a weak position. Overextending joints and muscles reduces the biomechanical effectiveness necessary for quick power application.

Catch Position

To initiate the catch, the rower must be in the correct catch position. In this position the slide is compressed to where the shins are vertical (see figure 13.1). The body has pivoted at the hips and swung forward enough for the chest to lightly touch the thighs. The shoulders are high and the back and arms are straight.

In a sweep boat, the chest is turned slightly so that it is parallel to the oar handle. The shoulder closest to the rigger is slightly behind or toward the bow of the outside shoulder, which is further extended toward the stern. In sculling the body stays almost square to the boat. If the sculler rows with the left hand slightly higher and closer to the stern than the right hand, then the left shoulder is slightly closer to the stern than the right shoulder (see figure 13.2). This position helps the athlete with the hands at the crossover position. Other scullers sometimes take the catch with the right arm bent to help with hand position at the crossover. This puts the body square to the centerline of the boat at the catch. When scullers row with one hand directly on top of the other, the shoulders are square to the centerline of the boat, but the height difference of the hands is quite substantial.

Once everything is in place, the rower is ready to concentrate on blade entry. Only the hands and arms put the blade in the water. They move independently of the shoulders, like independent suspension in a car. As the athlete approaches full extension the handle moves up, bringing the blade down toward the water. The blade is still traveling toward the bow as it begins to enter the water. The moment the tip of the blade enters the water the hands must move quickly to cover the blade fast and to the correct depth. At this moment the blade begins to travel toward the stern on a flat, horizontal path.

The blade begins to enter the water while the athlete's body mass approaches the stern. This movement enables maximum length in the water and occurs at the moment

FIGURE 13.1 Body position to initiate the catch.

FIGURE 13.2 Sculler at the catch.

when the athlete's body reaches full extension and the legs reach maximum compression. Good entry timing, full body extension, and maximum leg compression help minimize boat check; if a rower performs the catch properly, the boat will have the least negative acceleration and pitching in the stern. The blade begins to enter the water while still moving toward the bow, not while moving toward the stern (see figure 13.3). The moment the tip of the blade touches the water the athlete can apply power. This movement needs to be very quick and the rower needs to place the blade at the optimal depth. It is challenging because entry can greatly decrease the run of the boat and reduce the effectiveness of the crew's stroke length.

The end of the catch occurs when the blade is completely immersed. At the correct depth the top edge of the blade is just covered (see figure 13.4). Placing white tape

FIGURE 13.3   Proper hand and body movement for correctly guiding the blade into the water.

FIGURE 13.4   Blade at the correct depth.

on the shaft 20 and 40 centimeters from the blade can help the athlete and coach recognize when the blade is at the correct depth. The water should hit the shaft somewhere between the two tape marks. Tape marks also allow a coach to see if the blade remains at a constant depth and therefore has a horizontal path, which is the most efficient.

Once blade entry begins, rowers initiate the power phase by pushing back hard with the hips, using the legs and then a strong opening of the upper body. Correct entry at the catch creates a splash that is a perfect V (see figure 13.5a). Too much backsplash means the blade entry is checking the boat run (see figure 13.5b). No backsplash means the blade has moved toward the stern before entering the water (see figure 13.5c). When there is no backsplash, the pressure applied on the footstretcher before blade entry checks the boat run.

FIGURE 13.5 *(a)* Perfect splash on the blade at the catch. *(b)* Too much backsplash. *(c)* Not enough backsplash .

Coaching the Catch

Slow-motion video allows coaches to show their crew proper blade entry. Blade entry is a matter of good seat and hand timing. The seat should arrive at the frontstops at the same time as the blade is entering the water.

The catch should always be thought of as the end of the recovery phase, not the beginning of the power phase. Rowers should not apply power until the blade has started to enter the water. If the blade is not locked in the water or is driving in the air, power applied to the blade through the footplate transferred by the handle affects boat propulsion negatively.

Again, before you can work on the catch, rowers have to know the correct sequence out of the finish. As a coach, you have to check the following:

- Is the finish angle correct and is everybody at the same angle? (This is particularly important for crew boats!)

- Does the athlete use the correct sequence away from the finish? The correct sequence is as follows: The hands start the recovery, followed by the body until the hands clear the knees. The seat moves in a smooth, connected sequence. These movements should not be mechanical, with full hand extension and then full body swing followed by seat movement. The three movements should blend together; they do not all happen simultaneously but in the sequence. So for a short period the hands are still extending while the body is starting to swing. At this point the knees are still locked. The body is still swinging over when the seat first starts to move.

- At the finish, are the knees locked down and the hips firm, with body weight on the back or bow end of the seat?

- Does the body swing from the hips once the hands have started the recovery? Athletes should think about tilting their pelvis forward toward the stern. Many athletes have poor posture and hunch their shoulders to get body length. It is easier and more efficient to achieve body length by sitting tall and swinging from the hips.

- Are the shoulders in front of the hips when the knees break? The objective is to complete the body swing by half slide. Through the first part of the recovery the body weight moves from the back of the seat to the front of the seat.

- Is the seat speed steady?

- Is the oar angle marked so the athletes know the correct position to take the catch?

- Is the blade carried one full blade-width above the water during recovery? Blade and hands must remain in the same plane during recovery.

- Is the blade squared before the catch begins? The blade must be squared as the handle crosses the footstretcher (see figure 13.6). In a sweep boat a good point of reference is the footstretcher, while in a sculling boat a good point of reference is when the handles are 20 centimeters apart moving into the catch. The more skilled the crew the later they can square the blade. The later the square, the more difficult the catch will be.

FIGURE 13.6   Properly squared blades approaching the catch.

Moving the boat from point A to point B faster than the next crew is what our sport is all about, so you need to understand how to move that boat and what principles are involved. A simple lever, the oar, moves the boat. You might know from high school physics that with levers there is an effort, a resistance, and a fulcrum. In rowing the effort is applied to the oar handle, the resistance is the drag on the boat, and the fulcrum is the blade in the water. If the blade is not in the water, the lever has no fulcrum and therefore cannot work. The efficiency of the lever depends on how well the blade enters the water and how much effort is on the handle.

In theory rowers try to lock the blade in the water at the catch position and lever the boat past that position. Obviously the blade does not really lock in the water but moves in a pattern.

The fulcrum moves, but it is always near the tip of the blade. It is what propels the boat. The object is therefore not to move the blade through the water, but to move the boat through the water.

Setting Oar Angles

The angles of the oar handle at the catch and finish relative to the perpendicular line between the pin and the centerline of the boat are critical. You can see these angles when you observe the inboard relative to the side of the boat at the catch and finish. Setting these angles so that everybody is at the same position is an important part of getting a good catch. Marking the catch angle on the gunwales with tape and straws will help your crew get better positions. You only need to set the catch angle; the rowers' finish angle is fixed when the footstretcher is properly set longitudinally, but in the catch it is a help to have a marker to reach for. The recommended catch angle for a sweep boat is 50 or 55 degrees. The recommended finish angle for a sweep boat is 32 to 35 degrees. Depending on the speed of the boat, the finish angle is larger or smaller. The faster the boat, the smaller the finish angle, so the finish angle for an eight, for example, is 32 degrees. In a sweep boat, a crew rowing good length swings through an arc of approximately 90 degrees.

In sculling the boat is more difficult to mark because the catch and finish angles are larger. A sculling boat has an arc of approximately 110 degrees. At the catch the oar handles are outside the gunwales, so marking the angles is difficult and doesn't help the athlete. Table 13.1 shows the distance from the centerline of the boat to the pin for the angles.

Using a line down the center of the boat, such as a fixed string, and the distances from table 13.1, you can mark the finish and catch angles with tape on the gunwales of the sweep boat (see figure 13.7). The next step is to set each athlete's footstretcher for the required finish angle. Rowers should sit at the finish position with the oar handle just touching the chest. The coach should check that the tape on the side of the boat lines up with the back of the oar.

Table 13.1 Distances From the Rigger Pin to the Center of the Boat

			DISTANCE FROM PIN TO CENTERLINE OF BOAT FOR RESPECTIVE SPANS LISTED BELOW								
	Angle from pin to centerline	Cosine of angle	83.0	83.5	84.0	84.5	85.0	85.5	86.0	86.5	87.0
Angle in front of pin	55	0.5736	144.7	145.6	146.4	147.3	148.2	149.1	149.9	150.8	151.7
	54	0.5878	141.2	142.1	142.9	143.8	144.6	145.5	146.3	147.2	148.0
	53	0.6018	137.9	138.8	139.6	140.4	141.2	142.1	142.9	143.7	144.6
	52	0.6157	134.8	135.6	136.4	137.2	138.1	138.9	139.7	140.5	141.3
	51	0.6293	131.9	132.7	133.5	134.3	135.1	135.9	136.7	137.5	138.2
	50	0.6428	129.1	129.9	130.7	131.5	132.2	133.0	133.8	134.6	135.3
Angle behind pin	35	0.8192	101.3	101.9	102.5	103.1	103.8	104.4	105.0	105.6	106.2
	34	0.8290	100.1	100.7	101.3	101.9	102.5	103.1	103.7	104.3	104.9
	33	0.8387	99.0	99.6	100.2	100.8	101.3	101.9	102.5	103.1	103.7
	32	0.8480	97.9	98.5	99.1	99.6	100.2	100.8	101.4	102.0	102.6
	31	0.8572	96.8	97.4	98.0	98.6	99.2	99.7	100.3	100.9	101.5
	30	0.8660	95.8	96.4	97.0	97.6	98.2	98.7	99.3	99.9	100.5

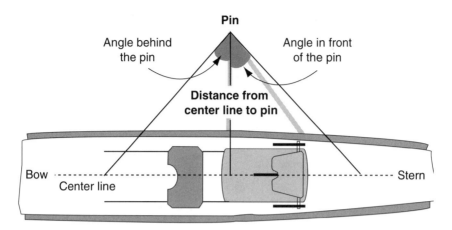

FIGURE 13.7 Taping the gunwale of the boat.

After setting the crew on the same finish angle, the crew must strive for the same catch angle. You can mark the correct catch angle on the side of the boat with a straw. The straw should be high enough that the handle can touch it at the catch. If the handle passes the straw as the blade approaches the water, the blade will be in the water when the handle passes the straw again. Thus the accurate catch position is right at the straw. If the handle only reaches the straw and not past it, the effective catch position is slightly less than the marked angle.

Coaches have to watch closely and use video to judge the correct catch angle in a sculling boat. However, they can mark the finish angles for sculling boats in the same way as for sweep boats. Marking the finish angles will help the crew set up in the correct position.

It is important to set the finish angles and make sure each crewmember is set to that same position. I always set the finish angles first and coach a crew from the finish position. The finish position is important as it is the one position that is fixed by the position of the footstretcher. You can coach a longer or shorter catch angle by having the rowers adjust body swing or compression, but it is very difficult to coach a longer or shorter finish angle without changing the footstretcher position. More body layback at the finish can lead to inefficient use of power and energy, as it has very little effect on the finish angle.

Conclusion

Now that we have analyzed the catch, here's a story that illustrates what can happen when rowers emphasize the wrong part of the catch. I was part of an Australian national team preparing for the world championships. During training we were struggling to improve our times. We had extremely fast catches, or blade entries into the water. We had been working on quick entry for a long time but were not seeing any improvement in boat speed. Eventually we noticed from video analysis that although we had fast blade entry, we had slow power application. Once the emphasis expanded to include speed of power application, not just speed of entry, but boat speed improved dramatically. A fast catch is not how fast the blade enters the water but how fast you apply power to the face of the blade. This power should be initiated with the leg drive, and it must be smooth and fast. If you remember this and the other tips in this chapter, you'll see your catch improve.

chapter 14

Leg Drive

Richard Tonks

I learned the value of sliding seats the hard way, when I was a schoolboy out training one hot summer's day. The wheel undercarriage of my seat broke, making it impossible to use my legs. Seven miles of swinging the body and pulling the arms made it a long trip home. It also made me realize just how much work the legs do in rowing.

Without leg drive we would be back in whaleboats and fixed-seat racing boats. The introduction of sliding seats, or sliding riggers, for that matter, brought the power of the legs into the picture. Using the legs allows athletes to row faster and farther over a longer period of time.

The sliding rigger and the sliding seat allow rowers to use the legs to propel the boat. The sliding rigger also keeps the body mass still and reduces pitching, allowing the boat to run flat. This is beneficial because pitching of the bow and stern slows the boat's forward movement through the water.

Leg drive pushes the boat forward and gives timing to the stroke. The best crews move effortlessly (see figure 14.1). There is no rushing on the slide on either the recovery or the drive. The size of the puddle and speed of the boat demonstrate the rower's work.

Effortless movement is the result of perfect timing between rower and boat. If a crew looks to be working hard, its timing and coordination are off. The rowers are trying to work beyond their ability, breaking the coordination of the muscle groups. This leads to jerky, sudden movements that require extra effort from one muscle group and a lessening of effort from another.

FIGURE 14.1   A world-class sculler's drive.

The timing between pedals and wheels on a bike is a fixed link and cannot be broken. The wheels can't move faster than the road is moving beneath and the pedals can only drive as fast as the wheels can move on the road. The relationship remains even when the bike is turned upside down and the pedals turned. Rigid cranks and a solid chain fix the link between pedals and wheels.

There is no rigid connection between the oar and the boat. The seat can move back and forth faster or slower than the boat, but such motion affects the boat's movement. Proper timing and control of the seat motion can increase boat speed. Control of the seat is the sole responsibility of the rower, as the legs control the speed on the slide.

Leg Drive Phases

The four phases of the leg drive are catch, drive, finish, and recovery (see figure 14.2, a-d). Because the stroke is cyclic, every phase depends on the previous phase. The catch depends on the recovery, the recovery depends on the finish, the finish depends on the drive, and the drive depends on the catch. Many coaches believe that the finish is the most important phase because without it a rower can't achieve good catch.

FIGURE 14.2 *(a)* Catch, *(b)* drive, *(c)* finish, and *(d)* recovery.

Boat balance is very important. To maintain balance rowers have to keep the blades off the water during the recovery. Just as it's easier to balance on a bike when it's in motion, movement can make balancing the boat much easier. A good lock-up, drive, and send create momentum that helps make balance and timing easier.

Rowing is a continuous, fluid motion. The boat is always in motion. The rower is always in motion. The blade is always in motion. There are increases and decreases in speed, but never any stopping or hesitation once the stroke begins.

Catch

The catch is the hardest part of the stroke. It takes a great deal of coordination to get the blade into the water as the rower comes forward on the slide and then pushes off with the feet while holding the back muscles steady and keeping the boat balanced at the most unstable part of the stroke.

Rowers must be relaxed and balanced as they move up the slide (see figure 14.3a). They should visualize connecting to the boat and moving it forward. As the seat nears the frontstops the rowers square the blade and the hands move forward and up. The blade's entry into the water must be as fast as possible. As the blade touches the water the legs push against the footstretcher.

The catch is a small, tight movement controlled by the legs. If rowers time the catch right and place the blade into the water correctly, the rest of the stroke will follow naturally (see figure 14.3b). The change of direction and the switch from relaxed

Photos on this page by Richard Tonks

FIGURE 14.3   Catch phase.

recovery to full power make this a difficult part of the stroke. The body swings over into the catch position at the start of the recovery, so it must not swing forward after the slide reaches the front. The seat rolls to the front of the slide and is instantaneously driven back by the legs.

The catch occurs when the rower comes onto the feet, not when the shoulders move forward. The body remains in the catch position. By coming onto the feet rowers transfer their strength and weight to the oar handle and the boat moves forward. It is the anchoring of the blade in the water that makes this motion so hard to perfect.

Timing at the catch requires coordination of the hands and feet, hips and shoulders, and blade and water. Good timing means the blade locks into the water at the catch and the boat moves forward. A strong back coordinates the hips and shoulders to hold the boat and helps translate leg drive into boat movement.

The leg movement locks the back and arms so the upper body does not move. The rower does not want any wasted movement at the catch, because any movement at that point that doesn't move the boat forward—it simply slows it down.

Drive

Rowers who train on a river know that leg speed at the catch depends on whether they're rowing with or against the current. Two crews rowing with the current at the same speed may have different speeds when they turn around and row against the current. This shows which crew has mastered the ability to get onto the feet at the catch and drive off at the required speed to connect with the boat at the frontstop. Training on a river can help beginners improve the catch.

Lifting the body up out of the catch position at the front of the slide makes it harder for the back to catch the speed of the boat. The back has a limited range of motion that must not be wasted. The back muscles' strength also should not be wasted trying to lock the blade in the water. Only the leg muscles are fast enough to match the speed of the boat going through 1000 meters at 36 or more strokes per minute.

At the frontstops of the slide rowers immediately push off the footstretcher. They must keep the shins and thighs relaxed to avoid stopping, and they must watch out for any last-minute pulling with the legs. If the legs are tight the seat will stop at the front. At the catch the boat is running at its slowest, and any delay getting the blades into the water results in slower boat velocity. The slower the boat the more time and energy it takes to get back up to speed.

The legs should pack up freely in time with the boat moving underneath. When the feet are set too high it affects the pack-up. The feet should be set up to enable a straight leg drive, but the setup also has to allow the legs to compact like a compressed spring. Once the legs are fully compressed, they spring out with life and quickness. Reduced leg movement in this phase is the result of tension.

Rowers come into the front relaxed. The legs compress as the hands roll forward and up. Immediately the rowers come onto the feet and lock the blades into the water at the farthest point, meaning they place the blades as far ahead in the water as they can comfortably reach. The tip of the blade must connect with the water exactly as the slide reaches the frontstops. Everything locks from the feet through the body to the tip of the blade.

The strength of the legs drives the body backward and the back muscles hold against the legs, forming a rigid connection between oar and boat. Because the blade is in the water the boat moves forward. The strength of the legs and torso dictate how fast and far the boat will go.

The leg drive off the front carries the body and the boat (see figure 14.4). It is easy for rowers to clench the muscles and feel as though they are pushing and working hard, but tightening the muscles actually impairs movement. The muscles must contract freely. The rowers may feel that they're not working hard enough, but they have to learn to recognize full power and not try to do more.

FIGURE 14.4   At the catch, the blade locks into the water and the legs drive the boat forward.

The legs, back, and arms must work together for the greatest possible acceleration, and progressing from the strongest to weakest muscles will help achieve this (see figure 14.5). Of the three groups, the legs are the strongest, dominating from the catch through the drive. Body movement is small at the beginning of the drive but increases as boat speed picks up. Although in the beginning it feels as though the torso is being left behind, movement increases through the stroke and the torso finishes at the same time as the legs. The arms are the weakest of the three and start to draw after the legs and back have accelerated the boat. The arms may bend slightly at the elbow at the catch but should stop bending after the catch. Rowers must be careful not to draw the arms early because this reduces power output from the legs and back.

Photo by Richard Tonks

FIGURE 14.5   Legs initiating the drive.

This is not a one-two-three movement—move the legs, now the back, now pull with the arms. At the catch all the muscles work but the strongest dominates. The body and arms try to swing and pull but don't come in until boat speed picks up. The arms should never take over for the legs or back, and the back should never take over for the legs. Instead they all must work together.

You can easily experience the principle of biggest to smallest using a hand-sized weight such as a shot put. Keeping the legs and body still, throw the shot forward with just the arms. Then throw the shot using the torso and arms. The shot will go farther than with the arms alone. Now throw the shot using the legs, torso, and arms. The legs start from a crouched position and push upward, the body swings up and forward, and the arms add to the speed built by the legs and torso. Give it a final push to increase speed and you've thrown it as far as you possibly can. The legs, torso, and arms work together to increase the speed of the shot, just as they work together in rowing to produce the greatest possible speed.

Using the three muscle groups in the wrong order slows the boat. In addition, the rower needs force to move from the feet to the blade. This force cannot be contained in the hands, forearms, or the shoulders. Using these muscles incorrectly results in reduced force on the pin.

The legs must initiate the drive. The body must not take the catch by lifting up off the thighs, which occurs when the seat pauses and the rower doesn't use the legs at the frontstops.

From the moment the blades touch the water the boat must accelerate. If there is no acceleration, this shows that the pressure of the blade pushing against the water is lessening. Even when a crew applies very light pressure the boat will still accelerate.

The catch pressure, light or heavy, must be maintained to the finish. The old saying "Only the best crews can paddle" (to paddle meaning to row with light pressure) remains true today.

The legs and back should maintain catch pressure through the end of the stroke. Maintaining the same pressure helps rowers achieve the maximum boat speed possible for that amount of pressure, while changing pressure during the stroke causes many problems. Maintain the catch! Finish the stroke! Think about the next stroke! There is no possibility of increasing the pressure once the stroke has begun. Rowers who are trying to work harder usually go to their arms, which takes weight off the back and legs. Although this satisfies the rower's desire to give his best, it ends up slowing the boat. Once the legs and back lock up at the catch the stroke should continue without interference from the weaker arms.

The pressure must be straight and parallel to the water. There should be no lifting after the blade is submerged—it's a waste of energy to try to lift the boat up out of the water. Once the blade drops in the water it doesn't move in a circle, going deeper and then lifting throughout the stroke to the finish. Instead it moves flat just underneath the surface of the water. This is the point where the legs are the most important. The drive must be constant and powerful from the frontstop until the legs are down.

Once the rowers are on their feet and start squeezing off the front, they must keep the pressure on the footstretcher constant. The legs should feel like they're accelerating throughout the entire drive phase. The hands can sense the leg drive and ensure that it remains constant throughout the drive. The legs are so strong that if rowers drive them as hard as they can, the back is unable to take the pressure, causing the rowers to shoot the slide. Novices with poor technique and weak torsos often have this problem. Slippage can be so bad that the power of the leg drive is lost for the entire stroke. This occurs when rowers drive the seat all the way down the slide with no connection to the boat's movement.

Rowers must not drive off the front at a greater speed than the boat is moving forward, because the back must be able to hold the leg drive. The catch cannot be too aggressive. The blade should not hit the water so hard that it bounces or the movement stops, because the boat must accelerate from the moment the blade hits the water. Crews and single scullers can see this acceleration by watching the stern.

It is possible for rowers to jump onto the feet so hard that the pressure seems to be against the stern and the run of the boat. Rowers can feel this when they push the catch extra hard during a good row. They feel the extra effort, but the boat is heavier and slower and the rowers lose their sense of timing.

Rowers can improve coordination between the catch and drive by rowing into a headwind. The wind slows the boat's speed, making the rowers work harder to connect at the catch. The wind also makes the rowers work harder driving out of the catch. This allows them to feel and analyze the opening of the legs and back more easily because it happens in slow motion.

When rowing with a tailwind, the timing at the catch becomes more difficult. The faster acceleration of the stroke doesn't allow rowers enough time to rectify a bad catch, and the leg drive has a shorter time span. If timing and coordination aren't right, the rowers lose more slide at the beginning of the stroke and more water under the blade at the catch. Less experienced crews will feel as though they are chasing the catch all the way through the drive and are never in control of the boat or the stroke.

Stroke length is shorter when stroke rate is lower. Sudden pulling on the feet or throwing the body forward are not the way to get full length. Instead, take length off the relaxed pack-up. The extra length will come with a higher stroke rate.

Rowers must avoid stiffening at the catch. Rowing is a sport of suppleness, and even under pressure rowers need to stay relaxed. Relaxation allows the muscles to contract freely and to their maximum ability. But relaxing doesn't mean rowers don't work hard—it means they work hard and have the right timing.

The body moves very little between catch and finish. The legs have to carry the body from the catch position to the finish position to maximize effectiveness.

Finish

At the finish the legs and back finish together. The legs lock to stabilize the end of the stroke (see figure 14.6a). With the hips locked and the back braced, the arms can pull strongly to finish the stroke (14.6b). The legs remain down until the body swings forward. The legs and hips must hold steady to stay balanced as the body swings over to begin the next stroke.

a

b

FIGURE 14.6   Legs locking to hold the finish.

Photos on this page by Richard Tonks

Recovery

As rowers comes forward the body relaxes in the catch position. The arms extend forward, straight but not rigid. The body is centered and balanced and the rowers control the blade for good balance. They must feel the weight of the blade balancing on the gate.

Rowers don't come up the slide, they let the boat flow beneath them, visualizing themselves sitting still and allowing the feet to come toward the seat. They keep their legs relaxed and they are aware of the stern coming forward. They think ahead as they approach the catch position. When weightlifters bend down to pick up a weight off the ground, they prepare their torso for the weight. Rowers don't have an opportunity to stop and set their torso muscles before driving off, so they must prepare their back muscles for the coming strain as they approach the catch.

If the legs are tense during the recovery, the rowers will stop at the catch before engaging leg drive. The legs need to be perfectly relaxed so the boat runs out under the rower. Tension makes it difficult to feel the boat run and results in stiff, jerky movements. The entire recovery should be relaxed and flowing, the body balanced between seat and feet.

The legs must not pull the seat up the slide. Only experienced rowers should use the recovery to propel the boat forward, because faster recovery makes the catch even harder to time.

Drills for Strong Leg Drive

MOVEMENT THROUGH CATCH

This exercise shows the importance of not stopping at the catch. Stand with feet normal distance apart, squat down, and spring as high as possible. Repeat, this time stopping at the bottom of the squat. Notice that the spring up is not as quick or high.

RUSSIAN CATCH

To practice timing of the hands and feet at the catch, start at the frontstop with the blade in the water. Push back on the slide for the first 10 centimeters and drop the blade out of the water. Roll forward and take the catch. Continue rowing the stroke for 10 centimeters. Keep the arms straight the entire time and make sure the back does not move.

HALF SLIDE

To improve quickness of the legs at the catch, row using only half slide. Boat propulsion is more immediate with the blades closer to 90 degrees, requiring rowers to apply the legs faster than at the normal catch position.

PART BOAT

To feel the speed of the leg drive, start rowing an eight with the bow pair. After 10 strokes, bring in the three- and four-seat rowers. The boat speed picks up and bow and two have to feel the difference in order to apply the same amount of leg drive. After 10 more strokes bring in the next pair and so forth until the whole crew is rowing. Each pair adds to the speed, and each rower must adjust their leg speed or get left behind.

LEGS DOWN

To practice using the legs throughout the drive, add on to the Russian catch drill by pushing the legs down until fully extended. Keep the body still in the catch position, concentrating on timing the legs with the movement of the boat. As the legs go down, feel the boat moving through the blades in the water. Maintain pressure to achieve constant acceleration.

MOVING ERGOMETER

To coordinate hands and feet at the catch, practice on the RowPerfect or Concept2 ergometer on slides. This teaches correct timing and weight at the catch and throughout the stroke. (See figure 14.7.)

Photo by Richard Tonks

FIGURE 14.7   Ergometer drill on a Concept2 ergometer with slides.

RESISTANCE ROWING

It is important to carry the body and the boat with the legs throughout the stroke. To build the strength for this, slow the boat down. Make it heave! Tie a cord around the hull or tow a can behind the boat, anything that will increase resistance. The slower the boat moves the greater the work rowers will do with each stroke.

Georgina and Caroline Evers-Swindell—2002 and 2003 world champions—demonstrate the importance of training for a powerful leg drive.

As we've seen, the best training for the legs is rowing. However, rowers can also do supplementary training on land. Squats, squat jumps, leg presses, squats with weights, and all weightlifting moves requiring leg drive improve strength and endurance. Watch form and take care when exercises require the back to support heavy weight. Weight training can be the quickest way to improve strength, but carefully consider which type of weight training, strength or endurance, is needed, and check with an expert before starting a program.

The legs make the greatest contribution to boat propulsion. They make up the largest muscle group but must coordinate with the torso and arms. Study winning crews and you'll see that quick, strong, continuous leg drive is essential for success.

chapter 15

Recovery

Volker Nolte

When rowers describe what it feels like to move fast in the boat, they often say that the boat is flying. This expression depicts not only high speed but also a sensation of effortlessness. The idea that rowing feels effortless when rowers are pulling pretty hard seems contradictory at first, but this is what happens when rowers learn to preserve energy by performing movements smoothly and efficiently. It is during the recovery phase of the stroke that the boat flies, an uplifting experience that rowers will experiment long and hard to produce. Although the drive phase of the stroke is what creates boat speed, the recovery phase is what creates excitement for the rowers.

Recovery Goals

"The catch is defined as the position where the handle is closest to the stern of the boat, therefore having the smallest x-value for the handle. The finish position is defined as when the handle is closest to the bow of the boat and the blade is out of the water" (McLaughlin 2004, 8).

The recovery phase lasts from the finish to the catch, and the drive phase lasts from the catch to the finish. These definitions make it easy to identify and analyze the phases. For example, when you graph force, boat acceleration, and oar angle, you get curves like those in figure 15.1.

The oar angle in figure 15.1 is helpful for identifying the recovery phase, because the recovery starts at the largest oar angle (finish) and extends to the smallest oar angle

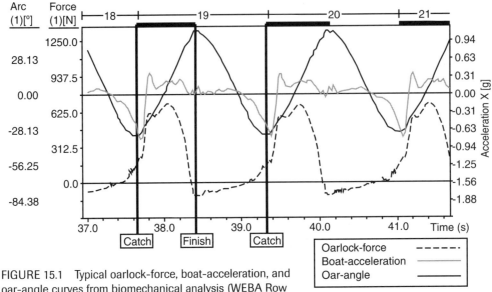

FIGURE 15.1 Typical oarlock-force, boat-acceleration, and oar-angle curves from biomechanical analysis (WEBA Row Expert System). This data is from the bow rower of a heavy-weight men's pair.

(catch). Thinking of the recovery in this way allows you to study different parameters during the recovery, because it allows you to distinguish each parameter during this phase (for example, the time for the recovery or the course of the boat velocity).

The main goal in rowing is to cover the race distance in the shortest time possible. To accomplish this, rowers have to produce force that overcomes resistance in order to propel the whole rower–boat–oar system. The geometry of rowing equipment only allows intermittent propulsion. Body movements occur through the flexion and extension of the joints; in rowing, whichever is stronger, flexion or extension, is what propels the boat. For example, the legs generate more force during extension rather than flexion, so leg extension becomes the drive. The more effective joint movements occur during the drive so rowers reach the finish at the end of force production.

The primary task in the recovery phase is to return to a position that allows the rower to begin a new power phase. In such a position the rower stretches the arms and flexes the hips and legs. Obviously, this can be done in different ways. However, since only resistance, not propulsion, occurs during the recovery, rowers need to complete this phase with the least reduction in the velocity of the whole rower–boat–oar system.

An often-overlooked task for rowers during the recovery is to produce the intended stroke rate. The recovery phase presents the rowers with a much greater chance to influence stroke rate than the drive phase.

The following are the tasks during the recovery:

- Move from the finish to the catch position.
- Minimize fluctuations in boat velocity.
- Minimize additional factors that increase resistance (i.e., rolling or pitching of the boat).
- Avoid any unnecessary resistance force on the oar (i.e., touching the water with the blades or improper feathering of the blades).
- Generate the planned stroke rate.

Strictly Science

How can rowers fulfill these tasks? We will be able to discuss practical applications after investigating the theory behind them. Biomechanics can help us outline the options for carrying out the best movements during recovery.

First we need to look at the forces on the rower–boat–oar system (see figure 15.2). Figure 15.2 excludes air resistance of the rower and the boat, since it only complicates the discussion without adding any information. Manipulations such as wearing specific clothing or shaping the boat influence air resistance, not rowing technique.

FIGURE 15.2   Rower–boat–oar system in the recovery with all acting external forces, including weight of the whole system (W); buoyancy (B); resistance of the boat (R); and air and water resistance on the oar (A).

Note that figure 15.2 shows the movement of the overall rower–boat–oar system, not just boat movement. Both forces in x-direction point to the left, meaning they slow the system down. As rowers move toward the catch, they exert force on the boat, which changes the velocity of the boat relative to the system, which leads to different velocities of the boat and the system. Figure 15.3 shows how these velocities interact.

Figure 15.3 shows that the velocity of the overall system decreases during the recovery phase, which supports the findings presented in figure 15.2. The only way to positively influence velocity is to reduce resistance forces on the boat and air and

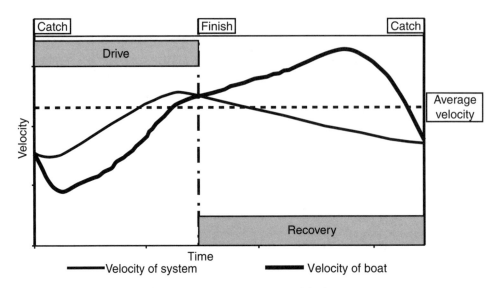

FIGURE 15.3   The velocity of the rower–boat–oar system and the boat.

water resistance on the oar. Rowers can achieve this through proper technique. They should not let the blades touch the water during the recovery, and they should feather the blades in a way that creates the least amount of air resistance—rowers should finish feathering the oars by the finish position and square them at the last moment before the catch. In addition, rowers can reduce resistance on the boat by moving their center of gravity horizontally as smoothly as possible, thereby reducing velocity changes of the boat when moving into the catch. Furthermore, rowers can reduce other resistance forces by minimizing rolling and pitching of the boat.

An interesting point for discussion is the influence of recovery movements on the stroke rate. Figure 15.4 illustrates that the duration of the drive phase varies little over

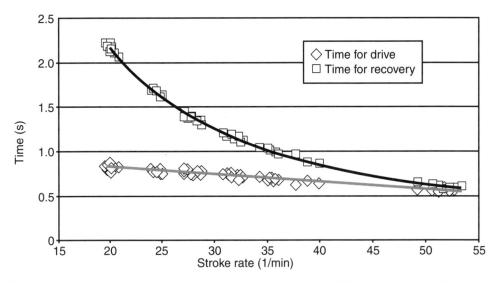

FIGURE 15.4   The amount of time needed for recovery and drive at different stroke rates. This data is from the stroke rower in a heavyweight men's pair (world champion 2003).

stoke rates, while the length of the recovery phase varies dramatically. The recovery has by far the greater influence on stroke rate. You could even say that the stroke rate is produced during the recovery. Several researchers have documented the phenomenon shown in figure 15.4 (Gerges 1977; Kleshnev 2003).

Finally, it is important to analyze hand movement during the recovery. The hand must move as shown in figure 15.5. First the hands move down to keep the blades off the water, and then they move smoothly and directly into the catch.

FIGURE 15.5   Hand movement during the recovery (white curve).

Practical Applications

During the recovery, rowers must do the following:

- Make movements feel light or effortless.
- Relax.
- Balance.
- Use the proper sequence.
- Move together as a crew.

After finishing the work of the drive phase, the boat must move freely underneath the rowers during the recovery phase. Rowers should feel the boat's speed and other sensations of an amazing run. To experience this they must relax during the recovery. They should execute movements during the recovery with the least effort possible, all while being prepared to react to unforeseen events such as getting hit by a wave or touching the water with an oar. This effortlessness and readiness is only possible when all muscles are relaxed, the rowers are comfortable in their positions, and the focus is on the boat.

Relaxed movements result in a balanced boat. Balance allows rowers to keep their blades off the water, keep the boat from rolling, and cost the least amount of work. When athletes start rowing on the water after a long period of training on the ergometer, they find that they have to exert more energy in the boat to maintain balance. Any rolling of the boat requires rowers to contract muscles not only to even out the boat but also to stabilize their bodies.

Performing the movements in the proper sequence puts all body parts in position to accomplish the tasks of the recovery. The arms have to move away from the body first so that the trunk can follow, and then the legs bend. Moving the arms away from the body first and keeping the legs locked down will allow the hands to finish the release at a level that keeps the blades off the water. Then, the movement of the upper body places the hands sternward of the knees so that the oars pass the knees at the correct level, off the water. The upper body actually finishes its sternward swing to get into position for the next catch before the legs start bending. When following this sequence, rowers do not need to swing the trunk even more sternward at the end of the recovery, and this prevents the dipping of the hands into the catch.

Finally, all rowers must move together during the recovery. If even one individual moves differently, it will cause extra work for all the other rowers in the crew, because the movement is against their momentum.

All these tasks are interconnected. Rowers cannot relax without balance, and they cannot feel light when their movements aren't together. However, when everything comes together, rowers experience flow—all movements feel intertwined and light, and the athletes feel like they can row forever. This is the peak of technical perfection, the sensation that all rowers strive for. This is when rowers feel like the boat is flying.

Drills for Recovery

An effortless recovery requires many kilometers of focused technique training. The following drills will help rowers reach this goal.

OPEN HANDS

Rowers position stretched hands on top of the handle. This emphasizes relaxed shoulders and arms.

RECOVERY PAUSE

This drill increases the feel for balance and working together. Rowers perform two or three normal strokes and then pause in the recovery of the next stroke. Every third or fourth stroke, the rowers pause for a few seconds at a specified point in the recovery (hands just past the knees, finish position, catch position). The bow rower or coxswain can help rowers start the motion again after the pause with their calls, but the rowers should be able to follow the stroke without external cues.

Pausing during every second stroke or even during every stroke increases the difficulty, as does performing an air stroke (keeping the blades off the water throughout the entire stroke cycle) instead of a pause.

CLAPPING THE BOAT

This exercise only works in sweep boats. The rowers clap the side of the boat with one hand during the recovery.

Clapping twice during the recovery makes this drill more difficult, especially when rowers perform the first clap with the outside hand and the second clap with the inside hand. The synchronized clapping of the crew improves rhythm and balance.

SET UPPER BODY

The focus of this exercise is setting the upper body, movement sequence, and balance. It is crucial to set the upper body's forward lean early in the recovery, and one way to learn this is to overemphasize the movement. In this drill rowers perform each segment of the recovery separately rather than together in one fluid motion. First, the arms stretch out of the finish. Then the upper body swings sternward until the rowers feel a stretch in the lower back. Finally, the legs bend. To increase the drill's effectiveness, add a small pause after each movement.

SQUARED BLADES

Rowing with squared blades is a universal and extremely valuable drill. It trains hand movement, balance, and crew coordination. Make sure rowers keep the blades fully squared, especially the new asymmetric Big Blades; otherwise rowers are cheating themselves out of the drill's full benefits.

FEATHER–SQUARE–FEATHER

Rowers perform a complete square–feather movement just after they take the blades out of the water with a normal feathering movement. The extra blade movement emphasizes balance, hand relaxation, and crew coordination.

STROKE-LENGTH PROGRESSION

Changing stroke length in any way improves balance and cooperation in the boat. Rowers can perform this exercise in many different ways:

- Row five strokes each: arms only, body swing only, quarter slide, half slide, three-quarter slide, full slide.
- Change movement length every stroke: body swing, quarter slide, half slide, three-quarter slide, full slide, three-quarter slide, half slide, and so on.
- Have the coxswain or coach call certain stroke lengths that the crew has to perform from the very next stroke on.

RHYTHM CHANGE

Repeating a sequence of very different strokes improves focus, crew coordination, and a feeling of lightness. Rowers can perform this exercise in different ways:

- Repeat a three-stroke sequence, such as two strokes body swing only followed by one stroke full slide. The short strokes don't require much effort but should be quick and fluent, while the long stroke requires a slow recovery to allow for preparation and a strong drive.
- Alternate half-slide and full-slide strokes.

- Perform 20 half-slide strokes while gradually increasing the stroke rate (up to 50 or more strokes per minute), followed by 5 full-slide strokes at maximum boat speed.

VARIED STROKE RATE

Change the stroke rate in a set fashion (every 10 strokes increase by 4 strokes per minute) or randomly (the coach calls random stroke rates).

By not giving the crew feedback about the stroke rate through the coxswain or a stroke meter, the crew develops a feel for the desired stroke rate. This exercise also trains coordination, flexibility, and teamwork.

Conclusion

Rowing in a boat that is flying is a magical experience. Rowers strive for this feeling, and even a few perfect strokes during a long row will keep them trying for more. Highly skilled crews obviously experience flow more often than less skilled crews, and great performances are usually connected with the sensation of flying. Skilled crews balance the boat perfectly and spend their energy effectively. Because they avoid all unnecessary movements, every bit of energy can be used to propel the boat; this is the prerequisite for fast rowing.

These sensations are more connected to the recovery than to the rest of the stroke, which is why the recovery is so important. In contrast to the energy and the power of the drive, the recovery is the result of relaxation, balance, and coordination. While the drive is the power of the stroke, the recovery is the art of the stroke.

chapter 16

Inside the Rower's Mind

Volker Lippens

Every rower realizes rowing technique differently. One hears the boat, another watches the blades, and another feels the forces on the hands or feet. The connection between the physical environment, or biomechanics, and the way athletes use this information can greatly influence rowing technique. We performed a complex analysis of movement by comparing physical data from rowing behavior with corresponding psychological data from the rower. This analysis can help athletes and coaches find connections between the biomechanically ideal technique and the athlete's psychological concept of technique.

This research came from my desire to validate different kinds of technique training. As a coach, I realized that some rowers need figurative descriptions, others prefer technical specifications, and a few are sometimes perturbed by a coach's instructions. There is more than one way to learn how to row faster!

This chapter makes a concrete proposal for bridging the gap between the movement that is produced by the athlete and the performer of the movement (the athlete). I present methods of movement analysis that encompass not only physical education but also psychological interaction between the athlete and the coach. First, I will introduce our study's theoretical approach and explain some methodological implications. Then I'll give two practical examples of our research that show the advantage of this research program.

Connection Between Athletes and Their Motion

What do athletes think and feel when they are in motion? In this section I'll describe internal perceptions using the so-called subjective theories, which assume that athletes are able to reflect on their movements and piece together new patterns on their own (Groeben 1988). Athletes cannot be aware of all parts of the subjective theories during the performance itself. However, we have developed a card-laying technique that enables athletes to use the theories' relevant aspects as completely as possible so that they can put together sport-specific contents and structures.

Human movement is a dialogue between person and world (Tamboer 1988; cf. Vereijken and Whiting 1990). On the one hand, the situation's demands and environmental conditions determine the movement dialogue; on the other hand, the individual's efficiencies determine the movement dialogue. The actual meaning is reflected in the contents and structures of the athletes' subjective theories about the specific performance. Therefore, this process of forming sport-specific contents and structures is a realization phase of motor learning in which athletes have to define their own experiences. This approach clearly differs from information-processing theories, particularly in its assumptions about human nature.

We consider the rower to be an autonomous, responsible person who, just like the scientist or coach, is characterized by "the central assumptions of reflexivity, potential rationality, the ability to speak, communicate, and act" (Groeben 1988). While there is an "illusion of autonomy" (Meyer-Drawe 1990), or the illusion that athletes learn independently, in reality there are both intrinsic and extrinsic influences on the athletes. Coaches must integrate the athletes' possibilities with a concrete analysis of the environment's requirements. When coaches are able to adapt their instructions to the athletes' learning styles, it often leads to a feeling of "being absorbed in action beyond boredom and anxiety"—the athletes experience flow (Csikszentmihalyi 1975). However, the necessary movement dialogue would not be possible without the basic premise of autonomy as an objective idea.

To teach rowing technique, Hacker (1994) proposes what he calls a shift from "extracting towards reconstructing concepts." This means that, instead of simply reproducing contents and structures of the rowing technique, coaches should be creative by applying appropriate methodological techniques and skillful experimental arrangements.

For this purpose we have made a complex movement analysis, and we have developed a way to represent the athletes' subjective theories by using sport-specific versions of the card-laying technique (Lippens 1996a). We created a basic vocabulary for technique experiences from previous interviews with athletes. Rowers reported, for example, when they felt their boat was well balanced, when they could extract the blades easily at the finish, or when they felt that the speed of the boat was high—"It sounds cool when the boat runs well." We recorded the experiences as subjective contents on index cards, which refer to the individual understandings of the skill the athletes are developing. During the experiment, immediately following a row we asked the rowers to arrange the cards according to the importance of their experiences. Thus, the contents and structures of the subjective theories can be related to knowledge structures, which offer the qualifications to enhance motor skills.

One of the first to recognize this relationship between the knowledge structure of the athlete *(Eigensicht)* and the performed skills in the boat *(Fremdsicht)* was Karl Adam, the famous German rowing coach and scientist. For example, he asked his sweep rowers to imagine the force pattern as rectangular, even though it is physically impossible to row in this manner. This mental image helped the rowers to perform properly shaped pulling forces.

The term *Fremdsicht*, or outside view, refers the visible behavior of motor performance, objectified by biomechanical data (Körndle and Lippens 1988). The term *Eigensicht,* or inside view, refers to all conscious cognition of the athlete, verbalized in the subjective theories. In short, the contents and structures of the athletes' subjective theories indicate how thoughts and feelings may change during the training process.

Since the movement of elite rowers is usually highly automated, access to all knowledge within the subjective theory is not always possible. How many times have you heard a rower say, "I've got the feeling for it, but I can't explain it in words"?

Answers to the question about creating the optimal run of the boat illustrate the problem of how to verbalize complex feelings. Studies into the subjective theories developed subtly differentiated statements about how rowers realize their technique; however, those do not always refer to physically measurable parameters. We can describe several indicators of proper rowing technique. We can quantify the vertical movement of the boat's stern through an analysis of the vertical movement of the rower's center of gravity. We can quantify the horizontal movement of the stern by measuring the acceleration of the boat and the propelling forces on both sides of the boat. We also know details about the blade and boat noises during the optimal run of the boat, which can play a significant role depending on the skill of the rowers. However, so far we have not discovered an objective, biomechanical model that completely describes the optimal run of the boat.

How to Find Athletes' Subjective Theories

In four steps athletes explore the contents and structures of their subjective theories. If possible, have the athletes perform the card-laying technique shortly after the actual movement.

1. First, each athlete selects the index cards with the statements about movement that best apply to the present motor performance. If important aspects are missing, the athletes can add specific criteria on blank cards. They can also correct the given criterion formulations. When the athletes have established a basic vocabulary, the first phase of the content recording is finished and they separate the stack of cards into applicable and rejected items.

2. Next each athlete arranges the chosen applicable items in theme groups, or categories, according to similarities.

3. The athletes classify the categories by general terms like "rhythm" or "relaxation." Arranging the items into categories reveals their connection to each other and their structure. For example, if relaxation were the main focus of an athlete, you would find several related items for this category, such as "There is a distinct contrast

between action and relaxation" or "There is quietness during the recovery." In addition, this step further develops the content since the terms in each category refer to the individual importance of the topics.

4. Finally, each athlete arranges the categories in a network according to their mutual dependencies. The primary category is placed in the center and the others at a distance, each according to its significance. The athletes define or assess the relationships on their own. This final structure is transferred into a chart, and thus the quality of their relationships is defined.

Synchronization Strategies in Coxless Pairs

In a crew performance, the coordination of each member appears in cooperation and is constituted by a "bipersonality of partner work" (Christian and Haas 1949). Rowing in a coxless pair can thus be modeled as a comprehensive dynamic system (crew) in which complex cooperative subsystems (rowers) have both to coordinate their individual motor performances and to synchronize them. Since a straight line is the fastest connection between two points, a crew that keeps its boat on a direct path from the start to the finish displays the better skill. This is particularly difficult in a pair where the two rowers have quite a different lever on the boat with the positioning of their riggers. The two rowers have to coordinate their movements to keep the boat moving in a straight line while applying maximal power.

For synchronization of group performances, there are two models of interaction between group members, direct and indirect (Troitzsch 1996). In the case of direct interaction, each rower follows the instructions of the member in the leading position. In rowing, the leading task is usually performed by the stroke rower. The bow rower tries to reproduce the stroke rower's individual movement coordination, minimizing the differences (see figure 16.1).

In the case of indirect interaction, all members focus on the expectations for their specific role in order to create the best crew performance possible, or the best run of the boat. Because of the asymmetric arrangement of the oars in a coxless pair, this can only be achieved by position-specific production of the individual coordination performance.

Hill (2002) presented more complex methods for analyzing inter- and intraindividual coordination. These methods allow a systematic investigation of dynamic movement synchronization. Hill suggests studying the force on the oar by identifying vertical or horizontal differences in form and area to quantify individual coordination of the movement. Hill draws a differential straight line over the concave segments of the force pattern. The area between the differential straight line and the actual force-time curves is indicated as shape difference in comparison with the area integral (value of smoothness = shape difference relative to total area under force curve [%]).

Another way to study coordination in a pair is to measure temporal movement synchronization (Lippens 1999). This method compares for each rower the times for certain parts of the stroke, defined by the oar angle. By evaluating the time differences of certain parts of a series of strokes, you can identify a coefficient of variability (standard deviation divided by mean). Rowers who repeat their strokes with more precision will display smaller amounts of coefficients. It becomes clear that the

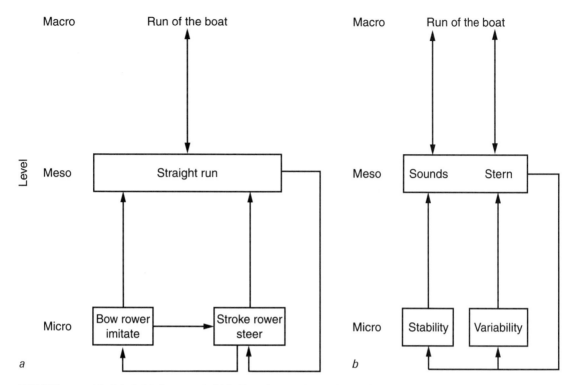

FIGURE 16.1   Model of *(a)* direct and *(b)* indirect interaction in the coxless pair.

stroke rowers alter their times for the drive phases much more than the bow rowers, affecting the whole stroke (see figure 16.2).

This research technique is based on the idea that movement performance is organized dynamically by self-assembled, smart mechanisms and not by fixed rules (Newell and Corcos 1993). For example, in one world-class crew the bow rower showed a relatively smooth pattern of pulling forces, while the stroke rower showed a larger variability in her force–time curve. In addition, over a series of about 60 strokes at different stroke rates (from 20 to 36 per minute), the duration of the bow rower's drive phase changed less than the duration of the stroke rower's drive phase. Nevertheless, there was a specific change in the coefficient of variability within the individual coordination performance when the crew changed to the highest stroke rate.

The crew performed a card-laying test after their row and identified "the run of the boat" as one category that described their present motor performance. Since the crew said the boat's best run in the series occurred at a stroke rate of 24 per minute, we investigated the crew's subjective theories for this run. The bow rower described her drive phase as very consistent, with almost no variation. To control her performance she listened to the sound of the boat. On the other hand, the stroke rower said that she adjusted her drive by watching the lateral movements of the stern.

Our measurements suggest that, because of the asymmetric arrangement of the riggers and the positioning of the rowers behind each other, it is best for bow rowers to reproduce their force application as accurately and consistently as possible. At the same time, stroke rowers should try to ensure a straight run of the boat by varying

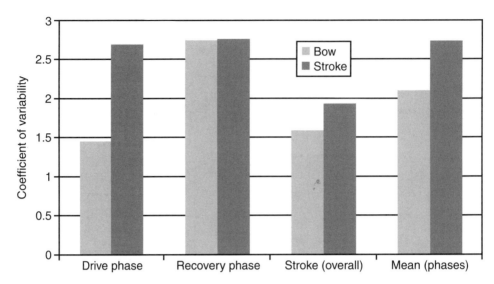

FIGURE 16.2   Analysis of the time for the stroke parts, as well as overall stroke for both positions in the boat (24 strokes per minute) (Lippens 1999).

Source: V. Lippens, 1999, "The temporal and dynamic synchronization of movement in coxless oared shells." In *Sports kinetics: theories of motor performance and their reflections in practice, vol. 2,* 1997, edited by P. Blaser (Hamburg, Germany: Czwalina), 39-44.

their force-time curves and the rowing angle. To accomplish this, stroke rowers watch the stern's lateral movements.

Based on their subjective theories, the rowers were concerned with the optimal run of the boat. If we interpret the force applications as a measure of the rowers to control this concern, we can see that both rowers applied individual strategies. This may indicate an indirect interaction between the rowers in pairs. The rowers in the bow position repeat their movements with the greatest consistency possible, while the crew partners vary their movements to adapt to the bow rowers.

This does not, however, correspond to the conventional task description for the stroke rower, which is to set the stroke so that the bow rower can reproduce it as identically as possible. However, such a rigid strategy would require more steering movements in order to keep the boat moving in a straight line. This example shows how rowers' subjective theories help us better understand motor performance. With this knowledge, coaches are better able to help athletes reach their peak performances. Coaches should not, for example, ask the bow rowers in a pair to simply copy their stroke, but to find movements that give them the feedback of an optimal run of the boat and repeat those with great consistency. The stroke rowers should try to apply their force on the handle so that the boat has the best straight run, which they can control watching the stern of the boat.

Technology and Technique Training

Providing athletes with information about their performance improves motor learning. But what kinds of instruction are particularly relevant for complex skills? Rowing consists of several movement sequences that have to be coordinated. However, we know little about how much or what kind of intervention is useful. Most coaches follow the biomechanically ideal rowing technique. They approach intervention through trial and error because they do not know how to use their athletes' perceptions of rowing movements.

In a complex movement analysis we compared physical data from the external movements with the corresponding psychological data from the rower's inner processes. The feedback for athlete and coach can be combined to close the gap between the biomechanically ideal technique and the rower's conceptual world.

Helping the Coach Close the Gap

We conducted a study where we gave a crew feedback based on our understanding of motor learning. The starting point of the intervention was a biomechanical technique analysis, for which we measured the force pattern of the stroke, the angle of the oar, and the speed of the boat. We classified physical faults in the stroke performance along with their negative consequences for boat propulsion. We could not find equivalent psychological data so easily, however.

We based our "coaching" on a model of hierarchically ordered schemata in the control of motor action. Zimmer and Körndle (1988) defined their concept of the schema as consisting of

- a series of basic parts that cannot be subdivided any further in the given context,
- a series of subschemata on varying levels, and
- a series of rules that organize the relations of the parts and the subschemata.

Skill, as a top-level schema and the final goal, is organized in an upward integration to reduce the complexity of the system (see figure 16.3). Therefore, a downward control is necessary and leads to semiautomated execution of the task. To improve performance, athletes need to modify lower-level schemata or even basic parts. To do this, the downward control on the lower level has to be removed.

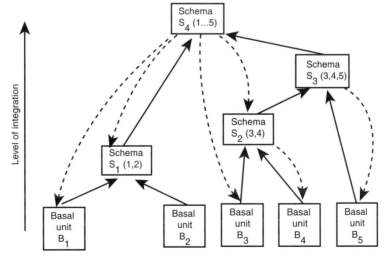

FIGURE 16.3 Example of an order of priority to integrate schemata for rowing skill (see figure 16.4) with the top schema being *run of the boat* and two subschemata being *sounds* and *pressure*. Pressure is downward constrained (see figure 16.5). The sets of basic parts (such as coordination of the legs or arms) on a lower level are not shown.

Applications for Technique Training

To start the coaching process, we conducted a card-laying test with each rower. This process revealed the rowers' subjective theories. Figure 16.4 shows the results for one rower regarding the run of the boat.

Then we tried to put the relevant coordination elements (such as "good feeling on the seat" or "harmony in the crew") into concrete terms, which directed us to a subschema for the drive phase (figure 16.5). This meant the rower needed to work on "good feeling on the seat" to be able to remove the downward control to the sub-schema *course of pressure* (see figure 16.4) and to include a new description of the schema: *behavior of pressure* (figure 16.5). This work gave the rower a clear direction to work on for improving rowing skill.

Further Developments

When describing their subjective theories, the rowers also reported emotional experiences, such as the feel of smooth movements, as well as physical experiences, such as a general good feeling (see figure 16.4). Those descriptions obviously exceed the possibilities of biomechanical measurements and fall under so-called meditative dimensions (see also Lenk 1985; Csikszentmihalyi 1975, 1990, 1999).

Our interviews often corresponded with the athletes' accounts. For example, we interviewed one rower during a test session. After the athlete had commented on his

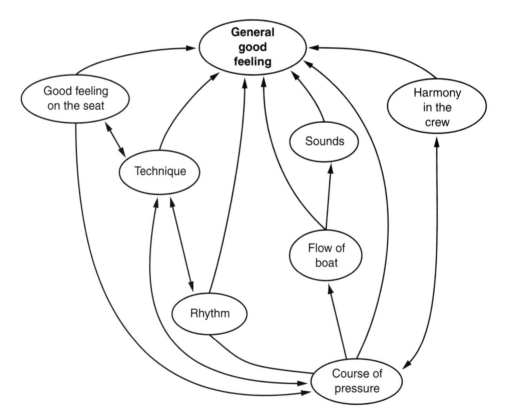

FIGURE 16.4 Causal diagram of one rower's subjective theory of the boat's optimal run.

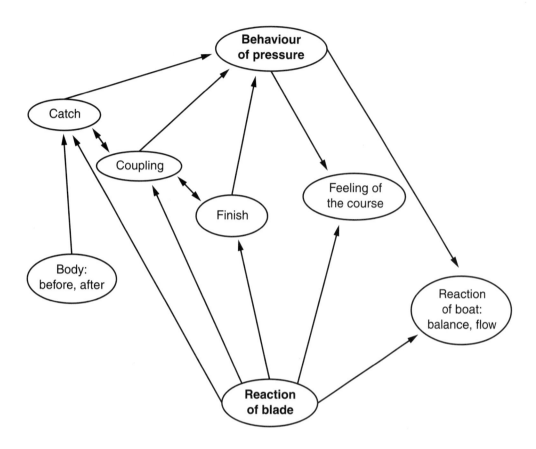

FIGURE 16.5 Causal diagram showing the revised subjective theory about drive.

movement for awhile via wireless microphone, he stopped rowing and reported, "I forgot the opponents for a moment, I simply thought, it doesn't matter, the boat is running, more than that isn't possible, so it is irrelevant what the others are doing now, at this moment this is really the optimum."

This phenomenon has always been a special topic with rowers. They describe the run of the boat in connection with acoustic feedback as "pleasant," a "great feeling," "fun," or "feeling the silence of the recovery." Rowers in a single or a coxless pair especially perceive this.

In the end, we have had to expand the schema integration. As part of our coaching advice, the athletes used mental training that helped focus their attention on certain aspects during technique training. This approach integrates the overall feedback sensations by putting the emphasis on reported experiences as a "good general feeling" when "the boat runs."

The emotional subsets of the subjective theories exceeded the motor-control criteria as a "smart mechanism" (Runeson 1977) and added a mental dimension to the training. The positive reports of the rowers lead us to believe that this experience may be what hooks the athlete searching for an optimal performance, because it creates excitement and integrates body, mind, and motion into a single amazing unit.

Potential of Subjective Theories

Our suggestion is that the athletes' subjective theories, put together over a longer time period using the card-laying technique, will indicate how thoughts and physical feedback sensations may change during the training process. In addition, the experience of kinetic sensations in smooth performances is an extraordinary motivation for the sport. This is a sign that the experience of sport motion by itself is undervalued and underestimated as a pedagogical goal, and therefore it should be adopted in modern physical education. However, the results should be evaluated in relation to concrete situations.

In addition, a long-term empirical analysis of possible intervention effects is needed in order to analyze how kinetic feeling becomes increasingly important for the subjective theories and to what extent it may contribute to self-confidence. Therefore, pedagogical experiments should be developed with the objective of contributing to "conditions which would allow us to be happy while being engaged in sport" (Court 1995, 242). Using underestimated potentials of traditional and of more recent sports, a pedagogic-oriented instruction might contribute to the development of a self-confident personality and the ability to act in sport and movement situations. Perhaps then the feeling of happiness resulting from the perfect performance (Lenk 1985) could be more often communicated to novice rowers (cf. Lambert 1998).

This may have motivated former German world champion in the single, Peter-Michael Kolbe, as well as Pertti Karpinnen, three-time Olympic gold medalist, to participate in our investigations: to learn more about how to row not only as a successful athlete but also as a competent performer. Their statements about how to row as a champion offer a great deal of inside knowledge we did not know before.

Our investigation revealed that Kolbe and Karpinnen paid attention to the sounds of their boats as well as the wake of the stern. When the wake opened symmetrically, it told the two scullers that their power applications were equal on both oar sides and the run was optimal. Derek Porter, who stroked to gold medals in the eight as well as in the single, had a different concept than Kolbe and Karpinnen. Porter's conceptual world contained a great deal of similarities but not the category of sounds. During a training session, Porter gave feedback about the sounds of the boat. He reported, "I'm sorry, but I only hear noise during the recovery, not sounds!" Nevertheless, some months later he won his silver medal in Atlanta.

The understanding of the subjective theories of athletes allows new insights on how rowers develop their skills. Coaches can learn to understand those connections and better provide an environment conducive to improvement. Obviously, it is not enough to provide outside feedback and instruction based on this. However, each athlete experiences skills individually, so the personal subject theories must be investigated and separate learning strategies have to be developed.

chapter 17

Ergometer Technique

Larry Gluckman

As rowing started to become popular, athletes started to build rowing machines to simulate on-water movement. Although these first rowing machines were far from today's ergometers, the basic features were there: simulation of the rowing movement and resistance to build a load for the athlete. These machines had two purposes:

1. To teach rowing technique with real-time feedback provided by mirrors, hands-on coaching, or visual review through photos and video
2. To allow physical training through simulated rowing when the weather prevented on-water rowing

The rowing machine has been a staple in the sport of rowing since the mid-19th century. Bill Miller of the Rowing Museum at Mystic Seaport and Northeast Rowing Camps reports that patents for rowing machines date as early as 1871. W.B. Curtis, one of the founders of the New York Athletic Club, designed and patented the Improved Rowing Machine on June 27, 1871. Kern and Laflin patented a hydraulic rowing machine in 1901. These machines were referred to as the Narragansetts because they were first built at the Narragansett Machine Company in Providence, Rhode Island. Rowers used these machines from 1900 all the way to the early 1960s, and they can still be found in college indoor training facilities. According to Miller, you can even spot a couple of the Narragansetts on board in one of the scenes in the 1997 movie *Titanic*.

In the early 1960s an Australian company built a large flywheel machine with leather belt resistance that they called an ergometer. The word *ergometer* refers to a device that measures work capacity (from Latin: *erg* means work, *meter* means measure). Dr. Fritz Hagerman, a world-renowned physiologist, tested many of the U.S. Olympic hopefuls in 1968 on this ergometer to determine their aerobic capacity. The only problem was that the machine's sensitivity to humidity and temperature influenced rowers' final performances.

In 1970, Gamut Engineering in California developed a rowing machine that was less sensitive to atmospheric conditions. The Gamut ergometer simulated sweep rowing with inboard-like arms that swiveled around a fixed axis and could be rowed on port or starboard. Through the 1970s and early 1980s it was popular in most college rowing programs.

The Modern Rowing Ergometer

Although the early ergometers were quite sophisticated, they were large and heavy, needed loads of maintenance, and were fairly expensive, all of which prevented them from becoming popular. Another major disadvantage was that the load on the handle was significantly different from the resistance that the water generates on a normal oar. Engineers continued to develop more advanced machines.

The Swedish engineer Gjessing accomplished a breakthrough at the end of the 1960s with the machine that was named after him. Not only did the machine very accurately measure the work of the rower, it also simulated the force curve and hand speed of on-water rowing with a snailshell-shaped gearing system (Nolte, Klauck, and Mader 1983). With proper maintenance, the Gjessing ergometer produced accurate and repeatable measurements and was therefore used by many national teams for research and training monitoring (including Norway, Spain, Italy, and Germany). Although the braking and measurement system was purely mechanical, the Gjessing ergometer was still quite bulky and expensive.

In 1981 the Concept2 Indoor Rower (C2IR) started its success story and has been a staple of competitive rowing ever since. Peter and Dick Dreissigacker, the designers and manufacturers, started with very interesting and ingenious ideas. First, they used air as the breaking system, which is a simple technical solution to the problems of simulating water resistance of the oar and measuring rowers' output. Similar to the blade in the water, the vent of the C2IR increases its resistance exponentially as the speed with which it is propelled increases. Secondly, the Dreissigacker brothers developed monitor devices that would give a rower feedback after every stroke, which was the starting point for indoor racing. These races became the foundation for the worldwide popularity of this ergometer type. Thirdly, they kept the C2IR affordable, durable, and reliable, so that now it is used literally in every boathouse in the world.

Over the years, the C2IR has evolved through four different models. The second model, called B, was the real breakthrough for Concept2. It had the first electronic monitor—the PM1—and the vent was built as a solid one-piece component. Concept2 competitors used this model as the base for a very interesting improvement. The Row-

Perfect ergometer combined all the benefits of the C2IR Model B with the simulation of the rowers' and boat's movements on the water. The footstretcher and the vent, combined as one unit, move freely on the same rail as the seat, so the rower's body literally stands still relative to the ergometer. You could call this model the "sliding rigger" of ergometers. The free movement of the vent and the seat requires proper rhythm and power application for the rower to produce a high power. Therefore, the RowPerfect ergometer is viewed by many as a more accurate simulation of the on-water rowing motion.

The Concept2 Model C became the standard in 1994, and the Model D has been available since summer 2003. With the exception of a few frame and seat redesigns, the Model C's only major change since its introduction is an upgraded performance monitor, from the PM1 to the PM2 or the optional PM2 + with personal computer interface and Internet capabilities. Both the PM2 and PM2 + have heart rate interface options. The Model D's main developments are a new performance monitor, the PM3, with a LogCard function for designing and storing workouts, force curve display, quieter flywheel enclosure, and ergonomic handle.

The rowing ergometer is used to simulate the rowing motion for training purposes. Electronic monitors allow athletes to control all aspects of their training: duration, intensity, stroke rate, and power application.

The C2IR set a standard for indoor rowing machines in durability, simulation of the rowing motion, and on-water feel. Besides upper-level racing, the C2IR is used for rehabilitation, group fitness workouts, and home fitness. Since the person using the C2IR can propel the resistance mechanism at any position of the handle, the machine allows for self-determined ranges of motion. The option of isolated parts or full-body rowing makes the C2IR a complete piece of exercise equipment.

Rowing is a superb conditioning activity for athletes at any level. Today's ergometers provide the full range of cardiovascular conditioning, from low-intensity to high-intensity aerobic and anaerobic levels. It also allows for rowing-specific strength development. Many people outside of rowing use the indoor rower to cross-train. The rowing motion involves many of the largest muscle groups, providing strength and circulatory training for muscles not exercised in the athlete's primary sport.

Rowing improves flexibility because it puts most of the major muscles through a wide range of motion. It is a nonimpact exercise, imposing less wear and tear on the body than many other activities. With ergometers, athletes can row indoors anytime, which is especially nice for sports that are affected by weather conditions. Finally, ergometers allow you to accurately monitor your level of conditioning and provide constant feedback during workouts. These advantages still motivate engineers to invent new models of rowing ergometers—some are built out of wood for aesthetic reasons, some use water resistance in specially-designed encased water containers. Nevertheless, Concept2 maintains its domination around the world—the official Indoor World Championships are rowed on this model.

The Monitor

Ergometers' functions increase with special monitors and computer connections. The Concept2 PM3 monitor has pace boat functions, Internet racing, power plot, multirower onsite racing, and data storage. It also lets rowers participate in an online ranking program and training forums. The computer adaptation increases the use of the C2IR and offers exciting ways to enhance the training.

The PM3 monitor allows rowers to program and store workouts by distance in meters, time in minutes and seconds, or just sitting down and rowing. The monitor displays stroke rate, stroke output per 500 meters, performance in watts, and estimated calories burned per hour. It also displays the load on the wheel, or drag factor, and has recall capabilities with adjustable split ranges to capture stroke information. Finally, the monitor gives feedback about the force curve.

The Slide

Inspired by the RowPerfect development, Concept2 developed their so-called slides. The slide consists of a base with two tracks and a carriage with wheels that runs on the tracks. It gives indoor rowing some of the same sensitivity as on-water rowing. The movement of the rower's center of gravity and the feel of "floating" are very similar to the feeling of being on the water. Miscues on the slide provide immediate feedback, which a stationary indoor rower does not offer. Two or more rowers can row slides together as a crew.

Rower Adjustments

Here are the steps for preparing the Concept2 ergometer for daily use:

1. Set the damper between one and three. The lower numbers give a light, lively feel. The higher numbers provide more resistance and feel like a slower boat. The indoor rower is self-paced, so damper setting does not provide a variety of resistance unless the rower's intensity is high enough to create drag on the wheel. In other words, the rower always controls the pulling power!

2. Adjust the monitor height to permit proper head positioning. Your head should be horizontal, and you should be able to see the monitor without restricting the flow of air from the mouth and nose through the head and neck into the lungs during any part of the stroke.

3. Before fixing the feet in the stretchers, place the handle in the handle hook so it's easier to reach. When the machine is not in use, store the handle against the chain guide to release the recoil mechanism.

4. To set footstretcher height, pull the toe piece toward you to release the foot piece from the two pegs. Slide the toe piece up or down to the proper setting, and then press the toe pieces back down onto the pegs. Begin by setting the footstretcher heel so that the strap crosses the ball of your foot. The best setting leaves the shin perpendicular to the floor at the catch. Lowering the heel permits more seat travel and raising it reduces seat travel.

Body Attachments

In addition to the footstretcher, there are two other attachments: the seat and the handgrip. It is critical to find a seat position that permits the widest range of motion in the pelvis and hip. Sitting toward the back of the seat is a good starting point, but some rowers prefer to sit closer to the front and use a foam pad or bubble wrap to slightly elevate the body.

The handgrip is also critical. The hands should reach the end of the handle with the pinkies over the top of the handle. The knuckles should be at 11:00 o'clock, which makes the wrists flat or slightly elevated. There should be a straight line from the knuckles through the wrist, elbow, and shoulder at the beginning of the stroke.

The Stroke

Rowing is a natural motion, and most people pick it up quickly. New rowers should have someone watch them row and compare their body position to those in their technique video or book. Table 17.1 is a sample form for evaluating position and form. Don't pull too hard until you've established safe, effective technique. During the learning phase the stroke rate should be about 20 to 22 strokes per minute.

Here are some tips for the different phases of the stroke.

Catch

- Extend the arms straight toward the flywheel.
- Keep the wrists flat.

TABLE 17.1 Rowing Ergometer Evaluation Form

Preparation	Description	E = Excellent S = Satisfactory NI = Needs improvement
1. Location on seat	Permits the body to pivot for body angle and lay-back. Avoids the pinching of nerves or blood vessels on the edge of the seat.	
2. Feet height	Allows the rower to reach a shin position perpendicular to the floor. Avoids hypercompression and hyperflexion.	
3. Damper setting	Permits a range of stroke rates without reducing length. Avoids turning rowing into a weightlifting event.	
4. Monitor height	Provides for a level head at the catch and finish for easy breathing.	
5. Clothing tucked in	Prevents loose-fitting clothes from catching in rollers.	
6. Location of water bottle	Fluids in easy reach of rower.	
7. Grip	Grip is relaxed, with the wrist straight or with slightly elevated knuckles. The knuckles and shoulders form a straight line during the early part of the drive.	
Position	**Description**	
1. Catch	Arms are long, shins vertical, upper body slightly compressed against thighs, shoulders relaxed, and lats engaged. The seat is 18-25 cm from the heels, hips are behind the shoulders, and head is up.	
2. Drive	Hips and handle move together, arms remain long for as long as possible, body engages as legs drive, and arms maintain speed of the handle. There is a 5-degree layback. The abdomen and lower back stay strong.	
3. Finish	Legs and seat are quiet, lower back is strong, elbows pass the body, head is level, hands are relaxed and active. Do not hit body, and avoid locking the knees—keep the legs long but relaxed.	
4. Recovery	The drive ends as the hands move past the shorts, and the arms pull the upper body forward until wrists are past the knees. The knees bend up into the window created by the arms, handle, and chest, squeezing into catch position without abruptness or dumping.	

Technique sequence	Description	E = Excellent S = Satisfactory NI = Needs improvement
1. Ratio	Time on the recovery is longer than time on the drive. Do not hesitate at either end—keep the handle moving. Use the correct ratio for the stroke rate.	
2. Rhythm	There is a flow that is consistent from stroke to stroke. The flow is fatigueless.	
3. Sequence	The press, pry, and pull sequence is established: legs, back, arms, arms, back, and legs.	
4. Shell compatible	The technique on the ergometer moves the boat effectively.	

- Lean the upper body slightly forward with the back straight but not stiff.
- Slide forward on the seat until the shins are vertical.

Drive

- Begin the drive by pushing the legs down.
- Keep the arms straight and the back firm to transfer leg power to the handle.
- Gradually bend the arms and swing back with the upper body, prying against the legs until you reach a slight backward lean at the finish.

Finish

- Pull the handle to within a few centimeters of the abdomen, drawing the elbows past the sides of the body.
- Keep the legs long and straight without locking the knees.
- The upper body should lean slightly back, about 5 to 10 degrees beyond the perpendicular.

Recovery

- Extend the arms toward the flywheel.
- Next swing the upper body forward at the hips to follow the arms.
- Allow the hands and wrists to pass the relaxed knees.
- Gradually bend the legs upward to slide forward on the seat.

Catch

- Draw your body forward until the shins are vertical.
- Lean the upper body forward at the hips.
- Make sure the seat is no closer than 15 centimeters from the heels.
- Fully extend the arms.
- You are ready to take the next stroke.

Common Technique Errors and Corrections

- The arms bend before the legs have pressed down (involving the arms too early).

  Correction: Keep the arms long and pry back as the legs press down until the hands approach the knees.

- The seat moves backward without the handle moving (shooting the seat).

  Correction: Use the upper body to link the hands and the hips. Tell yourself, "Hips and handle move together." The upper body should pry against the handle as the legs press down.

- The upper body is too erect during recovery (too stiff).

  Correction: Allow the hands and wrists to pass the relaxed knees before the knees bend upward. The upper body should lean slightly forward.

- The upper body leans back too far at the finish (too much "lean back").

  Correction: The upper body should not lean back more than 5 to 10 degrees past the perpendicular. Lean back about the same amount as you lean forward.

- You hesitate and lower the handle at the catch or beginning of the drive to the back of the machine.

  Correction: Keep the chain and handle parallel with the floor at all times. Once the seat stops moving at the end of the recovery immediately begin the leg drive.

Beginning Workouts

Resist the temptation to row for 30 minutes nonstop the first time on the ergometer. Do three to five minutes, then take a break to stretch and walk around. If you feel up to it, do four of these short intervals.

On the next row begin experimenting with stroke rate and power. Stroke rate is your cadence in strokes per minute. You should not exceed 20. Continue this experimentation for the following few workouts. For example, if you have no muscle soreness or stiffness, then go for a longer time, play with higher stroke rates, and so on. Contacting a coach or trainer for help with creating workouts would be a good way to start your program.

Before you move on to a more intense training program, check with your physician to obtain the proper training heart rate for your age and past medical history. Your physician will also indicate the best duration and frequency of training for you.

Since rowing is a complete body exercise, you may experience some muscle soreness in muscles that you don't normally work. If you do, consider reducing the duration, intensity, or frequency of training. Also be sure to have a pre- and postexercise stretch program. Finally, drinking enough fluids will help prevent muscle soreness.

You can follow some simple tips to make the rowing experience safe and effective. When selecting clothing, choose nonrestrictive clothing that allows you to bend freely at the hips, knees, ankles, and shoulders. Be sure that loose-fitting clothing does not hang off the seat and get caught in the seat roller. Snug-fitting shorts or pants that have a pad sewn into the seat are great for rowing. Footwear should allow flexion and extension of the ankle and keep the heel from rubbing against the heel support of the footstretcher.

You might also want a sport's glove, similar to a lifting or cycling glove. Sweatbands for the head and wrists are common, and the all-important water bottle is a must.

Rowing Ergometer Drills

ARMS ONLY

This drill teaches rowers to move the hands away before the knees bend upward. Also called the pick drill, it helps rowers learn to move "around the corner" at the catch and finish of the stroke.

Keeping the legs in the finish position and the back slightly behind the perpendicular, row with the arms only. The knees do not move upward. Allow the hands to float out until the arms are extended; keep the wrists relaxed. Be sure to pull the handle at the end of the drive to within 2 centimeters of the abdomen, halfway between the lap and the chest.

ARMS AND BACK

This drill shows rowers how the arms and back coordinate during the drive and recovery of each stroke. It begins the same as the Arms Only drill, but the handle moves past the knees as the upper body leans forward over the thighs, demonstrating proper extension of the arms and body before the legs come up. Change the direction of the handle by allowing the body to swing back. As the handle passes the knees, begin the arm pull as in Arms Only.

PARTIAL SLIDE

This exercise teaches proper body position and sequence at each point in the drive and recovery. Row each position continuously for 10 strokes, and then increase the seat travel to the next position. Continue until reaching the full slide position.

Quarter slide: Like the Arms and Back drill, but continue the extension forward with a slight bend of the knee.

Half slide: Same movement as the quarter but just a little more slide. Allow the seat to come halfway up to normal catch position.

Three-quarter slide: Allow the seat to come three-quarters of the way up to normal catch position. Fully extend the arms and pivot forward at the hips before the seat starts coming up the rail.

Full slide: Row full strokes, emphasizing full arm extension. Pivot at the hips before the seat starts coming down the rail.

LEGS ONLY

This drill teaches rowers that the legs, not the arms and shoulders, initiate the drive. Start at the catch position. Push the legs until the handle is over the ankles (pause a second and then recover). Come to the catch position and then drive again. Try to feel the pressure that can be generated without opening the back or pulling with the arms.

LEGS AND BACK

This drill is an extension of the Legs Only drill. Start at the catch position. Push the legs and pivot at the hips but leave the arms straight. Begin to move to the catch position by pivoting forward at the hips and then moving the seat up the rail with your legs. Keep the arms straight. Try to feel the pressure that can be generated without pulling with the arms.

ULTRASLOW MOTION

This exercise gets all of the body parts working in the right order. Row as low as 10 strokes per minute. Work on making deliberate movements and getting proper sequence on the recovery and the drive.

PAUSE DRILL

This drill involves full-stroke rowing with pauses on the recovery. A momentary pause at different times in the recovery lets the rower check the various recovery positions.

After each pause continue to full slide and take a drive by pulling through. Do five strokes, pausing at a specific position (such as the finish), then five strokes with a pause at a different position, and so on. This teaches rowers how to control body movement on the recovery. At each pause check body position in a mirror or by using a light reflecting against a wall to create a shadow.

Pause with the hands away from the body before the body swings forward.

Pause in the arm and back reach position.

Pause at each of the quarter-slide positions.

Pause at the catch.

AUDITORY DRILL

This drill teaches rowers to listen to the wheel and chain acceleration. As you row, feel the load against the body, see the immediate result of the different pull-throughs on the performance monitor, and hear the acceleration of the wheel during the drive and the deceleration of the wheel on the recovery. The heavy wheel will sound slow at first, but as the wheel accelerates and the pull-through becomes quicker, the humming of the wheel will become sharper and livelier.

Creating a Workout Plan

Each workout needs the same elements, including a goal, warm-up and stretching that are appropriate for the designated training, correct setup of the damper and performance monitor, workout details, cool-down, and notation of results.

• **Workout goal.** What is the purpose of a particular workout? A technique row focuses on safe and effective rowing. A moderate aerobic workout works the aerobic system but permits the rower to carry on a conversation. A vigorous aerobic workout focuses on heart rate, pace, and stroke rate. An anaerobic threshold workout stretches the aerobic system to its limits and begins to use a small portion of the anaerobic

Indoor racing on the Concept2 ergometer is very popular all over the world.

system. A high anaerobic workout challenges the cardiovascular system to its max and works the anaerobic power system so that it produces high levels of lactate.

Once you choose the goal of the workout, decide on duration, intensity, and frequency.

- **Duration** is the time, distance, or calories burned. Duration determines how long the rower will work out. Examples: 20 minutes, 5000 meters, or 300 calories.
- **Intensity** is the quality of the work output, the number of rest periods, the stroke rate, the damper setting, or the heart rate. Examples: 200 watts, 2:04 pace, 450 calories per hour, rest for 2 minutes between each 500 meters, 24 strokes per minute, or 132 beats per minute heart rate.
- **Frequency** is the rate of parts within a workout or of the workouts per time frame. Here's an example: six 2-minute intervals with 1 minute easy paddling

between intervals. The frequency in this example is 6 × 2 minutes hard. Or frequency could refer to repeating the above workout twice within a 14-day training cycle.

- **Warm-up and stretching.** Each workout should begin with a period of light exercise on or off the ergometer to raise the body's core temperature. Then do a series of static stretches for all the muscle groups involved directly or indirectly in the rowing motion, including hands, wrists, elbows, and shoulders. Also stretch the lower back, hips, hamstrings, quadriceps, and Achilles tendon.

- **Damper and performance monitor setup.** Note the damper setting, because it affects the workout's intensity and goal. The lower the damper setting, which permits less air to contact the wheel, the lighter and livelier the stroke will feel. As the damper number increases, the machine will draw in more air, making the stroke feel heavier. Set time and distance parameters for the workout on the performance monitor. Setting up the monitor properly includes selected recall of information for recording after the workout is over.

- **Body of the workout.** This includes the duration, intensity, and frequency of the workout. The workout body is the main part of the session. Pay special attention to choosing an appropriate workout body, but also make sure that your training is exciting and variable. For example, 2 × 20 minutes, with 5 minutes easy rowing, changing the stroke rate by two at the end of each 5 minutes, beginning at 22 ending at 28. Damper setting is 3.

- **Cool-down.** This is a period of moderate rowing for a set time or until you reach a certain recovery heart rate. Follow with stretching, particularly the hamstrings, muscles of the lower back, and Achilles tendon.

- **Recording workout performance.** Use a notebook or computer spreadsheet to record the results of the workout. First indicate the specifics of the workout, then record the results in time, distance, average watts, or calories. Note variation in stroke rate from the plan, average pace and workout heart rate at the end of each piece, and recovery heart rate taken at a prescribed interval from the end of the last piece. You might also want to note your impressions of the workout.

Maintaining the Ergometer

Maintaining the ergometer involves three things. The first is keeping the rail clean on a daily basis. Simply wipe the rail with a clean cloth or paper towel and water or commercial cleaner.

The second part is oiling the chain once a month for light use and once every two weeks for heavy use. Use lightweight machine oil, vegetable oil, or oil provided by the manufacturer. You need two people for this procedure. Moisten a clean cloth with the oil. Pull the chain handle out to the end of the rail. The person holding the chain walks the handle slowly back toward the wheel. The other person holds the oiled cloth so that the returning chain runs across it. Return the handle to the chain guide position, as you should always do when the indoor rower is not in use. This reduces the wear and tear on the shock cord.

Finally, you need to maintain the monitor. Be sure to keep the monitor in a place where it can't be hit by an errant handle. Clean the screen with a damp cloth to remove dust. Replace the batteries when necessary.

Learning to Pace

Learning to maximize fitness is key to athletic success. The machine's feedback allows rowers to analyze preparation as well as competition. Developing a personal strategy for competition lets rowers focus on their assets and not be distracted by a competitor's pace or race plan. Determining the best pace for you from your preparation enhances your chance of meeting performances goals. For example, you might estimate that 7:00 minutes or 1:45 pace for 2000 meters makes the best use of your preparation. Based on your training on the indoor rower, you would realize that rowing the first 500 meters at 1:40 might jeopardize that goal, so you would row the first part of the race at 1:46 pace, permitting your aerobic fitness to carry the early load. Then you could gradually reduce that split over the last 1000 meters, using anaerobic fitness as you get closer to the end. By maintaining control of the splits and understanding the energy systems, you perform closer to your fitness level than you would if you were drawn into an unsustainable pace.

Some general rules have become apparent from the performances of elite competitors. For example, a rower's 30-minute pace (time per 500 meters) is 5 to 7 seconds slower than the 2000-meter pace. The 60-minute pace is 7 to 9 seconds slower than the 2000-meter pace. By improving the 30- and 60-minute performances a rower can improve on the 2000-meters.

Other analysis suggests that collecting the times for 6 × 500 meters on the rower with 3 minutes rest between each 500-meter piece helps you predict a 2000-meter time. Take the six times and drop the fastest and slowest 500 meters. Add the remaining four plus 8 to 10 seconds. Divide this sum by four and the result is your pace for a strong 2000-meter performance.

Coaching Rowers on an Ergometer

Whether you are a rowing coach or a personal trainer, the indoor rower offers an opportunity to work closely with your athlete. It gives you the chance to "lay hands on" the athletes to help them better understand the motion and rhythm of the stroke. The ability to stop at any point in the stroke and reposition the athlete provides immediate feedback on a stroke-by-stroke basis. Nearly any drill on the water can be performed on the indoor rower, including timing, sequencing, certain technique points, and learning to accelerate from catch to finish.

You can add the slide component for team focus, helping the athletes work on matching their timing at critical points in the stroke. If timing doesn't match, the carriages will touch either the front or back of the slide, causing a loss of rhythm.

Whether you're a coach, trainer, on-the-water rower, or indoor rowing enthusiast, you'll find it helpful to develop a philosophy toward rowing on the ergometer.

- **Know why you prescribe the ergometer or why you row on it.** Is it to improve overall fitness, complement land training, build a strong rowing mentality, work on technique for on-water rowing, or compete at indoor rowing regattas?

- **Why do the testing?** Is it to measure improvements, qualify for the opportunity to row in a particular crew, learn how to pace and push yourself, or come up with a baseline to begin the process?

- **Create benchmarks for future athletes.** By keeping previous results, beginning athletes can compare themselves to athletes of similar age and size. Concept2's online ranking lets rowers compare themselves to others of their sex, age, and weight.

Conclusion

Indoor rowers have provided on-water rowers and indoor rowing racers the ability to develop both cardiovascular and strength fitness for over 20 years. The total body benefits of rowing are well documented, and the performance monitor has made exercising and training on the ergometer systematic and analytical. Serious rowers and fitness enthusiasts alike should take advantage of indoor rowing.

chapter 18

Technology for Technique Improvement

Valery Kleshnev

Sport science and biomechanics can help athletes and coaches achieve their best performance. But how? What exactly is sport science, and how can we make it more efficient? To answer these questions, I'll define a methodological model of sport science made up of three components: measurement, analysis, and feedback.

- *Measurement* is a component that produces information. It includes selecting and developing equipment and methods of data acquisition, processing, storage, and visualization.

- *Analysis* is a secondary component that produces knowledge. It includes collecting and studying measurements.

- *Synthesis* produces the expertise, in rowing's case the system of tools and methods, for improving technique and implementing knowledge into practice.

The pyramid model illustrates these three components (see figure 18.1). This model is useful not only for rowing biomechanics but also for any other applied science as well.

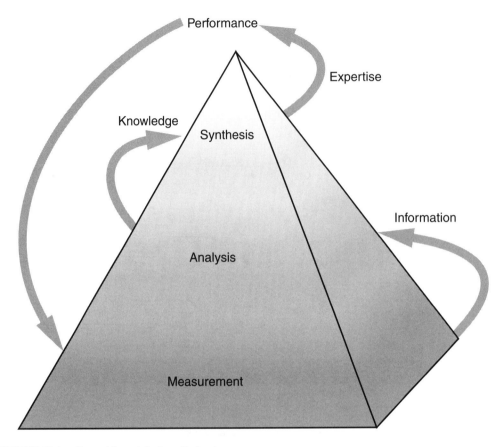

FIGURE 18.1   Pyramid model of applied science.

Biomechanical Measurements

We can classify biomechanical measurements by mechanical area (kinematics, kinetics, hydrodynamics) or their applied methods (contact and noncontact). We can measure kinematical parameters (displacement, angle, velocity, acceleration) with both contact and noncontact methods, but it's better to measure kinetic parameters (force, momentum) using contact methods.

The contact methods employ different transducers, which are placed at the measured object. Telemetry systems and data loggers collect the rowing data acquired with transducers. Contact methods usually take a lot of time to set up, but data processing is much quicker and the data is more accurate.

Noncontact methods use cine or video imaging and image digitizing to collect data. Also, radar guns, light gates, and GPS systems can measure the position and velocity of an object. Noncontact methods require more complicated and time-consuming data processing, but they're usually the only way to acquire data during competitions.

Figure 18.2 shows the main kinematical (light shading), kinetic (dark shading), and environmental parameters (striped) measured in rowing.

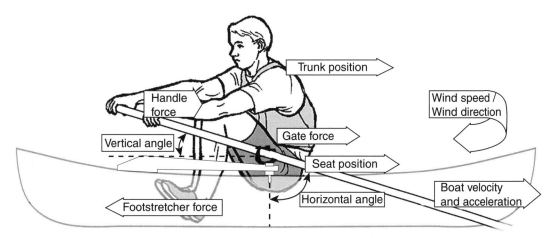

FIGURE 18.2   Biomechanical parameters in rowing.

Rowing Kinematics

Kinematics describes motion without regard to the force producing the motion. It deals with such variables as dimensions and angles, displacements and rotations, and velocity and acceleration.

Oar Angle

Since horizontal oar angle defines the phases of the rowing stroke, we'll look at oar angle first (figure 18.3). Researchers use two different coordinate systems of the oar angle: The first defines zero degrees as when the oar is perpendicular to the boat axis (Nolte 1985; Dal Monte and Komor 1989), and the second identifies zero degrees as when the oar is parallel to the boat axis (Cameron 1967; Zatsiorsky and Yakunin 1991). In our discussion we'll use the first coordinate system. In this system, the catch

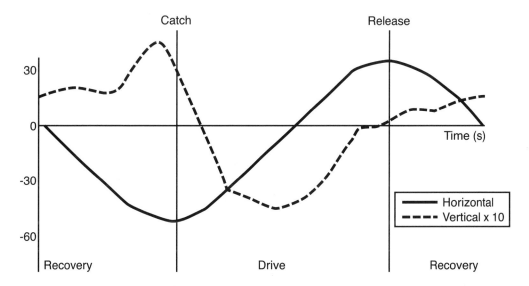

FIGURE 18.3   Graph produced by transducers measuring the horizontal and vertical oar angles with phases of the stroke cycle.

oar angle has negative value and the release angle has positive value. We'll define the start of the stroke cycle as the moment when the oar is at zero degrees during recovery (perpendicular). The catch angle is the minimal angle and release angle is the maximal.

The horizontal oar angle is a traditional rowing parameter, but we recently introduced the measurement of vertical oar angles using two servo potentiometers. The first potentiometer, mounted on top of the pin, measures the horizontal angle. The second potentiometer is attached to the first one and measures the vertical angle. It reads zero degrees when the center of the blade is at water level.

Boat Velocity and Acceleration

You can measure boat speed with different impellers and inductive sensors; we used an impeller from the Nielsen-Kellerman SpeedCoach and a custom-made electromagnetic pick-up gauge. We measured boat acceleration along the horizontal axis using a piezoresistive accelerometer.

We can derive the following parameters from the curves of boat speed and acceleration (figure 18.4):

- Average boat speed
- Minimal and maximal speed and acceleration
- Standard deviation of the boat speed and its coefficient of variation during the stroke cycle (ratio of the standard deviation to the average value)

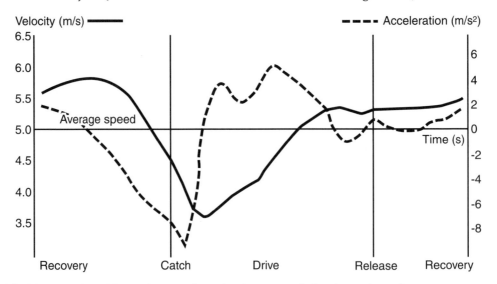

FIGURE 18.4 Typical boat velocity and acceleration curves during the stroke cycle.

Seat and Upper-Body Displacement

To measure the linear position of the seat and upper body relative to the boat, you can use a device that consists of a multiturn potentiometer, radial spring, pulley, and non-stretchable fishing line. Mount the device on the boat and directly connect it to the point of interest, such as the seat, or connect it through a pulley mounted onto a special mast at the same height as the point of interest.

These position data help us calculate linear velocity of the legs (seat speed) and trunk movement (difference between upper body and seat speed). To calculate trunk movement, we use the sternum and clavicle joint. To determine arm velocity, we subtract the velocity of the trunk from the linear speed of the handle. To calculate linear speed of the handle, we use the angular velocity and the inboard radius of the oar. The velocity curves of the legs, trunks, and arms (figure 18.5) are useful for defining different rowing styles (Kleshnev 2000).

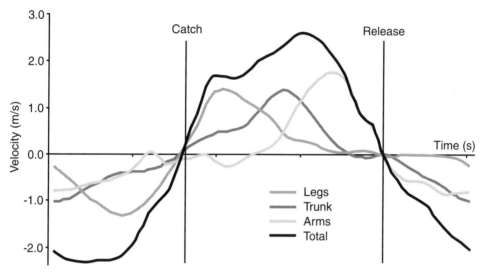

FIGURE 18.5   Curves of leg, trunk, and arm speed.

Other Kinematical Parameters

Today's technology allows us to measure a number of other kinematical parameters. For example, researchers have used microgyroscopes to measure the three-dimensional acceleration and orientation of the boat (Wagner, Bartmus, and de Marees 1993; Smith and Loschner 2000). These measurements help research efforts and help improve rowing technique.

Rowing Kinetics

Kinetics is the study of force, or the internal cause of any motion. Researchers have been measuring forces in rowing for more than a century (Dal Monte and Komor 1989). Force production is closely related to rowing power and boat speed, so it provides invaluable information about rowers' strengths and weaknesses (Secher 1993). Force production can be measured at three points: the handle, the gate, and the footstretcher. Each method has benefits and drawbacks.

Handle and Gate Forces

We determine handle force by measuring oar-shaft bend using either precise inductive (Gerber et al. 1987) or strain-gauged transducers (figure 18.6). One disadvantage of this method is that it requires calibration of each oar. Another is that in measuring oar bend we measure the moment of the handle force (torque M). We can derive a magnitude of the force if we know the length of the lever, but the point where force

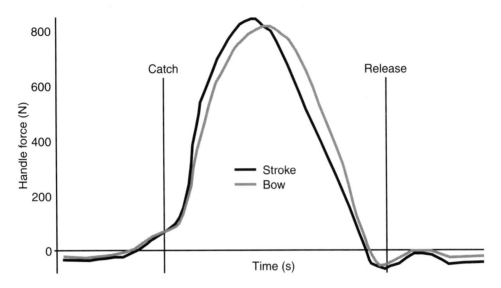

FIGURE 18.6   Sample data for a pair from strain-gauged transducer measurement.

is applied to the handle is not certain, especially in sweep rowing, where the rower can pull more with the inside or outside arm. This can create problems if we want to know the handle force (Fh) itself. However, this method does reliably measure rowing power (Ph) applied to the handle, because

$$Ph = w \times M$$

where w is the angular velocity of the oar. Handle power does not depend on the inboard; therefore it does not depend on the point of force application.

We can measure gate force using different instrumented gates (Nolte 1985). This method allows us to measure up to three force components (forward, lateral, and vertical) relative to the boat (Smith and Loschner 2000) or to the oar. Measuring gate force produces more accurate and informative data on the force applied to the boat, which can help us calculate the net propulsive force for each rower. However, calculation of the handle power (P) from the gate force (Fg) is not reliable. Power depends on the inboard (Rin) and outboard (Rout) levers, but we don't know exactly the points where force is applied to the handle and blade:

$$P = w \times Rin \times Fh = w \times Rin \times Fg \times [Rout/(Rin + Rout)]$$

The outboard lever (Rout) changes during the drive, since the point of application of the resultant blade force moves on the blade (Nolte 1985; Kleshnev 2002). Therefore, gate force is not an accurate estimation of the rower's power production.

Footstretcher Force

The force a rower applies to the footstretcher (Ff) is valuable for evaluating rowing technique and performance. It's difficult to measure footstretcher force because of the limited space between the footstretcher and the boat fittings and the importance of the footstretcher's position, height, and angle. In our work we use strain-gauged inserts in the footstretcher tube to measure the left and right forces separately (figure 18.7). A bottom fitting has a linear bearing for preventing force losses.

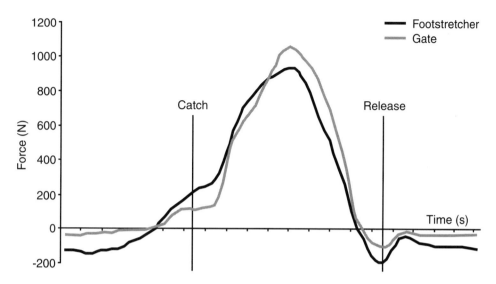

FIGURE 18.7   Sample data for a pair from footstretcher force transducer. Footstretcher force is positive toward the stern and gate force is positive toward the bow.

We can derive a net propulsive force for each rower (Fnet = Fg – Ff; see figure 18.8a) and total propulsive force, which affects boat acceleration and speed.

Footstretcher force allows us to more precisely calculate the rower's power production because it is less affected by unsteady movement of the boat (figure 18.8b). This method finds the power sum that rowers apply to the handle and footstretcher to be 16.8 percent higher than the traditional method, which uses only handle power (Kleshnev 2000).

We can derive instantaneous handle power (Ph) as

$$Ph = Fh \times Vh \times \cos(j)$$

where Fh is resultant handle force calculated as a vector sum of the normal and axial forces, Vh is resultant handle velocity calculated as a vector sum of the linear handle velocity relative to the boat and boat velocity, and j is the angle between Fh and Vh vectors.

Footstretcher power (Pf) is calculated as a scalar product of footstretcher force (Ff) and boat velocity (Vb):

$$Pf = Ff \times Vb$$

The rower's total power is derived as a sum of Ph and Pf:

$$P = Ph + Pf$$

Around 53 percent of total rowing power was applied at the oar handle (Ph), and the other 47 percent was applied at the footstretcher (Pf).

Other Kinetic Parameters

We can measure other kinetic parameters for technique assessment:

- Vertical seat force can reveal lifting of the athlete's body weight, important in rowing technique.

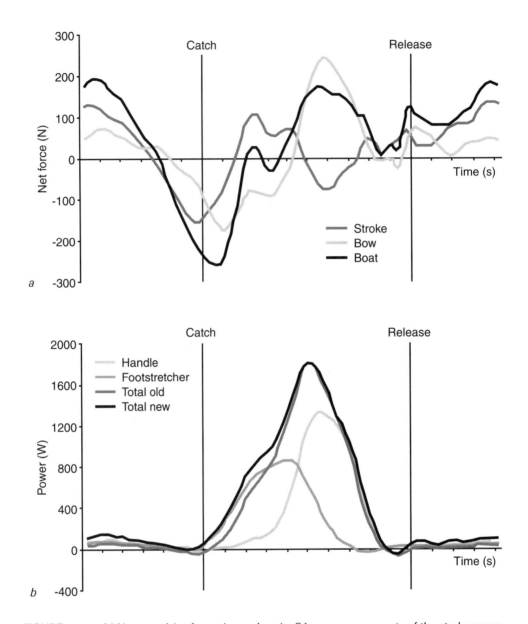

FIGURE 18.8   (a) Net propulsive forces in men's pair; (b) power components of the stroke rower.

- Blade force can provide information about the center of pressure on the blade. This may help rowers fine-tune the gearing and the selection of blade shape.
- Three-dimensional forces at the footstretcher can help researchers investigate the fine dynamics of rowing technique.

Environmental Parameters

Water temperature and wind speed and direction affect boat speed and rowing technique. In our work we continuously measure wind speed and direction using a microturbine and vane, which we attach to the shaft of the potentiometer and place on the boat canvas. We measure water temperature once during the testing session.

Noncontact Measurements (Imaging Technology)

Imaging technology, usually referred to as video analysis, is not easy to use in rowing because rowing is performed over a long distance that can't fit into a laboratory. You can't use standard camera setup and calibration routines, and you have to do all digitizing manually, making analysis very time consuming. In rowing, quantitative video measurements and analysis are generally restricted to research purposes and seldom used in daily training (Martin and Bernfield 1980). The development of automatic image recognition and related technologies will allow rowers to use quantitative video analysis more often.

Qualitative video analysis can be very useful. Usually, coaches shoot video footage from a speedboat and discuss it later with their rowers. In the future it may provide immediate visual feedback for athletes and coaches. Another use for visual analysis is capturing video on a computer, which is fairly easy with the latest technology. Rowers can replay and analyze captured video files on the monitor, print them as videograms, and store them in video databases for future review.

Biomechanical Analysis

Analysis is the process of converting information into knowledge. In this section we will discuss data processing methods, which are the basis of any analysis, and three kinds of analysis: statistical analysis, biomechanical modeling, and performance analysis.

Data Processing

Rowing is a cyclic sport. This means that athletes perform a number of stroke cycles during an event (around 250 during a 2000-meter race). While modern computer equipment makes it possible to process and output such copious information, it is of little use for rowers and coaches. Therefore, the main task of data processing is to normalize the data, or convert it into an easily understood form, such as a single representative stroke cycle (Kleshnev 1996). Figure 18.10 shows telemetry software structure and illustrates the data normalization process.

In our normalization algorithm, the following occurs:

- The software normalizes all data relative to the average cycle time over the sampling period.
- It chooses the stroke rower's cycle start as the trigger for the whole crew.
- It then calculates each set of normalized data to 50 data points. This number of points per stoke cycle is a compromise between data accuracy and volume.
- It derives the average value and its standard deviation for each point of each array.

This means that our program derives a normalized set of 50 data points for each measurement (oar angle, gate force, and so on) that represent average stroke characteristics. We have checked the validity of the algorithm by comparing the extreme values (catch

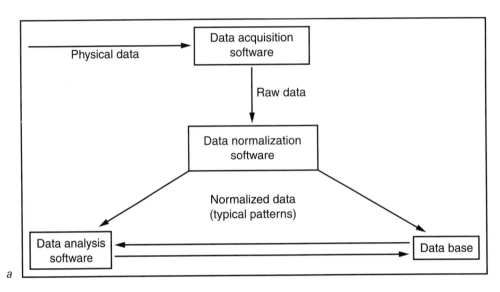

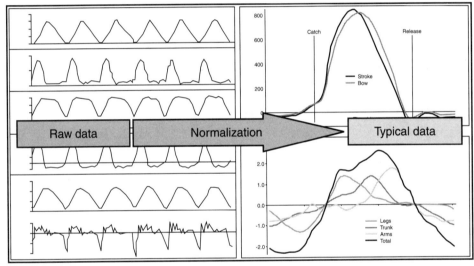

FIGURE 18.9   Block schemes of *(a)* rowing software and *(b)* data processing.

and release angles, maximum force, work and power, and so on), which we calculated using normalized data taken as an average from each stroke cycle. The differences are in a range 0.02 to 0.85 percent, acceptable for biomechanical analysis in rowing.

The software also derives selected parameters for each stroke (figure 18.10). This is useful in analyzing rowers' race performances.

Statistical Analysis and Evaluation

When you have a great deal of biomechanical information stored in a database, you can easily perform statistical analysis to compare each rower to a similar group of rowers. After three years of testing, our database has more than 400 session records, 1800 boat samples, and 6000 rower samples.

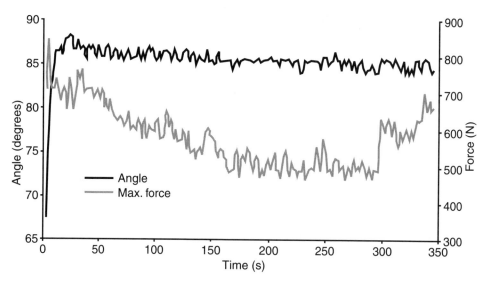

FIGURE 18.10   Total oar angle and maximum force over a rowing race.

Table 18.1 is a sample evaluation of biomechanical parameters. The values in the table are based on the average (A) and standard deviation (SD) in each rower's group. The very low interval is below A – 2SD, low is between A – 2SD and A – SD, high is between A + SD and A + 2SD, and very high is above A + 2SD.

You can also do a more sophisticated statistical analysis to correlate biomechanical parameters and assess their differences in groups of athletes. For example, we found that blade propulsive efficiency correlates with the shape of the force curve (Kleshnev 1998), and Kleshnev (1996) found that better rowers have more trunk power.

TABLE 18.1   Sample Evaluation of Biomechanical Parameters

Rower groups	Number of trials	TOTAL ANGLE (DEGREES)					MAXIMAL HANDLE FORCE (N)				
		Very low (less than)	Low (less than)	Average	High (greater than)	Very high (more than)	Very low (less than)	Low (less than)	Average	High (greater than)	Very high (greater than)
Men scull	519	102.8	106.6	110.4	114.2	118.0	593	680	766	853	940
Men light scull	161	99.5	103.3	107.1	110.9	114.8	579	636	692	749	805
Men sweep	1628	84.4	87.8	91.2	94.6	98.0	491	581	671	761	850
Men light sweep	808	81.0	84.5	87.9	91.4	94.9	467	528	590	652	714
Women scull	489	96.7	101.0	105.2	109.4	113.7	394	471	547	624	701
Women light scull	739	95.2	99.7	104.2	108.7	113.2	355	416	477	538	599
Women sweep	1708	80.0	83.5	86.9	90.4	93.8	345	412	479	547	614

Biomechanical Modeling

Biomechanical modeling is helpful for analyzing rowing technique. A biomechanical model is a system of mathematical equations that describes different components of the biomechanical system and connects them with each other. The biomechanical system in rowing is the rower–boat–oar, or RBO, system.

Modeling can be used for the following purposes:

- Predicting rowing performance (average boat speed)
- Determining what combination of biomechanical parameters (stroke rate, angle, force, power) is required for achieving a target boat speed
- Defining the extremes of the system (highest hydrodynamical efficiency, highest power output)
- Fine-tuning the crew and boat setup

Biomechanical modeling can be very simple or very sophisticated. Figure 18.11 is a very simple model of the effect of stroke rate on boat speed and stroke distance.

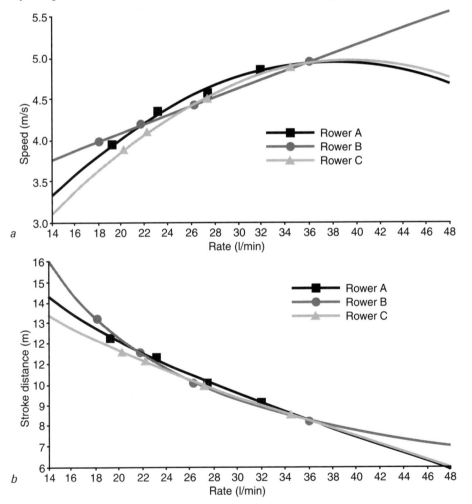

FIGURE 18.11 *(a)* Boat speed and *(b)* stroke distance relative to stroke rate for three different rowers.

We developed simple software that inputs the results of an on-water step test (boat speed and stroke rate of three or more pieces with increasing stroke rate), calculates regression equations, and outputs their graphs and numerical values. This software could be helpful in developing training regimes and assessing technique efficiency at different stroke rates.

Figure 18.12 presents a more sophisticated model that shows nonlinear regressions of the work per stroke dependence on the rowing angle and the average force in men's sculling and sweep groups. The surface shape is concave in sculling and convex in sweep rowing, which means that longer angles and higher force result in less work per stroke in sweep rowing but are more effective in sculling. This correlates with our previous findings that in sculling a larger distance per stroke brings more power and boat speed, but in sweep rowing stroke rate is more important (Kleshnev 2001).

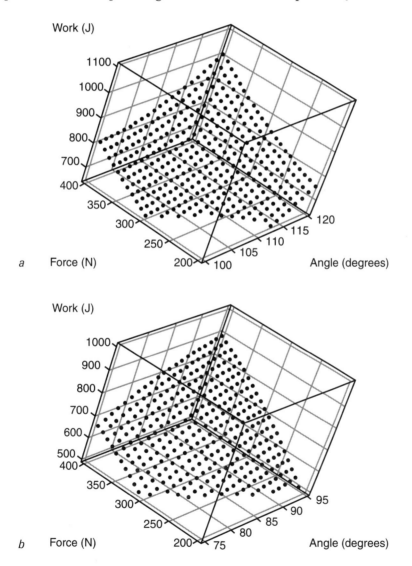

FIGURE 18.12 Model of work per stroke relative to rowing angle and average force in *(a)* men's sculling and *(b)* sweep rowing.

There have been attempts to build a mechanical model of the rower–boat–oar system, which could help optimize rowing technique (Dal Monte and Komor 1989; Atkinson 2000). However, lack of information on aerodynamic resistance prevents the model from reliably predicting boat speed.

Performance Analysis

We'll discuss the measurement and analysis of racing parameters separately because it is such an important subject and because data collection during a race has a special requirement—it can't interfere with the athletes' performance. Because of this, the parameters are basic: split times every 500, 250, or 100 meters, and stroke rate.

Analysis of race information, on the other hand, can be quite sophisticated (Kleshnev 2001, 1). Analysis can determine different patterns of race strategy and tactics. The typical race strategy in rowing is a fast start and first 500-meter section (2.5 to 3.0 percent faster than average) and slower second and third 500-meter sections (1.0 to 1.5 percent slower than average). The last 500 meters are at the average race speed. Seventy percent of winners show their advantage over competitors in the last part of the race.

Analysis of the racing stroke rate in different boat types shows a very strong correlation with boat speed (Kleshnev 2001, 2). We can predict racing stroke rates using the regression equation of the dependence of the stroke rate on boat speed and the predicted times for each boat type (see table 18.2).

Boat speed and stroke rate can help determine the distance that a boat travels per stroke (DPS). The correlation analysis of the rowers' performance, stroke rate, and distance per stroke shows that races can be won with both higher rate and longer distance per stroke (Kleshnev 2001, 2). However, the majority of winners show a larger distance per stroke than their competitors, especially in sculling.

TABLE 18.2 Prognostic Stroke Rates for Each Boat Type

Boat type	Rate (1/min)
W1x	35.2
M1x	37.3
W2-	36.2
M2-	38.3
W2x	37.0
M2x	39.0
M4-	40.0
LW2x	36.6
LM2x	38.5
LM4-	39.8
W4x	38.8
M4x	40.6
W8+	39.5
M8+	41.4

Biomechanical Feedback

The tools and methods for presenting biomechanical information to rowers and coaches are an important part of sport science. However, measurements and analysis are useless if the coach and rower don't know how to use them to improve performance. There are three levels of biomechanical feedback: traditional feedback, immediate feedback, and direct movement control. The two main concerns in feedback are shortening the delay between action and feedback and reducing the components of the feedback loop.

Traditional feedback is for the coach and takes anywhere from minutes to weeks. Immediate feedback is for the athlete and takes a few seconds. Direct feedback directly affects the athlete's muscles and takes a few tenths to hundredths of a second.

Traditional Feedback

Traditional feedback improves the coach's understanding of each rower's technique, although it can also be presented to the rowers.

Rowing test results come in the form of tables and graphs. For example, the x-axis can represent horizontal oar angle, which helps connect different parameters with phases of the stroke cycle (figure 18.13a). The curves in figure 18.13b are the course of the blade's center relative to water level, which has zero vertical angle.

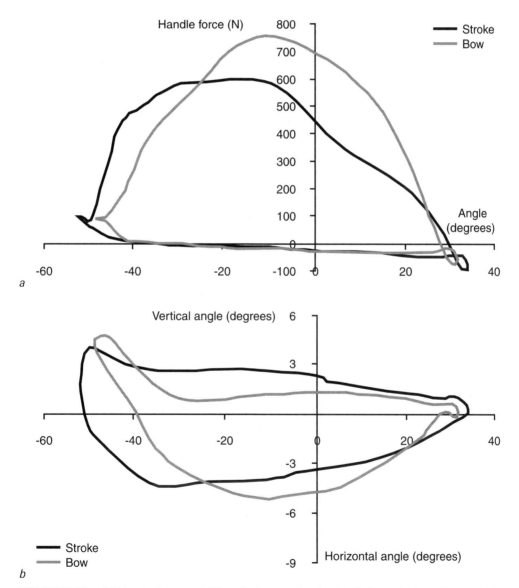

FIGURE 18.13 *(a)* Handle force and *(b)* vertical oar angle plotted relative to horizontal oar angle.

Overlaying biomechanical parameters and video footage is a useful form of traditional feedback. This method connects a visual image of the rower with internal biomechanical parameters. Computer animation can also aid understanding of the interaction of different parameters.

Immediate Feedback

Immediate feedback comes in the form of numbers, graphs, or images. Devices such as the Nielsen-Kellerman SpeedCoach provide numerical feedback on stroke rate and boat speed. The computer display during ergometer rowing (Hawkins 2000) and portable monitors mounted on the footstretcher provide detailed information on biomechanical parameters such as force and angle in both numerical and graphical form.

Mobile personal displays (MPD) provide feedback in numbers, graphs, and images in an easily accessible way. The simplest method is based on a mirror principle and consists of delivering an image of the rower in real time by means of a video camera and radio link. More sophisticated methods employ computerized telemetry systems, which acquire biomechanical data, process it, and deliver it in real time on a minimonitor. For this method to work, the rower has to understand the information. This must be done with the help of a coach and traditional feedback methods. For example, the coach can comment on the rower's technique during an immediate feedback session.

Direct Feedback

The next logical step of biomechanical feedback is to bypass the movement control centers in the brain and directly control the muscles. This is simpler than it sounds. For example, in the Soviet Union during the early 1980s I witnessed experiments involving electrostimulation of the leg muscles during rowing. Researchers stimulated the quadriceps at a specified moment in the leg drive and took the trigger signal from the seat position sensor. However, the experiments were not based on sufficient measurement and analysis of rowing biomechanics and failed to achieve their goal—reliable improvement of performance.

Current technology allows us to control the motor area in the human brain, which, in conjunction with microsensors and microprocessors, makes real-time technique optimization possible. Similar technology was once implemented in Formula One car races, but is now banned. Using this technology in competitions will probably be considered biomechanical doping, but it is possible that it may be used during training. Biomechanics faces the same ethical and legal problems in this area that biochemistry and other sport sciences already face.

Conclusion

Biomechanics has three aspects: biology, technology, and practical application. Rowing biomechanics works with other sciences in these three aspects. In its biological aspect it collaborates with sport physiology in defining rowing efficiency and methods of muscle training, and it works with psychology in improving feedback efficiency and methods of motor control. In its technological aspect it uses the latest microelectronic technology for measurement and analysis, applied physics, and mathematics. In its practical aspect it deals with the sociology and psychology of rowing coaches and their methods; rower behavior and culture; and the entire rowing community's rules, traditions, and culture.

These three aspects of rowing biomechanics easily fit in our pyramid model (see page 212), where technology is connected with measurement, biology with analysis, and practical application with feedback. This methodological setup puts practical aspects on the top of the pyramid, making them the most important part of the system and the first thing to consider in any research and development project.

part III

Racing

chapter 19

Selecting Athletes and Crews

Thor Nilsen

Selecting a crew always creates discussion and often creates irritation and conflict. Everyone has an opinion and a vision, and not even race results can prove that the selection was perfect. Everyone wants the strongest crew, and clear, sound selection principles and systems help make this happen.

In many cases the coach makes the final selection based on personal knowledge of the athletes' physical and psychological capacities. This can work in a smaller group that trains together daily as long as the coach or leader has the necessary knowledge to make the selection. This method does, however, run the risk that human relationships and subjective measures will influence the selection.

When selecting a crew within a bigger group it is important to have clear rules that everyone understands. One criterion that several American universities once used was height. They hung a board at a height of 1.90 meters across the door of the admission office. New students had to enter this office, and the rowing coach would contact those who had to duck to go in. Today crew selection is much more sophisticated of course, but this was a simple, easy-to-understand system for sorting out ability.

When selecting rowers for national team and international competitions, the system depends on the number of candidates and available data. The principle is to collect as much objective data as possible before making a final decision.

The data can be divided into the following categories:

- Health
- Physical characteristics
- Physiology
- Technical skill and biomechanics
- Psychology and sociology
- Field tests

Health, Physical Characteristics, and Physiology

If candidates are new to the system, it is necessary to start with a thorough checkup, even if they've already had a physical. This checkup must include a complete blood analysis to identify possible iron deficiency, dehydration, and other problems. Iron deficiency and dehydration are especially common among lightweight candidates, who often cut weight through dehydration without thinking about the consequences. The checkup should include a body-fat test. Also, creatine phosphokinase (CPK) and urea measurements are possible indicators of overtraining.

TABLE 19.1   Physiological Laboratory 6-Minute Test Data From an Olympic Champion

Time (min)	Work (W)	Rate	HR	BF	VE (1/min)	VO_2 (1/min)	VCO_2 (1/min)	RQ	VO_2 (ml $\times$ kg^{-1} $\times$ min^{-1})	EQ-O_2	EQ-CO_2	MET
0:30	480	38	173	68	141.0	3.96	3.60	0.91	44.5	36	39	12.7
1:00	460	35	174	69	202.6	5.73	5.38	0.94	64.4	35	38	18.4
1:30	440	34	177	69	215.9	5.78	5.93	1.03	64.9	37	36	18.5
2:00	410	31	178	62	219.4	5.90	6.17	1.05	66.3	37	36	18.9
2:30	430	32	179	62	213.1	5.93	6.04	1.02	66.7	36	35	19.0
3:00	410	31	180	62	223.1	6.12	6.24	1.02	68.8	36	36	19.7
3:30	420	33	179	65	226.4	6.20	6.20	1.00	69.6	37	37	19.9
4:00	420	32	182	64	230.0	6.25	6.30	1.01	70.2	37	37	20.1
4:30	440	34	182	69	230.8	6.15	6.17	1.00	69.1	38	37	19.7
5:00	440	34	183	69	235.5	6.22	6.22	1.00	69.9	38	38	20.0
5:30	480	36	183	75	238.0	6.13	6.23	1.02	68.9	39	38	19.7
6:00	500	40	183	75	240.0	6.02	6.34	1.05	67.7	40	38	19.3
Max	500	40	183	75	240.0	6.25	6.34	1.05	70.2	40	39	20.1

There are several systems for measuring physical characteristics. Standing height, sitting height, arm length, and body weight reveal important information about physical differences that helps coaches decide who to seat where in the boat and what equipment adjustments to make.

Physiology includes all factors related to physical capacity:

- Maximum strength
- Muscular resistance
- Maximum oxygen uptake
- Endurance
- Flexibility
- Coordination

Simple tests make it possible to evaluate strength, flexibility, and coordination. Muscular resistance and oxygen uptake have to be tested on a rowing ergometer, as only laboratory equipment correctly measures oxygen uptake, breathing frequency, ventilation, and so on. This is valuable information that helps provide a complete picture of an athlete's capacity (see table 19.1).

Several national teams use the six-minute or 2000-meter maximum ergometer test. It is a race simulation with a full warm-up, a full start, and a sprint at the end (see figure 19.1).

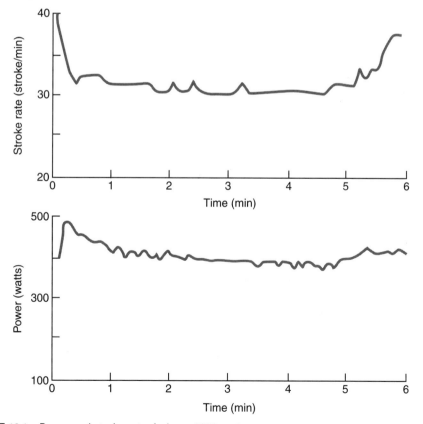

FIGURE 19.1 Power and stroke rate during a 2000-meter ergometer test.

Some national teams also use short, full-out maximum ergometer tests (such as for 45 or 90 seconds). A rower's test results over a period of time reveal maximum anaerobic capacity as well as strength development (see figures 19.2 and 19.3).

An ergometer also allows for an extended, progressive, incremental submaximal test for anaerobic threshold (AT) and lactate analysis (figure 19.4).

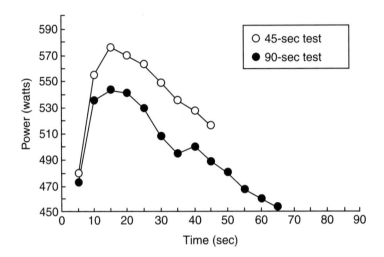

FIGURE 19.2   Power during short full-out pieces on the ergometer.

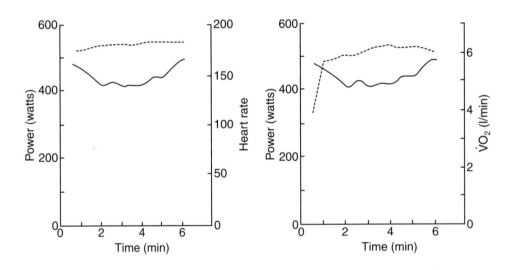

FIGURE 19.3   Power, heart rate, and oxygen uptake during a simulated 2000-meter race on the ergometer.

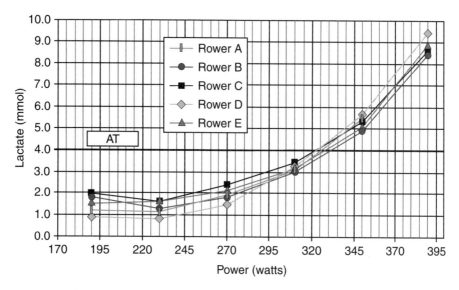

FIGURE 19.4 Lactate measurements during submaximal, incremental ergometer tests of different rowers.

Technique and Biomechanics

Rowing has many systems of technique analysis based on biomechanical measurements. The problem is that each system produces an enormous amount of information, and it can be difficult to determine what information is relevant for improving performance.

Measuring force on the oarlock gives a force curve, length, and working angle, tools that are valuable in creating a homogenous crew. However, the instrument most used in technique analysis is the video camera. The slow motion, frame-by-frame, normal speed, and double speed features give an overall impression of rowers' technique and their ability to adjust and cooperate. It is important to use an established protocol of specific camera angles, distance, and order of the movements for consistent results.

Psychology and Sociology

We want to find winners, but it is not always easy to tell how the candidates will behave during stressful situations such as championships. The goal is to find rowers who give the most and the best at the right moment, but who also show the right mentality in training and outside of rowing.

Without a psychiatrist's or psychologist's help, it is difficult to obtain an objective psychological profile of your rowers. Fortunately, this isn't necessary. The goal is to find rowers who are motivated, self-confident, and able to meet the demands of high performance. Winning rowers are also result-oriented and can focus their psychological energy on maximum performance even when under stress.

There are different ways to get an idea of a person's character and personality. One common method is the questionnaire. These surveys can profile candidates to a surprising degree of accuracy, even if they aren't specifically designed for athletes. There are also systems specially designed for elite athletes, such as the SPCS Program (Sport Psychology Consultation System) designed by the Australian researcher Brent Rushall in 1987. His system helps coaches better understand the athletes by providing several observations that coaches can use along with their own observations.

While psychological data focuses on athletes' behavior as individuals, sociological data focuses on athletes' behavior as members of a group.

In the last few decades sociologists have done various studies on rowers. For example, Lenk did sociometric examinations of the Olympic gold medalists from 1960 and the world champions from 1962. These rowers answered questions about which persons from the group they did or did not prefer to row with, live with, and so on. Lenk used the information to make a sociogram (a diagram that shows the social connections between members of a group—for example, which member respects which other in the group or could share a hotel room with another member during camps or travel) and to settle potential conflicts before they occurred or affected group unity.

How far to take sociological mapping depends on group size and composition and how long the athletes have known each other. Here are some generalizations to consider:

- A crew with strong internal unity can tolerate greater tension.
- A crew without internal unity is often inefficient.
- Internal antagonism does not necessarily weaken a crew's performance if the performance satisfies the individuals' motivations.
- Crew members who see the other members as equal in ability are more successful. But if the similarity is too great it can make role distribution difficult.

Remember, the crews who are socially well adjusted do not always perform the best.

Sociology and psychology also include the coach or leader's place in the group. This is a question of self-analysis that is not always easy to accomplish, but the answer is valuable. For example, if a coach knows how his athletes view him, it is easier for him to communicate, because he knows the level of respect and responsiveness the team has to him. Or if he knew that the team members did not respect his position, he could develop strategies to improve the relationship.

Field Tests

A field test is vital for final crew selection. The other variables are important, but as long as championships are raced in boats on the water and not in laboratories, it is necessary to find the candidates with the best boat-moving capacity (boat movers) and sort out the candidates who only move the water (water movers).

Tests are often where rowers face the biggest frustrations. Strong, well-built candidates may be cut in favor of less well-built rowers. Ideal body weight and height plus a high oxygen uptake do not always mean a fast boat. Strong rowers often misuse their strength in the catch because they produce more power than the boat can absorb.

Tests range from participation in regattas with different crew combinations to special test regattas of 500 to 2000 meters. U.S. and Canadian rowers use a great deal of seat-racing, testing individual candidates in pairs, fours, or eights against each other. The number of candidates and open slots determine which system to use. In any situation where some candidates are guaranteed a seat, there is a risk that those with guaranteed seats might manipulate the selection by regulating their own effort depending on whom they are rowing with.

Use the following tests for selecting scullers from groups with 12 or more candidates:

1. **Test regatta over 2000 meters in singles.** Row twice within two hours. Time is decisive and is awarded points after placing. The 12 best continue on.

2. **Test regatta over 2 $\times$ 1000 meters in double sculls.** Race in both directions, with two to three minutes rest between races. All boats row against each other. Points are awarded after placing. This tests needs six double sculls, making 11 races of 2 $\times$ 1000 meters.

3. **Test regatta over 2 $\times$ 1000 meters in quadruple sculls.** Race in both directions with two to three minutes of rest between races. The best double combinations row all races together. This test needs three quadruple sculls, making 5 races of 2 $\times$ 1000 meters.

The rests must be equally distributed and the boats of the same quality. It is also important to use the same regatta course under the same conditions for all crews and boats. Three days are sufficient for this test. It gives a good overview of the different boats, their internal ranking, and the best combinations.

It is difficult in sweep rowing to determine individual ranking in big groups. In most cases, you have to start building fixed pair combinations and then leave the two rowers together to work as a unit during the test races.

If there is enough equipment you can use the following system:

1. **Test regatta over 2000 meters in straight pairs or coxed pairs.** This test requires six boats. Race twice within two hours. Time is the determining factor and points are awarded for placing. Additional points are given for physiological capacity and laboratory test results. The 12 to 16 athletes with the most total points continue on.

2. **Test regatta over 2 $\times$ 1000 meters in coxed fours or straight fours.** Use the same system as with the quadruple scull (see number three above). This selection system gives a good overview of different crews' possibilities. It also shows who can withstand psychological and physiological stress.

These test regattas are a model for training and prepare rowers for future competitions.

Countries with small rowing programs often let clubs create the crews for international championships. They establish certain criteria, such as minimum results in bigger regattas. This simplifies the work of the rowing federations, but it seldom creates the best national team.

In today's competitive rowing climate it is necessary to work systematically and analyze each candidate to create the best crew. The methods in this chapter are not necessarily the absolute best, but they are simple enough for the participants to understand, and they are objective.

chapter 20

Setting Race Plans and Tactics

Mike Teti and Volker Nolte

In 1996 when I was coaching freshmen at Princeton, I had a really good crew. We had won the freshmen championships the previous two years, and the team had gotten even better. We were fast, but we still lost by nine seconds against Brown University before the season's championships. We rowed faster than we ever had before, but Brown University had four athletes in their boat who rowed internationally and had won either world championship or Olympic medals: Jamie Koven, Xeno Müller, Denis Zvegeli, and Igor Boraska.

One week later, we had to race the same Brown crew in the Eastern Sprints Championships. What was I going to tell my crew before the race? "If you race well and row over your heads, you can win"? No, I couldn't say that, especially since these athletes were very bright students. I told them: "You are the second fastest crew in the country. You have to go out today and make sure that you become second! And if Brown makes a major mistake, you could put yourself in position to win."

Everyone wants to win. No one likes to lose! For this reason it is important to respect your competition. The crews that you compete against are coached well, especially in international rowing. Their skill is often equal to your skill, so on any given day anyone can win. You need to know how to use any information you have about the crews you'll compete against to create a winning strategy.

Psychological factors ("I like to see my competitors!"), physiological factors (optimal usage of energy supply systems), and physical factors (necessity of the start, drag, weather conditions) influence the speed profile that a crew and their coach decide on for a race.

If you define *strategy* as a skillful plan to reach a goal, the crew and coach can lay out a plan for winning a race: "Let's lead the race at 500 meters!" *Tactics* are the means to implement the strategy. Once they've come up with a general plan, the crew can decide on the details: "After the start, we'll keep the stroke rate over 40 and emphasize the catch until the 500-meter mark." There are endless factors to consider (weather conditions, competition level, importance of the race) and consequently, the race plan possibilities are endless. Nevertheless, you can learn from the experience of other coaches and the knowledge that we now have thanks to technology that allows us to study race dynamics.

Adapting the Race Plan to the Crew

The most important factor in choosing a race strategy is your athletes. What's your crew's level of fitness? How experienced are they with the level of racing they face in the next competition? Do they like to take charge or would they rather come from behind? How confident are they about their ability and the situation they will face? Can they handle a complicated race plan?

A high school crew obviously needs more attention during a race. It is hard for young athletes to focus over a longer stretch, so you have to give them tasks that they can concentrate on for every 250 meters. These could be technical: "At 750 meters we'll do 20 strokes with clean finishes." They could also be power-related: "When we're 500 meters into the race we'll push hard with our legs for 15 strokes." Elite athletes, on the other hand, can focus on the feel of the boat's run and can even vary tactics depending on how the race unfolds.

You can only have a sophisticated race plan if you have a sophisticated crew. Sometimes rowers want to plan small details or even play around with the tactics during the race. This can backfire if the athletes are not ready for it, but it can be very helpful if they know what they're doing. For example, seasoned rowers who have raced many times and trained many kilometers know how fast they can go from point A to point B. These rowers know exactly how well they're doing in a race. If they know they're doing well and a crew is leading them at the 1250-meter mark, they are confident that either the leading crew will die a slow death or the leading crew is the greatest that has ever rowed. Such rowers know when to let a crew go ahead and when to chase them immediately, and they can plan for this freedom in their strategy.

Winning a bronze is much better than racing for victory and coming in fourth. We experienced this with the women's quadruple in 2001. Our American team was leading against Germany (a gold medalist for many years) to the 1300- to 1400-meter mark when suddenly we were rowed through not only by the Germans but also by Great Britain. Watching all the heats, we realized that it seemed impossible for our crew to beat Germany or New Zealand. However, it seemed quite possible that we could beat Great Britain if we rowed well.

Coach Kris Korzeniowski told them, "As Americans, it seems to be in your blood to go out and try to win, and it is quite difficult as your coach to tell you differently.

But today, I want you to go out and race for the bronze medal. It will be difficult the way it is! Therefore, I will propose the stroke rate that you should row and where you should spend yourself. Remember, the U.S. team has not won a medal in this event for many years, it is a great accomplishment to win any medal at the world championships, and you have athletes in the boat who will row for the first time in their life on this level, so it will be an even greater accomplishment if you win a medal!" The women listened, went out, and executed the race plan perfectly. They cruised along for the first part of the race, attacked at 800 meters into the race, rowed through Australia and Great Britain, and won their bronze medal.

In comparison, in 2002 we won all our races in the men's eight before the final of the world championships. Although none of these were comfortable wins, we thought that we had a chance to win the final and the gold medal. After our victory in the World Cup in Lucerne, we came back to Princeton and felt that we made some improvements. At the world championships, we won our heat easily and had a great week of practice after that. The Canadians raced better than expected in the finals, as did the Germans, so we came in third. Our athletes rowed hard, and although it may not have been their very best piece, it was definitely not a bad race for our crew. After the race, I met the crew at the dock. It is not important to meet your crew at the dock after a win, but it is extremely important to meet them after a loss. I wanted to be there to let them know that for six of them it was their first medal at a world championship, and they had to realize that these medals are very hard to come by.

The same idea applies to ergometer tests. Say you have a previous performance of 20:00 minutes in a 6000-meter ergometer test. This performance has an average of 1:40-minute splits per 500 meters. You should not try to row 1:36-minute splits the next time you do the 6000-meter test, because you will only last 3000 to 4000

© Joel W. Rogers

It's important for coaches to pick their crew up psychologically and help them put performances—both wins and losses—in perspective.

meters. You should row the first part of the test at a pace that you know you can hold. If you then come to the 5200-meter mark and feel you're doing well, you can crank the splits down and reach a personal best. You can then walk away from the test feeling really good.

An approach like this is intelligent and you should support your athletes' use of brainpower. At the end of the test or race they should know that they maximized their performance and the outcome was worth the struggle.

Setting Realistic Goals

If everything indicates that your crew has no chance to win, you have to set a realistic goal in order to motivate the rowers to do their best in the race. For example, if this is your crew's first race at a certain level, you shouldn't say, "If you have a great race, you can win!" You have to have a measured goal that is realistic. Instead you might say, "The fastest we ever went over the 2000-meter course is 6:00 minutes. Today we have a tailwind out there, so let's try to row 5:59 minutes—this is our 'gold medal' for today!" This is a goal that the crew can go for. They won't just go through the motions. They'll feel good when they accomplish a significant goal.

The first year that I coached the freshmen crew at Princeton, we raced Harvard University along with MIT (Massachusetts Institute of Technology). I was in the coaches' launch with the MIT coach and their sport information officer who followed the race. Harvard and my crew went off and were leading MIT by a huge margin. At the end of the race, I saw the flag go one–two in short order and then I saw the MIT coach and officer watching their stopwatches. The second MIT crossed the finish line, the flag went down and the two MIT guys high-fived each other and hugged each other in joy. "This was the first time that we were under 20 seconds to Harvard!" they said.

Instead of agonizing over a major defeat, they were happy to achieve their goal of coming in less than 20 seconds behind Harvard. For these novice athletes, it was a great accomplishment to score this way against the larger rowing schools. They realized that 19 seconds behind is better than 20 seconds behind; 10th place is better than 11th! All these are good achievements for a developing crew.

Preparing for Races

Most race preparation is done in training before the competition. You've already figured out the crew's most efficient stroke rate. However, you shouldn't focus too narrowly on a particular stroke rate. You shouldn't say, for example, "The magic number is 38! We can't go any higher or lower."

You may have found that 38 strokes per minute is the most efficient rate for the crew, but you still have to factor in the adrenaline that comes in a major race. The athletes may feel really good and a stroke rate of 40 per minute feels comfortable, but 40 strokes per minute probably won't still feel comfortable with 400 meters to go, when they have to shift gears. This is where the coxswain or the experienced bow person in coxless boats plays a major role. If the crew is within one stroke per minute of the preferred stroke rate and they are moving well, there's no problem. But if the crew is stroking 42 per minute, the coxswain has to make an adjustment.

The first step is coming up with the basic race strategy. You have to do this at home as part of the training process. Through months-long training, you've determined your maximum pace, which start you want to do, and where you want to do your lift. This does not mean that your strategy should be carved in stone. You may have to change tactics according to what happens in the heats. Therefore, the more races you do, the better, and the more information you have, the better.

My belief is, it's never a bad thing to win the heat. You have to be decisive, especially in international rowing. You can't go through all the possible scenarios in training or discussions. For this reason I think it's good to go out and try to win a heat. This can be risky, because if you win you may not have races for several days, but the advantage is you learn about yourself and your competition.

If you want to build special bursts into your race plan, you have to plan ahead. Special bursts are only effective if they are a decisive attack that changes the race. Such an attack has to be compact, which means that 20 strokes are too long and 10 strokes are not enough. To make a difference in the race, you need 15 strokes. To be potent, they have to be rehearsed. The crew needs to know exactly what to do in terms of technique (stroke length, force application), stroke rate, and the actual beginning of the burst.

Sometimes you can make only one of these shifts in a race, sometimes two. I have never done more than three shifts. However, these shifts are the most important tactic you can use. I don't put the most rhythmic rower in the stroke seat, I put fast athletes in six, seven, and eight seats who can shift gears.

You have to start working on the race plan months before the race. First, the crew has to learn what commitment to a race plan means. Then they can rehearse the race plan. The race plan is technical, physiological, and psychological. This is what the 15-stroke bursts are all about! You have to practice how to do these moves during training. We do these rehearsals just about every practice. If we do a 500-meter timed piece, we rehearse the 15 strokes during that piece. If we race for 1000 meters, we do the burst in there, and we rehearse the focus bursts in a 3-mile test race. Since we rehearse it so often, everyone knows exactly what to do and what it is going to feel like. The real test, however, is to put everything together in a 2000-meter race. Making a potent attack after starting at a high stroke rate or when you are already fatigued is when the 15 strokes are the real test.

We always try to make some tactical attacks during a race. The more experienced a crew, the more flexibility they have to adjust to a situation. The coxswain may want to hold off on a move when the crew has a great rhythm so as not to interfere with this rhythm. Be sure to rehearse this kind of flexibility during training. A less experienced crew, on the other hand, needs to have a rehearsed, set race plan. You increase the confidence of such a crew when everyone is on the same page.

In 1999, we had the best crew of all the world champions from 1997 to 1999. We executed our basic tactics in the heat, and we went out for a big lead after an incredible start. We were leading by more than a length 700 meters into the race, but soon the Romanians were coming after us. We only won the heat by 0.1 second. However, several good things happened in this race. First, our basic tactics worked and we won the heat. Second, we had about a week to rehearse what to do differently in the final, the potent shift with 500 meters to go.

On the Friday of that practice week, we believed that we needed to try out our move under racelike conditions. So, we decided to do a 1750-meter piece with a PaceCoach (now known as the SpeedCoach). Everyone wanted to try out our tactics when we were fatigued. The PaceCoach showed that the crew nailed it down. Now the crew was confident that they could execute the plan, and the plan worked out perfectly in the final. We got out to a lead, were passed by the British crew in the third 500 meters of the race, and went right back through them in the last 500 meters.

I asked the crew a few months after the race, "What went through your head when Great Britain rowed through you?" They told me that they knew they were in trouble, but they were positive that they had one more chance. The crew was not sure that they would win with 500 meters to go, but they were confident that they could get back into the race.

Collecting Information

At many regattas nowadays you receive official results and sometimes split times (every 500 meters). You can also take stroke rates from the shore, and with the SpeedCoach you can get feedback about the speed and stroke rate of every single stroke of your crew. You have to interpret and use this information to the best of your ability.

Let's say your four crew tells you after their heat, "We only lost by half a length, so we'll be able to beat them in the final if we stay in front of them at the 500-meter." At the same time, the official split time shows that the winning crew was leading at the 500-meter by three seconds and at the end by six seconds. Your crew is still confident and optimistic, but the actual numbers indicate that it would be better for the crew to focus on maximizing their performance.

You can use stroke rate and speed data for smaller increments to find the most effective stroke rates for your crew in different race situations (cruising or sprint). You also have to consider one other factor: The other coaches also study the race results. You can't say, "Since you went through a crew in the last 400 meters of the last World Cup Regatta, you'll be able to do it again." Put yourself in the position of the coach of the crew that you just beat. You would certainly have worked on the crew's ability to sustain the last 400 meters.

In 1988, the Germans completely changed how to row an international eight's race. They introduced the tactic of simply going for it. They would just go and then hang on. The Canadians picked up on this; the crew of 1992 is a good example. Today the way to race an eight is to generate a lot of speed in the first 500 meters. Then you have to be able to continue at 38, 39, and even 40 strokes per minute all the way.

In an international eight's race you always have to be with the leaders because it is difficult to get big margins back, though you don't necessarily have to lead. You also can't let a crew lead by one length at the 1000-meter mark, because you don't want them to be able to think, "I only have to hang on for another 2 minutes and 38 seconds." Don't let them get brave.

You want to be in a good position right from the beginning in an eight's race, but it's a little easier in a single or pair to come back after not leading at the 500-meter. You also want different race profiles in the heats and the finals. First, you don't want to show all your cards, and second, after you have the lead, you're pretty much defending.

In the final, leave nothing to chance. You go, then you go, and you go again! As a coach, the longer you have a crew, the easier it is to prepare attacking tactics. For example, college coaches work with their athletes for more than half a year and have the chance to race several times.

The heats of the world championships are often the first race as a crew. Even though you get results and split sheets from other regattas, you haven't seen the other crews yet. Our approach is, "Well, we have all kinds of information about the other crews. We didn't race them, but they didn't race us either." We know what we can do, but they don't. They may assume that we are quick, but they don't know. This is not necessarily a bad situation.

If you ask athletes, they'll say that their most memorable race is when they rowed even splits at the beginning of the race and then rowed hard through all the competition at the end to win the race.

My philosophy is, "Get out with a good start and possibly lead the race. Then try to make the lead slowly bigger and cruise and win the race comfortably." If you can avoid the drama, avoid the drama! However, this is in theory. In practice, you are limited to what the crew can do.

Studying Races

Klavora (1980) published one of the earliest studies on race strategies. He examined the 500-meter split times of international races, especially from the 1976 Olympics. Over the last few years, researchers have published more and more analyses of race times and split times (for example, Schwanitz 2000, Kollmann 2000, and Kleshnev 2001). These studies discuss so-called gold-medal standards, race profiles from 500-meter split times, and profiles relative to average race speed or gold-medal standards.

From statistical analysis of race results over many years, the following has become clear:

- The relative speed of the different boat classes remains constant (for example, the men's single scull races at about 81 percent of the men's eight).
- In general the race times in international races get faster every year.

Therefore, most rowing associations redefine their gold-medal standards every four years. This means they predict the time of the gold-medal winner at the next Olympic Games under favorable weather conditions. Gold-medal standards help rowers and coaches set goals (times for training pieces), compare boats of different categories during training (relative speed of different boat classes), select teams (an association with limited funding can rank boats of different categories), judge race conditions at a regatta after the first race, and so on. Table 20.1 lists gold-medal standards from Kleshnev (2001).

TABLE 20.1 Gold-Medal Standards

Boat type	W1×	M1×	W2–	M2 –	W2×	M2×	M4–	LW2×	LM2×	LM4–	W4×	M4×	W8+	M8+
Gold-medal time (min:s)	7:12	6:32	6:53	6:14	6:38	6:02	5:44	6:46	6:11	5:48	6:06	5:34	5:54	5:20

Reprinted, by permission, from V. Kleshnev, 2001, *"Racing strategy in rowing during Sydney Olympic games,"* Australian Rowing (1): 20-23.

For many years now FISA, the international rowing association, has required official 500-meter split times for all participants in FISA-sanctioned regattas. The split times are measured at the 500-meter points of the 2000-meter course. These split times give athletes and coaches an idea of the competitors' speed distribution throughout the race. FISA has discussed requiring split times for 250 meters or even 100 meters, but at this point such an undertaking would be too costly. However, technological developments (laser technology or GPS) will certainly make this possible in the future.

If you study the 500-meter split times you'll find four approaches: even split, fly and die, classic optimum, and conservative (see figure 20.1).

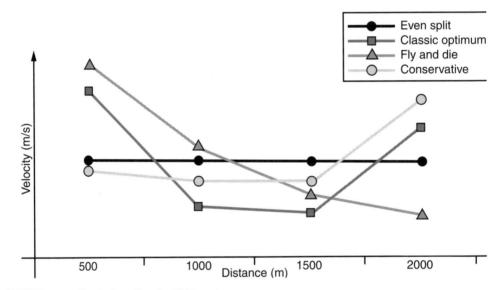

FIGURE 20.1   Tactical profiles for 2000-meter races.

From a theoretical hydrodynamic point of view, the even split is the most efficient approach, because drag increases exponentially with speed and any change in speed expends extra energy. Even splits are splits that do not differ more than 1 percent from the average split over the whole race. However, this profile is never really found in racing, because it does not take into account other factors (physiology and psychology) and it is impractical (it doesn't provide for the start). Nevertheless, many coaches promote this profile for pedagogical reasons, although in practice their crews perform quite differently. Even splits may be useful for explaining certain situations to a crew, especially when they start their races too fast or slow down too much at the end. A coach could then ask the crew before their next race to "try to split more evenly."

Crews use the fly and die quite frequently, especially in eights, very fast tailwind races, or heats. However, the crews often do not actually "die" at the end of the race (an expression for when lactic acid production forces a significant slowdown); they deliberately reduce speed. They give up their full effort to preserve energy because they are so far behind or because they are leading comfortably. Crews that use the fly and die are able to watch their competitors and control the race.

The conservative strategy lets the crew focus on technique during the first part of the race and save energy for the final sprint. On the other hand, the crew may lose contact with the leading boat and need considerable confidence not to panic. This tactic can be quite successful in races with strong headwinds where often the last 500 meters are sheltered from the wind, and in securing a place in the middle of the field, such as racing for the bronze medal.

The classic optimum strategy is by far the most common. This is understandable, because it makes the most effective use of the body's energy systems. The classic optimum strategy uses anaerobic alactic energy along with some lactic energy at the beginning of the race and anaerobic lactic energy at the finish, resulting in higher speeds in the first and last 500 meters. In addition, it has psychological advantages—the rower feels in the middle of the action and in control—and allows for technical focus and the final sprint.

Kleshnev (2001) analyzed all the races from the 2000 Olympic Games. He was able to compare the races since weather conditions were favorable and consistent throughout the week. Kleshnev was the first to examine the profiles of the different races (heats, repechages, semifinals, and finals), and in doing so he found some interesting differences.

Figure 20.2 shows that speed increases with the importance of the race, from heats to finals. This is logical since the slower boats don't make it to the finals. With an overall increase in speed the difference between split times decreases, which makes sense because there is less room for variation. Nevertheless, there is almost a 4 percent difference in split times in the finals.

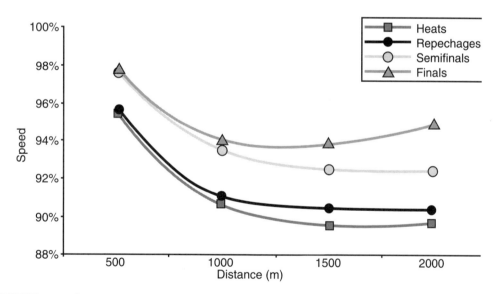

FIGURE 20.2   Average race profiles from the 2000 Olympic Games relative to the gold-medal standard (Kleshnev 2001).

If you analyze split times relative to average speed over the race (figure 20.3), you can see that the races get closer to the classic optimum race profile as they become more important. All data supports this argument except for the final 500 meters of the semifinals.

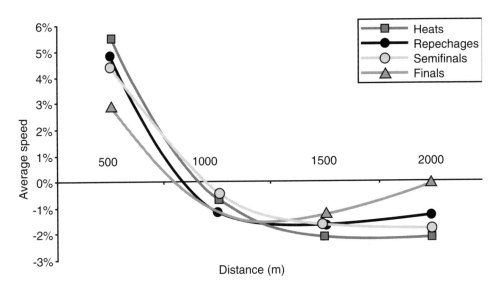

FIGURE 20.3   Average race profiles relative to average race speed in the 2000 Olympics (Kleshnev 2001).

It is possible to record more data from races of your own crew, such as the average speed for 100-meter splits (see figure 20.4). If you compare this data with the official 500-meter split times, you'll see that the splits differ more than 10 percent. These results support the idea that even splits are impractical. In addition, more detailed analysis actually shows the tactical moves of a crew (1100 meters), as well as problem areas (1500 meters). Such detailed analysis is valuable for the crew and their coach, but you can't see the same analysis of the other crews.

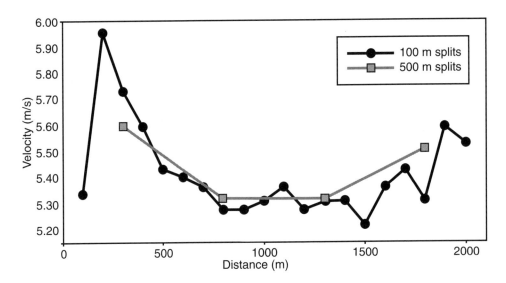

FIGURE 20.4   Comparison of official 500-meter split times with 100-meter split times from Nielsen-Kellerman SpeedCoach (Lucerne 2000; Canada LM4-; Final).

Conclusion

As a coach you have to be able to make adjustments. You have to stick with what works for your rowers, but you also have to be able to add to their repertoire.

When we won the men's eight in 1997, we got all kinds of praise. However, it wasn't an easy victory: We came in third in our heat, we were second in our repechage, and less than one second away from not making the final. In the final we were able to plan adjustments, and the athletes were able to execute those adjustments.

We had a great start in the heat simply because we emphasized the start in training. We had the lead pretty much up to the 1750-meter mark until two crews rowed through us. Of course, I watched the race and saw what happened, but it is important to get the crew's perspective, so I sat down with the crew after the race to hear what happened from their point of view. Their assessment was that the planned approach for the sprint was too complicated. Because they felt their cruising speed in the middle of the race was fast enough and the official split sheets agreed, we set a goal for the next race to do the 15 hardest strokes they ever did at the 1750-meter mark. Stroke rate was not important, only pulling harder than ever. These tactics brought us through the repechage and gave us four days to work on our new tactics.

For the next four days, whenever the crew rowed on the course they rowed the first 250 meters as they would in the final race. Then they paddled to the 1750-meter mark to do the all-out sprint to the line. They practiced this over and over again: first 250 meters, last 250 meters, turn around, first 250 meters, last 250 meters, and so on until everyone in the boat knew how to approach these phases of the race. In the end, the crew executed this plan perfectly. More than anything else, it was our carefully planned strategy that helped us win the championship.

chapter 21

Relaxing and Focusing on Race Day

James Joy

> *To practice quieting and focusing your mind, it's usually quite helpful to quiet and relax your body and your environment . . . The general instructions for teaching people concentrative meditation are first, get in a quiet place . . . The second part of quieting your environment is to reduce the time pressure of a hurried, scheduled life.*
>
> **Charles Tart**

In his preparation for championship fights, Muhammad Ali valued his daily four hours of quiet time with his Spanish masseur: The masseur spoke no English and Ali spoke no Spanish. As Ali found, planned periods of quiet allow athletes to regenerate and optimize their potential by increasing self-knowledge. The benefits of relaxing quietly and focusing include heightened mental awareness, flow, and ability to remain in the moment.

Along a similar line of thought, Chicago Bulls coach Phil Jackson expressed his admiration of Michael Jordan: "In becoming a great athlete Michael has attained a quality of mind few Zen students ever achieve. His ability to stay relaxed and intensely focused in the midst of chaos is unsurpassed" (Jackson 1995, 174). If the success of Michael Jordan and Phil Jackson is any indication, meditative training has great practical value for athletes and coaches.

Yearly Plan

A five-stage meditative practice in a systematic yearly plan is the best way to develop relaxation and focusing (see figure 21.1). The program includes quiet sitting, visualization, relaxation, concentration, and mindfulness.

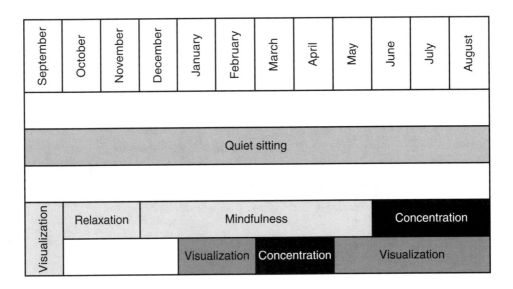

FIGURE 21.1   Yearly mental training cycles (assuming the main competition is in August).

When you integrate this mental plan with physical and technical training, it becomes part of the fabric of the program. Over time, the consistent reinforcement of relaxing and focusing becomes evident in the racing stroke and in the athlete's overall performance. For a sample program, see table 21.1.

The ability to relax and focus on race day requires systematic training and intensive involvement by both coach and athletes. When coaches participate with their athletes during mental training sessions on land, it reinforces the importance of the practice. Regular training follows a natural progression from quiet sitting, visualization, relaxation, concentration, and mindfulness to flow and peak performance.

From the beginning of training, the objective is flow. Flow is the effortless swing, or stride, or stroke, and in rowing flow produces effective shell run. Flow involves being totally integrated, mind, body, and environment. Phil Jackson refers to this as the "power of We rather than the power of me" (Jackson 1995, 35). I witnessed this power in 1984 with coach Neil Campbell and the Canadian men's eight. The Canadian eight that year was of one spirit, and they won the gold medal. Oneness of body, mind, and spirit allows rowers to relax, focus, and enjoy the competitive moment.

TABLE 21.1 Sample Mental Training Program

Meditative method	Practice on land	Parallel practice on water
Quiet sitting • Seated on floor in relaxed posture, eyes closed • Yoga stretching	Practice 5 times a week, 3-5 min per session Yoga 10 min daily	Long-distance steady-state rowing without body tension Minimal communication from coxswain and coach; maintain silence
Visualization • Rowing-simulation exercises on land • Visualize an object • Repeat until object is clear in your mind	Practice 3 times a week, lying down, 10 min per session Integral yoga (breathing, concentration, posture) 10 min daily	Eyes closed while rowing Focus on person in front (visualize bladework) Feathering rowing for body work
Relaxation • Progressive relaxation techniques • Tensing and relaxing specific body parts	Practice 3 times a week, lying down, 10 min per session Tensing and relaxing arms, legs, and so on; relaxed breathing; experience the effects	Tense and relax stroke cycle Row at 90% effort Easy speeds (30 strokes)
Concentration • Check for good posture • Count breaths or concentrate on a small object • Let go of thoughts • Stay present • Integrate body, mind, and spirit	Practice 3 times a week, 8 min per session Integral yoga (breathing, concentration, posture) 10 min daily	Intensive drills for entry, drive, release, recovery
Mindfulness • Body scanning • Present moment has full attention	Practice 3 times per week, 10 min per session Yoga 10 min daily Rowing simulation exercises	Slow-motion rowing, Quarter slide slow-motion rowing, back end or a miniature whole stroke

Incorporating Meditative Practices

 At the start of the season, the group had barely been able to watch 5 minutes of a game tape without getting so restless that they couldn't concentrate. Slowly, however, I was able to build up their endurance so that by the playoffs they were able to view entire ball games with full attention. Initially I introduced them to 3-minute periods of meditation and gradually stretched them out to 10 minutes. The constant practice of awareness and concentration certainly made the group easier to coach.

Phil Jackson and Charley Rosen

It took Phil Jackson two years to convince the Chicago Bulls to do group meditation. Jackson writes, "The first time we practiced meditation, Michael (Jordan) thought I was joking. Midway through the session, he cocked one eye open and took a glance around the room to see if any of his teammates were actually doing it. To his surprise, many of them were" (Jackson 1995, 173).

When you integrate meditative practices into physical and technical training, mental training becomes ordinary and fundamental, and the athlete does not view it as something extraneous from the "real" training (see figure 21.2). In fact, physical and technical training provide the necessary focus for intensive mental training.

Team spirit is an important byproduct of the team sitting together on a regular basis. With daily practice, the team's power of awareness increases dramatically along with mindfulness, or the ability to remain in the present moment.

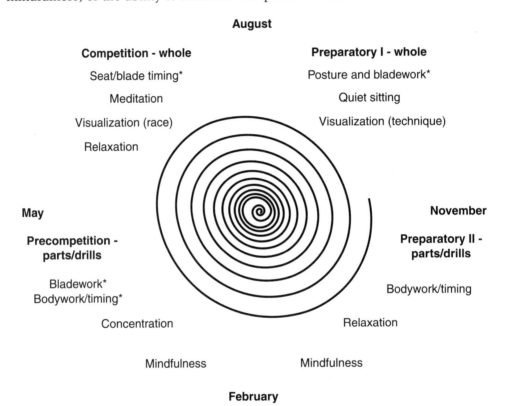

August

Competition - whole

Seat/blade timing*

Meditation

Visualization (race)

Relaxation

Preparatory I - whole

Posture and bladework*

Quiet sitting

Visualization (technique)

May

Precompetition - parts/drills

Bladework*
Bodywork/timing*

Concentration

November

Preparatory II - parts/drills

Bodywork/timing

Relaxation

Mindfulness   Mindfulness

February

FIGURE 21.2   Mental and technique (*) training.

Meditation Techniques

Meditation may seem foreign to the athletes at first, but in most cases they've already experienced meditation, just not in a systematic way. Here are a few practical methods that coaches and athletes can try on their own.

Quiet Sitting

The most effective introduction to meditation is five minutes of quiet sitting in each training session. In the beginning, body posture is relaxed. With practice athletes begin to acquire an erect posture.

The team learns to slow down and be aware of the present moment, including physical feelings, sounds, objects, and breathing. Quiet sitting is like a warm-up for advanced meditation, so schedule it throughout the year. You can alternate quiet sitting with yogic stretching and systematic breathing. Quiet sitting and yoga help the team recognize the need to slow down from the fast pace of daily life.

You can incorporate quiet sitting into on-water training by using long-distance silent rows and concentrating on timing and technique. Slow motion rowing on the ergometer or on the water also improves the athletes' awareness and accuracy of each stroke. Quiet, slow motion is the tai chi of rowing and can be used at any time during the training session.

Visualization

As Phil Jackson explains, "Visualization is an important tool for me. Coaching requires a free-ranging imagination, but during the heat of the season it is easy to get so wound up tight that you strangle on your own creativity. Visualization is the bridge I use to link the grand vision of the team I conjure up every summer to the evolving reality on the court . . . Before each game I usually do 45 minutes of visualization at home to prepare my mind and to come up with last minute adjustments" (Jackson 1995, 121).

To practice visualization, sit in a comfortable position and place a small two- or three-dimensional object in front of you such as a watch. After concentrating on the object for a few minutes, close your eyes and try to create an image of the object. If any part of the object is not clear, open your eyes and correct your observation until the mental image matches the original object. Advanced visualization involves imagining the rowing stroke. To practice this, close your eyes and see, feel, and hear the stroke at various speeds.

Dwight Stones, the 1976 Olympic high-jump champion, says of visualization, "I see a translucent image of myself coming out of myself. I watch to see if I will make it. Many times I don't. I have to concentrate harder" (McCluggage 1983, 95). Before an actual attempt, he would stand with closed eyes, going through every step of his movement. You could see him nodding his head as he visualized the jump.

Introduce visualization early in the training process through simulation exercises for improving technique and later in the training process through race simulation (see figure 21.2). In simulation drills the rowers go through the different parts of the stroke. The coach assumes the role of choreographer, simulating the blade action. Then the athletes try to match the coach's movements. They internalize the movement pattern and improve their ability to perform the action on the water.

In *The Centered Skier* (1983), Denise McCluggage says, "It is your nervous system, not your musculature, that determines the pattern, sequence, and timing of your movements. When you imagine an activity you are, as far as your nervous system is concerned, actually doing it" (106).

This visualization in rowing is similar to shadow boxing in boxing, taking practice swings in golf, or shooting free throws without the ball in basketball. On the ergometer, rowers perform parts of the stroke cycle without the oar handle. The coach demonstrates the movements for the rowers to mimic and monitors the rowers' accuracy. The coach must be skillful so that she can demonstrate the stroke accurately for the rowers. These demonstrations also strengthen the coach–athlete relationship.

Simulation drills improve individual coordination and group timing. If the crew does three weeks of daily drilling, when they begin the spring water workouts they'll find the balance of the shell has improved. I first used these exercises in 1969 with the Yale lightweight team. They were skeptical at first, but after one year they realized the drills greatly improved their rowing. Simulation helps athletes internalize the stroke cycle. The technique becomes part of the athletes' mind, body, and spirit. It is also an excellent form of cross-training.

An on-water simulation drill rowers can do is feathering, or air-stroke rowing. Rowers keep the blades feathered as they perform the rowing stroke. When they become more proficient, they can balance the blades off the water.

Race simulation, a second type of visualization, comes later in the training cycle. Use short pieces, such as 500 meters, and designate a focus for each piece, such as stroke rate, rhythm, shell run, or race plan. Insist that the athletes take a moment to establish their focus before starting.

The next step is total race simulation. Kenneth Doherty, long-time track coach at the University of Pennsylvania, wrote, "An excellent method of 'mental training' a few days before competition is to cover the exact distance of one's race at a slower pace during which one concentrates on simulating the race itself. In so doing, play the role of how you feel as well as what you do" (Doherty 1964) Total race simulation includes every aspect of race day, including weigh-in, meal times, race plan, and cool-down. Crews should do total race simulation at least two or three times, usually on days when a 2000-meter time trial is scheduled. As a result, when the athletes arrive at the regatta they are well prepared mentally, physically, nutritionally, technically, and emotionally. They "take ownership" of the regatta site without feeling distracted or intimidated. It helps if the coach lets the athletes determine their schedule.

Relaxation Techniques

Relaxation involves lying on your back for 10 to 30 minutes at the end of practice. With your eyes opened or closed, systematically tense and relax the different parts of the body. Move through the body from toes to head, up and down each side of the body. Then tense and relax the major segments of the body. Finally, spend a few minutes in total relaxation with your eyes closed.

You should introduce relaxation techniques early in the preparation phase to help refine technique and later during the competitive phase to help release tension in order to race effortlessly. On-water practices for relaxation include slow-motion rowing, part-stroke rowing, rowing at 75 percent effort, and relaxed-grip rowing and sculling.

Another on-water drill is doing a set number of strokes with the body completely tensed followed by the same number of strokes with the body completely relaxed. Encourage the athletes to feel the difference, especially the increased run of the shell and the longer stroke length during the relaxation strokes. This drill also helps develop awareness and concentration.

Concentration

Concentration is important for improving focus. It is a difficult practice that requires both patience and perseverance. It involves sitting on the floor with the spine erect, which allows the athletes to slow down and experience stillness with a relaxed yet strong mental focus. You can use three methods: focusing on an object, counting breaths, or doing a set routine of yoga postures. In the first method, place a small object about half a meter in front of you. Keep your eyes open and focused on the object. Don't let your thoughts wander. This practice is called one-pointedness because your concentration is fully focused on a single object (Goleman 2003). This one-pointedness translates to rowing when you focus on the neck of the person in front or look over the stern from the stroke seat. Your concentration is on your immediate environment.

To count breaths, assume a comfortable sitting position with your eyes either open or closed. Take full, deep breaths that originate from the abdomen. Breathe in for six counts, breathe out for six counts. Make it rhythmic!

The third method for concentration is integral yoga, which the athletes can do as a team. This practice combines posture, concentration, and breathing, and is therefore called integral yoga.

On water, you can practice concentration by holding a particular focus, such as bladework, for a number of strokes or minutes. Coaching-intensive technique days are another excellent method for improving concentration. Choose a quiet stretch of water 1500 to 2000 meters long. Have the crew do multiple sets of drills focusing on different parts of the stroke cycle, positions, and movements, such as rowing with a fixed body angle, straight arms, or quarter slide. Perform each set for the length of the course. Closely monitor the performance, increasing the crew's concentration level and helping them realize the importance of accurate drilling. The frequent turning around is a welcomed pause in the athletes' focus. Include this practice in both the preparation phase and precompetition phase as the emphasis shifts from "training to train" to "training for performance."

Concentration can be practiced on the water as well as off the water.

Concentration expands awareness of body, thoughts, and emotions. Eventually these three become one. The athletes make no attempt to suppress their thoughts, they simply let thoughts come into the mind and go out. This awareness is important because as psychologist Charles Tart explains, "Ideas keep us living in an abstraction instead of the actual sensory reality" (2000, 59).

Concentration is the process of letting go of thoughts and observing your own mind. When you reach this stage, your concentration practice is moving toward mindfulness.

Mindfulness

Mindfulness means paying attention on purpose, in the present moment, and in a nonjudgmental way. This kind of attention nurtures awareness, clarity, and acceptance of present-moment reality (Kabat-Zinn 1994). Athletes such as Wayne Gretzky and Michael Jordan exemplified this skill by being fully aware of everyone on the ice or the court and the location of the puck or ball at any given moment. Ice skater Brian Boitano and Chicago Bulls coach Phil Jackson both attribute their championship success to an ability to remain in the present moment. Mindfulness training begins with consciousness of the body that then works outward to include the surrounding environment.

The formal technique for practicing mindfulness is the body scan. Lie on your back with your eyes closed. Focus your attention on the different parts of the body, beginning at the feet and progressing up one side to the head and back down the other side. As you scan the different body parts, make no judgment. Feel the targeted area and make note of any pleasant, unpleasant, or neutral sensations. When you finish, your whole body is integrated with its immediate environment.

A parallel situation occurs in the shell during slow-motion rowing. The more the athletes slow down, the more improvements begin to surface in awareness, accuracy, and control of the movements. Ken Wilber, author of *The Eye of Spirit,* refers to this quality as the "ever-present awareness" (1997, 286).

Encourage the athletes to work in silence and focus on the present moment, whether in the shell, on the ergometer, or in the weight room. This highly developed state of personal mindfulness is the common thread between all of the crew's training methods. It is the spirit by which they should approach all training and racing.

For effective racing, the athletes focus only on their own shell in the present moment. At a coaching conference in 2000, Canadian coach Al Morrow spoke about this mindfulness in McBean and Heddle, his 1992 Olympic pair: "They maintained focus with only a half-length lead on their competitors. They remained in the present moment, focusing on their own performance of the stroke cycle—an excellent example of stroke-by-stroke racing."

Mindfulness practice helps the coach and athletes step outside their hectic lives and learn from the stillness of their minds. This is the ever-present spirit. We move from the quantitative and busy to the qualitative and essential. We realize how routine our lives are. Self-awareness helps us become more spontaneous and more creative, and it regenerates our mind, body, and spirit. We also experience a significant shift from the purely thinking or rational mode to a clearer intuitive mode. Athletes have to make decisions quickly from moment to moment and intuition is a very beneficial skill. For any physical skill to be effective, it must eventually evolve to this intuitive or nonthinking stage. In rowing, the execution of the stroke cycle is completely reflexive and spontaneous. This is the beginning of flow.

Flow

In the foreword to the *Tao Te Ching*, Stephen Mitchell beautifully illustrates flow: "A good athlete can enter a state of body awareness in which the right stroke or the right movement happens by itself, effortlessly, without any interference of the conscious will. The game plays the game; the poem writes the poem: We can't tell the dancer from the dance" (1988, vii-viii).

In *Awakening Earth*, Duane Elgin observes, "Flow consciousness has long been recognized by athletes when they achieve a high level of concentration and synchronization" (1993, 188). Flow consciousness is paradoxical in that it often requires great effort to achieve a seemingly effortless and spontaneous result. With effort we move beyond effort and find stillness. Here is how Steve McKinney describes his experience of breaking the world downhill ski record: "I discovered the middle path of stillness within speed, calmness within fear, and I held it longer and quieter than ever before" (188).

Csikszentmihaly succinctly explains flow in his 1975 article, "Play and Intrinsic Rewards." I have included examples from rowing in parenthesis. "We experience [flow] as a unified flowing from one movement to the next (continuity in the stroke cycle) in which we feel control of our actions (absolute control of the balance), and in which there is little distinction between self and environment (the rower is one with the equipment); between stimulus and response (the oars are applied and the shell responds beautifully); or between past, present, and future (focus is on each present stroke)" (43).

Regular meditative practice improves the body's flow. The smooth, effortless action of the body represents the refined inner consciousness of the athlete's mind. The spirit of training inextricably links all five meditative steps and flow (see figure 21.3).

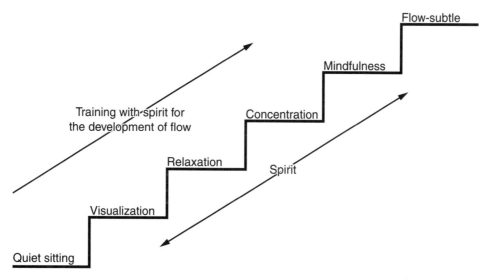

FIGURE 21.3   The five meditative training methods for developing flow.

Flow is an important product of mental training. When the athlete's mind and body are relaxed, focused, and in the present moment, fluid movement, or flow, occurs. We can see this flow in the athlete's movement—a stroke, a swing, a stride. In rowing, flow is total integration of body movements with the shell, blades, and water, along with a heightened awareness and concentration.

In addition to systematic mental training, the critical factors for achieving flow include posture, relaxation, timing, economy, and refinement. Coaches and athletes must constantly practice and monitor these qualities. With experience we become more aware of what we are doing while we are doing it. When we combine high levels of skill with equally high levels of consciousness (mindfulness), we can achieve flow and experience peak performance.

Feldenkrais, an expert in the field of movement, stated that athletes must learn how to turn strenuous movements into effective, smooth movements. This requires miles of rowing and hours of intensive drilling. With a relaxed focus, rowers are able to feel the fluid movement of the body and the endless run of the shell. As flow develops in the parts of the stroke, it carries over into the whole stroke, and it carries over from practice into races, which is the ultimate goal.

Great rowers are able to experience flow under competitive conditions and even under stress. Take for example the winning performances by Ekaterina Karsten in the 1999 world championships, by Peter Haining in the 1994 world championships, and by Xeno Müller in the 1996 Olympics. Through fluid and coordinated movement during the first 1500 meters of the race, these athletes preserved energy that allowed them to accelerate past their competitors in the final 500 meters.

Summary

For both coaches and athletes, the major task on race day is focusing and relaxation. It is easy to say that you're going to meditate, but it is difficult to discipline yourself to be patient and keep up your daily practice. Do not look for immediate benefits! The body and mind do evolve with consistent training: Physical movements become refined and the mind reaches higher levels of consciousness. These developments accelerate when you integrate the meditative practices into technical and physical training. The dynamic posture improves; movements become more economic, automatic, and intuitive; and breathing becomes systematic. You know what you are doing with your body while you are doing it, and this mindfulness becomes part of you.

Make time each day for some form of mental practice, integrating it into the overall training plan. Mental training should be part of every aspect of your training program. Remember, the first step is recognizing the need to slow down and experience quiet time. This develops our ability to listen and observe.

As race day approaches you must be sure that meditative practices are carefully planned and integrated into the physical and technical training. The coach should orchestrate the training so as to minimize internal anxieties, frustration, anger, and fear. Neil Campbell, coach of Canada's 1984 Olympic gold-medal eight, told me that he never made a negative comment to the crew in the last two months before the Olympic final. Consequently, the crew was confident, spirited, and determined.

Mental training as an integral part of the overall training starts with quiet sitting through visualization and simulation exercises. Next comes relaxation, then intensive concentration, then mindfulness practice, and finally mental and physical flow.

As our body flows, our mind becomes more intuitive, and our spirit becomes an integrative force in our practice and racing. Mental training enhances the flow and power of physical movement by allowing efficient release of energy. With mental training, the athletes are ready for racing.

chapter 22

Coxing

Lesley Thompson-Willie

If you ask coxswains how they started coxing, you will hear many different stories. There are coxswains who started because they wanted to be part of a team, because they were too small to be a rower, or because they were the younger brother or sister of a rower and happened to be light enough. No matter how you became a coxswain, though, in the end you have to want to be in the coxswain's seat.

I was a university gymnast who got injured. A month after knee surgery, my university's rowing team recruited me to be a coxswain for the spring rowing season. I was light, aggressive, athletic, and not too tall. My first crew included members who had rowed with the national team, so my learning curve was steep. Once my knee healed, I coxed a lot, rowed a lightweight single, and did a bit of sweep rowing. However, lightweight rowing was not contested internationally at the time, I was on the short side to be an elite rower, and I liked coxing. I remember thinking I could be "good at this coxing thing" and set out to make the national team. Not everyone aspires to the national team, but we all aspire to be the best coxswains we can be.

Basic Coxing Responsibilities

Just as rowers and scullers must acquire an aerobic base and basic technique skills, so must coxswains develop some fundamental skills. The rowing stroke is cyclical; novice rowers usually learn the entire stroke cycle at once and then spend years refining their stroke. The approach to coxing is slightly different. Learning to be a coxswain requires sequential skill mastery that begins, of course, with the basics.

Communication

Before any crew goes on the water, have meetings to discuss and clarify the basic commands. All the athletes must understand what each command means, for safety reasons as well as for smooth practices and race plans.

Communication between the coxswain, crew, and coach is extremely important. As the coxswain you have been entrusted with a position of leadership, and you must support the program and the coach. The crew is looking to you to fulfill the responsibilities of your position, not to order them around. One of a coxswain's most important skills is listening to your coach and teammates. If a difference of opinion surfaces during a workout, acknowledge that person's opinion and then discuss the matter after the workout.

The entire crew needs to know what's going on. If you are discussing a workout on the water, make certain that the crew can hear you and the rower's response. Be careful not to continually talk to your stroke and block out the opinions of other crew members. Also, limit discussion on the water. Realize that you may have to wait to speak with the coach before and after practice. Accept change and acknowledge your limitations and then work on them. Finally, you should project a positive attitude even when you don't feel like it.

Steering

Steering is the first on-water skill that a coxswain needs to master. In the beginning it helps to focus only on starting, steering, stopping, and turning the shell around.

Steering straight is difficult to master, especially in wind or current. Place your hands on the gunwales and lightly hold the steering loops or toggles. Steer the shell with smooth hand motions. To maintain speed, try to steer as little as possible. When racing on straight courses, assuming there is minimal wind, start your steering correction just after the catch. If you are making a small course correction, use the least amount of the rudder over several strokes and slowly bring the shell back to the center of the lane. The boat's greatest resistance to changing course is when the blades are in the water, because the blades act as stabilizers during the drive. Although the boat is much easier to steer when the blades are out of the water, drastic steering can disrupt the shell's balance and slow its run. Do not drastically change the rudder position, and try not to keep it on during the whole stroke, although there will be instances when you may have to have the rudder on slightly during the recovery, as this slows the shell speed. The smoothness of your steering motions is key. Always straighten the rudder gently.

For large, sweeping turns start steering as early as you can, using the smallest rudder angle possible. For sharp turns you will have to use a large rudder angle throughout the entire turn. If the rudder is not enough to make the necessary correction, you can have the port or starboard rowers adjust the pressure they are applying. When making major steering corrections, I usually tell the crew that I am steering.

Coxswains must plan their course well in advance and adjust for wind, current, and other shells. Pick a landmark far ahead of you and aim straight for it, making small corrections as you go. If you are racing on a 2000-meter buoyed course, use your peripheral vision to help you steer. Try to look three or four buoys ahead to check that you are in the center of the lane. You should see the same number of buoys on each side if you are centered in the lane. As long as you're going straight, it may not be necessary to go back to the center if you have gone off course. However, you also do not want your crew to worry about hitting the blade on a buoy, so you might decide to return to the center.

Check for wind or current by looking at the water ahead of you. Flags can indicate wind direction on the course. Try to identify surface-water patterns. You want to correct to one side of the lane before you hit the wind gust or current. In strong wind or current, especially if you are in an eight, your bow might push to one side of the lane more than the stern. In these cases you may find yourself going down the course sideways. Try to anticipate this and correct your steering early. You may have to steer the stern back in line with the bow and then try to edge the bow back to the center. I try to let the crew know if we are coming into any strong headwind or tailwind gusts. These winds do not affect your course as much as a crosswind, but they can give you a tactical advantage.

A shell is more responsive the faster it is going. Shells that have a large rudder or one directly under the coxswain also tend to be more responsive. If you are rowing with arms only or in pairs in an eight, the shell will not turn as quickly because of the slower boat speed.

When steering bow-coxed shells, there is one rudder bar that you push to the right or to the left. I steer with my dominant hand, using my other hand to brace myself. The advantage of a bow-coxed boat is that you can see directly in front of you. However, you will not be able to see the blades as easily. It will take a little while to get the feel of the width of the blades and boat behind you.

Make sure you know where to place the rudder toggles or loops to bring the rudder back to straight. You can use tape to mark the spot for your hands on each gunwale to ensure that the rudder is straight. Over time the rudder ropes or loops may stretch and you will have to adjust your markers. I like to hold the steering ropes lightly in my fingertips so I don't oversteer. Before practices and races the coxswain should always check the steering system and fin to make sure there are no problems.

Basic Commands

Coxing commands must be clear and concise. Basic commands differ from program to program, so in this section we'll discuss some of the commands I have used with the Canadian national women's program.

Starting

To get the crew in the right position before we start, I say "Sit up," or indicate where on the slide I want the crew to be. If I say "Sit up," the crew knows to go to a particular position on the slide and put their blades in the water. They will be ready for the start command. Commands to start the crew rowing can be as simple as "Ready go" or "Ready row." I use "Attention go" to start the crew.

Make sure everyone knows the starting sequence, stroke rate, and pressure. Decide how you will approach rowing away for steady-state workouts, rowing into pieces, controlled rate starts, or workouts with another crew beside you. To simulate the start of a race as much as possible, I have the crew start with the same sequence of strokes we would in a race.

In the mid- through late 1990s the national women's eight and lightweight men's four did a lot of shared workouts. Before the two crews went on the water, I would meet with the bow of the men's four and discuss rowing away together in terms of pressure, rate, and number of strokes. This helped keep the crews side by side for steady-state work and guaranteed a fair start in competitive pieces. If one shell was slightly ahead or behind we would adjust the timing of the build to allow the other boat to pull even. The goal is to have all crews go through the marker at the same time and at the required speed or rate.

Stopping

Commands to stop the crew should be clear and simple. "Easy," "Let it run," or "Weigh enough" are common examples. "Easy" is a good command because it is one word, but you have to be careful that the crew knows that "Easy" means they should stop, not row with less pressure. When you want the crew to row with less pressure, you can use "Light" or "Row light." I use "Easy" to tell a crew to stop, starting the command at the catch of the stroke.

The crew must be clear on how you wish to stop or slow the shell. I ask the rowers to finish the stroke until their hands are away from the body. Then they lock their knees and keep weight on the oar handles to stay balanced. The tone of my voice tells the crew if we need to stop quickly, and I might add, "Hold hard." Review your commands and exactly how you want the crew to stop a shell.

Turning the Shell

Once you have given the stop command, the blades will be off the water and the shell will continue to glide forward. When I use the command "Blades" or "Blades down," the crew drops their blades to the water. The crew should perform this together in one smooth motion. When the momentum has slowed, call a particular side to hold water. The rowers on that side will turn their blades partially onto the square and dig them slightly into the water. This swings the bow of the shell in the direction you want to turn. It also swings the stern to the opposite side, which you need to remember when you are turning the shell into a buoyed lane.

When the shell is partially turned in the correct direction, I give one command, "Ready turn." In most cases the crew knows that we are turning, and they know which side needs to back (push the blade forward) and which side needs to row. Time the final command, "Easy," so that the shell drifts to the position you wish to start from.

Novice crews need a little more instruction. You may want to tell each side what to do to turn the boat ("Port to back, starboard to row, ready back" or vice versa). The shell should be balanced while turning around. The crew should not take a water break or adjust clothing until they've turned the boat.

Coxing Norms and Clarifying Calls

The crew should know how you are going to call rate and pressure. How will you call stroke-rate transitions? How many strokes will it take to get to the desired rate? How does a crew interpret "Up in two" versus "Up over two"? Coxing norms prevent this kind of confusion.

Say you are rowing steady state at 24 strokes per minute. You're to go to 36 strokes per minute for one minute, drop to 32 for two minutes, and then increase to 36 for one minute, which is the finish of the piece. You might make the calls as follows: "36 up over 3," then "Up now," saying "up" at the finish of the stroke and "now" approaching the catch, or simply "36 up" if the crew knows what piece they are doing. At the minute mark you would call "32 power now," saying "32" at the catch, "power" at the finish, and "now" at the catch of the next stroke," or simply "32 now" with "32" at the finish and "now" at the catch. For the next transition you might call "36 up." At the end of the piece, call "Down." You can make calls at various times during the stroke cycle. It doesn't matter how you place your calls as long as the crew knows what you expect. Make sure you call drills in and out the same way so the crew understands how to execute them properly. Through practice you'll determine which calls produce the desired results. There is no single set of norms, but it is important to set yours either as a program or as an individual crew.

Advanced Coxing

After the basic skills come more advanced skills, including positioning correctly in the shell; calling time, distance, and place; motivating the crew; knowing race-day responsibilities; maintaining weight requirements; and understanding rowing technique for coxing.

Positioning in the Shell

When getting in the shell, make sure you place your foot in the center of the coxswain's seat. This will ensure you do not damage the seat. Some coxswains lean forward and sit very low in the shell to minimize wind resistance, while others sit straight up. Sitting straight has some advantages over leaning forward. If you are sitting up, your back can touch the shell. You can brace yourself between the back of the seat and the footboards so you don't move around as much, especially during a racing start. Whatever you decide, make sure that the toggles or loops are at the right distance.

Coxswains must master the sequence of the skills so they can guide rowers.

When your back is lodged firmly against the back of the shell, you get a better kinesthetic sense of the speed of the shell. If you put your hands on the gunwales, you can get a feel for the shell's balance. Coxswains can often feel the water running underneath their seat as the shell is going along, and experienced coxswains can usually tell by the feel of the water beneath them if something catches on the fin or rudder. For example, at one world championships we were doing our warm-up and we weren't hitting our race rates as easily as we should. When I looked behind me, I noticed that the wake was larger than usual. I stopped the crew and reached under the shell to check the fin and rudder, and I found some weeds. Now I always check for weeds or debris on the fin when we are in the starting gates.

In a bow-coxed shell you must be able to get out of the shell easily in case it flips or fills with water. You should be able to brace yourself against the headrest, the bottom of the shell, and a bulkhead. If the bulkhead is too far to the bow, you can build up the area with plastic foam and move the headrest. How low you are in the shell depends on individual preference; however, you shouldn't get so low that your vision is impaired. Make adjustments just as rowers change footstretcher height or placement. I prefer to have my head and shoulders above the deck so I can easily see other shells. If you are in a coxed pair, I suggest a lower position so as not to disrupt the sensitive balance of a pair.

Calling Time

Once your steering skills are competent you can begin to call time, distance, and place. During a workout you should time both the work and rest intervals using a timing device such as a CoxBox. Decide with your coach and crew if the build into higher rate pieces is part of the rest or part of the work. Some crews like to hear when they are halfway. During long pieces some crews like to hear the time at two-minute intervals. However, don't overload the crew with information by calling every two minutes of a long steady-state piece. Experiment with different calls and let the crew decide what they prefer.

Many rowers will time the pieces themselves. If you are working out with another crew make sure you coordinate your watches. When you are doing a shared workout on an unmarked course and you are doing the row in pieces rather than from a standing start, you can set your timing devices together. One person can call out, "Ready to set watches, three, two, one, now." Decide when you will start to row. For example, call "Row away at 30 seconds, crews to build over three starting the piece at one minute for four minutes."

Some crews use time in addition to distance markers to call tactical moves. You may wish to call a technical point at two minutes into the race or start your final sprint at a specific time. If you are going to use time for certain calls during a race, make sure you account for wind and water conditions. A tailwind can shorten a race and a raging headwind with waves can make the race much longer.

Calling Distance

If you are calling distance, be sure you know where you are on the course, be it a waterway, a 2000-meter racecourse, or a course for head races. Review the flow pattern and then identify the distance markers on the course. Focus less on technical points during the row and concentrate on your location on the course. Look for buoy markers, significant landmarks, and any flags on the course.

Ask the crew how they want you to call distance on a 2000-meter course. If I make a distance call, I use this sequence: 500, 750, 1000, 750 to go, 500, 250. It gives the crew a psychological boost to count down the meters to the finish line. You don't have to use the 500-meter markers; I have used race plans where I call distances such as 350, 900, 600 to go. FISA courses and some national courses use the Albano buoy system. In this system the buoys are often 10 meters apart so it is easier to call odd distances.

Calling Place

Decide with the crew how you are going to call placing during races. For example, at the 700-meter mark I might call "Second by a deck" and then a tactical move. This means there is one crew ahead of you and your shell's bow ball is a deck's length behind the other crew's bow ball. If I predict that the other crew is strong during the middle of the race but might fade at the end, and we tend to have an even pace throughout the race, I wouldn't make this call the same way. I might modify it and say, "Second by a deck, stay with them," and then add a tactical call such as "legs now" to keep the crew moving at the same or a slightly quicker pace. Later in the race, perhaps with 500 meters to go, I'll make the "Let's go through them" call, if everything is going according to plan.

Calling what place you are at in a race can be difficult when you have six crews very close to each other. You don't want to become preoccupied with one or two crews. You may forget about the crews behind you or in far away lanes. If you make a call to move, tell the crew whether you have pulled closer or ahead of other crews. If you make a call to move and nothing happens, then you have to stay on the crew and stay as positive as possible. You may have to adjust your race plan or make a planned call earlier. You will probably want to warn the crew about the change.

When does the crew expect to hear where they are in relation to other crews? Each individual may want different information. It is up to you to have the crew come to a consensus on what information you will provide and when you will provide it. Newer coxswains may want to stick to a set plan. Once coxswains have earned the trust of the crew and coach, they can add or eliminate distance and place information or change the timing of their calls as they see the race unfolding.

You should call place during side-by-side competitive and group workouts. In a noncompetitive workout such as a steady-state workout, be careful not to turn it into a competition by constantly calling the workout like a race. The coaches will probably want you to keep the boats together and keep the crew from falling behind. Don't let the crew fall so far behind that they don't know where they are in relationship to the other crew.

Motivation

Everyone likes encouragement, and motivation is an integral part of coxing. Some rowers want a lot of external motivation and others do not. How you motivate your crew depends on crew consensus and your personality. If an individual is doing something well, tell them. If you make a technical call to a rower, let them know whether or not they have fixed the fault.

You must give accurate information to the crew; your credibility lies in the balance. If you are a full length behind another crew, don't say you are three-quarters of a length, because the crew will know the difference. Crews want to know where they are, and then they expect to work to move up on a crew. Giving feedback that you are moving on a crew is extremely motivating. When you are falling behind, identify what is happening and then try to make a change. The tone of your voice can let the crew know how they are doing. Sounding excited about what's happening can be inspiring.

Some coxswains curse to motivate their crew. Swearing isn't appealing to spectators, it is offensive when used constantly, and it ultimately becomes ineffective. I have sworn in races, but only as a last resort or to emphasize an urgent point.

I believe in racing to win and being realistic about your performance. If you find yourself in fourth place, you don't want to dwell on that fact. You want to work on moving through other crews to get your crew into the best possible finish position.

Racing

On race day it is critical to be aware of weigh-in and race times. If you have to carry weight, be sure to take it in the boat with you for the race. At some regattas the coxswains have to attend a coaches and coxswains meeting before the racing starts. Have your tools and your fully charged amplification system with you. If you are racing multiple races, find out where you can charge your system between races.

I always check with the coach that all the riggers are properly set and all nuts and bolts are secure. Check that the rudder, fin, and rudder ropes are secure. If it is hot, consider taking water with you.

I spend a fair amount of time visualizing the race. I go over the race plan, possible scenarios, and corresponding calls. Finally, I check the race conditions with the coach to determine any tactical changes.

The warm-up can be stressful. You have to be extremely alert for oncoming boats. Trying to do your warm-up pieces on a crowded course requires nerves of steel. Look to see what races are before and after you to get an idea of what boats will be warming up around you. You also want to know exactly when the race before you is in the starting gates. Turning the shell around in lanes can be tricky if the crews at the blocks beside you arrive at the same time. Give yourself enough time to account for any wind that might blow you off course as you back into the gates. Know the rules of racing.

Once we're in the starting gates I check the fin for weeds, and if it is right behind me, I make sure the rudderpost is secure. I also tell the crew when all the crews have locked onto the starting gates. If the crew is experienced, I ask the bow pair to help keep us straight in the lane. They can touch or back the shell as they see fit unless I tell them to stop or give them a specific command. I find that they keep on top of alignment, and their reaction time to wind is usually quicker when they don't have to wait for me to tell them what to do.

I reset my CoxBox once the rowers are sitting and ready to go. I like to have a running time of the race. You have to make sure that your stroke doesn't go over a stroke-rate sensor, as this starts the timing device before the race begins. If this happens, reset the timing device. Also, I often have a tape recorder in the shell for taping the race. The tape helps me to analyze my calls after the race and even listen together with the team to identify calls that worked and those that did not.

Try to stay calm before the start. Let the crew know beforehand if you might change the plan during the race. I don't say very much at the beginning of a race, because talking fast and talking a lot distract the crew. The crew knows what they are doing and usually can't go any harder than they already are. I check to see if we have come out of the starting blocks straight, and I make corrections only when absolutely necessary. I try to feel what the boat is doing, if the rate is too high or too low, if we are spinning our wheels, or if we aren't being aggressive enough.

You must get the number of strokes in your start sprint correct, because some, if not all, of the rowers will be counting the number of strokes until the transition to race pace. Some crews time their start sprint instead of counting strokes. Calling the transition to race pace and into the final sprint is extremely important. The crew must understand exactly how you will call the transitions.

Work on getting the correct number of strokes to the finish line, and tell the crew approximately how many more to go to race through the finish line. Never let the crew ease off before the finish line; add strokes on if you have miscalculated. Finally, know the flow pattern and where the cool-down area is, which may be different from practices.

Weight Requirements

The international minimum weight limit for coxswains is 50 kilograms for women's boats and 55 kilograms for men's. A sound nutritional plan to achieve that weight is important. You should not go to extraordinary measures, especially at the last minute, to reduce your weight. More weight will slow down the boat by creating more water resistance, but an athlete should never dehydrate, especially in a hot environment. Even a little bit of dehydration can influence reaction time and judgment. It is also unhealthy to drink a lot of fluid to bring your weight up to the minimum.

Don't overlook exercise. I believe that being fit helped me handle stressful racing situations and hot, humid conditions. I was a decent weightlifter from my gymnastics background, and I took great joy in trying to outlift my crewmates based on strength to body-weight ratios. This helped my credibility when I asked the rowers to give that extra effort.

Coxing Rowing Technique

You need a good understanding of rowing technique and style. You will be expected to learn, teach, and reinforce proper technique.

Educate yourself by taking technical courses, talking and listening to your coach, doing video analysis, learning program directives from your club or association, doing some rowing yourself, spending time in a coach boat as an observer or as a coach, and being open to new ideas. Coxing technique is more important in steady-state practices, although you may make technique calls during races. Stay with the theme of the row and do not talk while the coach is talking. Do not jump to another technique point just after the coach has spent time on a particular element of the stroke. Check the following technique points, but always account for wind, swells, and other environmental factors.

Motivating the crew is a part of coxing.

Timing

You want the crew's blades to enter and exit the water at the same time. Assess timing at the catch and the release. Is anyone skying, or missing, water? This may make them late. See if everyone is squaring up at the same time and that they are feathering at the same time. Blade entry and exit are usually based on the stroke's blade. Strokes are sometimes late when you attempt to control stroke rate or slide control. One of the first things I do is judge the timing. I start by making general timing calls if I see errors. I try not to pinpoint one rower at the beginning of the row unless the coach or rower has asked me to do so. Start by looking at the stern pair's timing and make timing corrections down the boat from there.

In most cases I do not tell the rowers what they are doing incorrectly; I call a correction instead. If five's blade is going into the water late because of skying, I call the rower's name and say, "Hands up at the catch." Calling "Susan late" is too general. There are many possible reasons why she is late. I might say "Susan skying" if she knows how to make the technical correction. Let rowers know a couple of strokes later whether or not they have made the correction. Later on in the workout you can tell them that they are rowing well or that they are on time. Technical changes are difficult, so try to acknowledge any positive changes the rowers make.

Angle of Entry

Ideally, all angles are the same at the catch and the finish. Look at the blades' angle of entry. Incorrect angles may be due to the placement of the footboards; a different span, inboard, or blade length; or the rowers' body type, flexibility, or technical ability. Discuss incorrect angles with the coach.

Blade Height

Check blade height off the water before the catch and at the release. Is the blade clearing the tops of the puddles? Look at the height of the blades off the water during the recovery. Are they all at the same height? Let the rowers know whether to move their hand level higher or lower.

Blade Depth

Inspect blade depth from the catch through the finish. If the blade is too deep I might call "Horizontal." Listen carefully to the coach so you can make connections between corrections the coach has asked the athlete to make and what the blade is doing. If you observe the blade going deep and the coach has mentioned to the rower that he is lifting his body too early and not using his legs soon enough, you can use this information to make calls. You could use the calls "Horizontal," "Legs," or "Push" for that athlete.

Does the blade sit still at any point during the drive? If the blade wavers through the water, it may indicate incorrect power application. A rower who is going shallow lessens power on one side. Look to see if the rower's inboard is lower than the rest of the crew and if the blade is coming out of the water early. Often the puddle looks very large with a lot of top water or froth.

Body Position

Make sure everyone is over the keel of the shell at the release and then again at mid-drive. Determine if each rower has an equal pivot out at the catch. I use the call "Pivot" to get the crew to reach at the catch. Note if anyone is dropping the outside or inside shoulder.

During the 1991 rowing season, our crew had not been rowing with a lot of pivot, so there was less length at the catch. Amazingly, during the warm-up for the final of the world championships the crew relaxed and started to pivot out of the shell at the catch. I could see straight down the middle of the shell. I could see past all the rowers when they were at the catch. The crew was over the keel again mid-drive through the finish of the stroke. At this point I knew we were going to have an amazing final, and we eventually won.

Hand Technique

Although you shouldn't lean out of the boat, sometimes you can look down the gunwales to see who is using improper grip. You may be able to see why a rower is feathering in the water or washing out by observing the rower's wrist action. In an eight you may not be able to see the bow section and you will need to ask the coach to give you feedback. Look at their grip to see if they are using the outside hand incorrectly during the release. Watch for the hand sliding down the oar, the hand coming off at the catch, a pinkie finger over the end of the oar, a thumb on top of an oar, and so on.

Balance

Check the gunwales to see if one side is higher than the other. Check to see if the port or starboard oars are higher than each other. You can always use a small level. Use both the height of the blades off the water and the height of the inboard to make corrections. Rowers often complain about the shell's balance. Because they have an oar in their hand, they know how easily they are getting their blade in or out of the water. Coxswains might not notice the shell's balance as easily as the rowers. I often could tell if the boat was down slightly to one side because my back would start to hurt on that side. To correct the balance, start by correcting the rowers whose hand levels aren't the same as the rest of the crew.

Rhythm and Ratio

A crucial element of advanced coxing is acquiring a feel for the speed and rhythm of the shell. One of the best ways to work on crew rhythm is to spend time working with the stroke. Ask the crew to change the speed or ratio of various parts of the stroke ("Speed up the hands" or "Slow the swing," "Lock down the knees slightly longer" or "Break the slide with a touch more control"). Part of good rhythm is the correct ratio of time on the slide in relation to time the blade spends in the water. You can compare the speed of the slide and the speed of the swing away by looking at the speed and timing of the inboards coming toward you. Getting a feel for what is fast depends on stroke rate and pressure. I check puddle clearance at various rates and pressures. The boat will have a certain glide beneath you that is hard to describe and that you learn to recognize with experience. Using a SpeedCoach can help you associate the feel of the shell with the pace you are going. Eventually this feel will become instinctive.

Sometimes you recognize that, based on measurements on a marked course or with a calibrated SpeedCoach, you are going very fast, but the boat doesn't feel that great. I call this "rowing on the edge." As a coxswain, it is important to recognize this feeling. The last thing you want to do is slow the shell down in order to have a more controlled or smooth-feeling boat.

Don't overlook the importance of sound. It gives clues as to how the blade is entering and releasing, how the shell is running, whether someone is pulling away from the oarlock and needs more inboard pressure, or whether someone is too hard around the release, causing the shell to rise and fall.

It is important to look at puddles and how much splash is produced at blade entry or release. Note what the puddles look like and how far you are clearing them at a given stroke rate (puddle separation). "Clearing puddles" refers to the distance between the puddle of the last stroke and the puddle of the seven-seat at the next stroke. At lower rates there is more puddle clearance than at higher rates. You want as much puddle clearance as you can get since the more clearance you have at a given stroke rate, the faster the boat is traveling. Puddle clearance provides insight into power application, technical faults, fatigue levels, and speed away from the line. During a racing start in an eight, rowers will be rowing in the puddles of other crewmembers in the shell. You want the rowers to get out of each other's puddles as soon as they can. Generally you don't want the stroke rate to be so high that the rowers are rowing in others' puddles.

I rely on the feel of the shell above all. Sometimes I briefly close my eyes to feel the balance and glide of the shell. This feels like your body absorbing the catch all at once. Then you want to feel a horizontal surge of the shell forward as the rowers push back toward the bow. At the release you want to feel the momentum of the shell continuing at the same pace as much as possible. The blades come out together and there isn't a sensation of one side dragging the blades out, unbalancing the shell. The shell glides underneath you and the water runs evenly off both sides of the stern. The rowers come forward at a constant speed, and just before the boat slows down and drops, the rowers pick up the shell at the catch. There are a few times when I have felt this in a race. The 1992 Olympic final, which we won, was one race where everything felt perfect.

Reflecting upon my many years of coxing experience, perhaps it all comes down to remembering that you are an important member of the crew. You must keep the crew and shell safe at all times. The challenge is to steer straight, say the right thing at the right time and place, and help the boat go fast!

bibliography

Chapter 1

Affeld, K., K. Schichl, and A. Ziemann. 1993. Assessment of rowing efficiency. *Int J Sports Med* 14:S39–S41.

Alexander, F.H. 1922-26. The theory of rowing. *University of Durham Philosophical Society* I.III: 160-179.

Kleshnev, V. Propulsive efficiency of rowing. Coaches' Infoservice, www.sportscoach-sci.com (accessed March 29, 2004).

Martens, R. 2004. *Successful coaching*, 3rd ed. Champaign, IL: Human Kinetics.

Nolte, V. 1984. *Die Effektivitaet des Ruderschlages*. [The efficiency of the rowing stroke.] Berlin: Bertels and Wernitz.

Sands, W.A., and J.R. McNeal. 2000. Enhancing flexibility in gymnastics. *Technique* 20, 5.

Schwanitz, P. 1991. Augewählte Beiträge aus der Biomechanik für die Leistungsentwicklung im Rudern. [Selected biomechanical topics about the development of the rowing performance.] Presentation at the FISA Coaches' Conference, Athens, Greece, 1991.

Schwanitz, P. 1995. Entwicklung der Bootsgeschwindigkeiten und Fahrzeiten—ihre Relation und Prognose. [Development of the boat velocity and race times—relations and projection.] *Rudersport* 32:859–861.

Chapter 2

Carey, P., M. Stensland, and L.H. Hartley. 1974. Comparison of oxygen uptake during maximal work on the treadmill and the rowing ergometer. *Med Sci Sports* 6 (2): 101-103.

Cunningham, D.A., P.B. Goode, and J.B. Critz. 1975. Cardiorespiratory response to exercise on a rowing and bicycle ergometer. *Med Sci Sports* 7 (1): 37-43.

Di Prampero, P.E. 1981. Energetics of muscular exercise. *Rev Physiol Biochem Pharmacol* 89: 143-222.

Hagerman, F.C., M.C. Connors, J.A. Gault, G.R. Hagerman, and W.J. Polinski. 1978. Energy expenditure during simulated rowing. *J Appl Physiol* 45 (1): 87-93.

Hagerman, F.C., G.R. Hagerman, and T.C. Mickelson. 1979. Physiological profiles of elite rowers. *Physician and Sportsmed* 7 (7): 74-81.

Hagerman, F.C., and W.D. Lee. 1971. Measurement of oxygen consumption, heart rate, and work output during rowing. *Med Sci Sports* 3 (4): 155-160.

Hagerman, F.C., M.D. McKirnan, and J.A. Pompei. 1975. Maximal oxygen consumption of conditioned and unconditioned oarsmen. *J Sports Med* 15 (1): 43-48.

Hartmann, U., and A. Mader. 1996. Variability of energy supply and possibilities of interpretation. In *Current Research in Sports Sciences*, ed. V. Rogozkin and R. Maughan, 179-185. NY/London: Plenum Press.

Jackson, R.C. and N.H. Secher. 1976. The aerobic demands of rowing in two Olympic oarsmen. *Med Sci Sports* 8 (3): 168-170.

Mader, A., U. Hartmann, and W. Hollmann. 1988. Der Einfluß der Ausdauer auf die 6 minütige maximale anaerobe und aerobe Arbeitskapazität eines Eliteruderers. [The influence of endurance on the 6-min maximum anaerobic and aerobic capacity of an elite rower.] In *Rudern: Sportmedizinische und sportwissenschaftliche Aspekte*, ed. J.M. Steinacker, 62-78. Berlin: Springer.

Mader, A., and H. Heck.1986. A theory of the metabolic origin of anaerobic threshold. *Int J Sports Med* 7 (Supplement 1): 45-65.

Mader, A., and W. Hollmann. 1977. Zur Bedeutung der Stoffwechselleistungsfähigkeit des Eliteruderers in Training und Wettkampf. [Regarding the importance of the metabolism capacity of an elite rower in training and competition.] In *Informationen zum Training: Ausdauertraining,*

Stoffwechselgrundlagen und Steuerungsansätze (Supplement to Leistungssport, Vol. 9), ed. Deutscher Sportbund, 8-62. Frankfurt.

Mickelson, T.C. and F.C. Hagerman. 1982. Anaerobic threshold measurements of elite oarsmen. *Med Sci Sports Exerc* 14 (6): 440-444.

Secher, N.H. 1993. Physiological and biomechanical aspects of rowing. Implications for training. *Sports Med* 15 (1): 24-42.

Secher, N.H., O. Vaage, and R.C. Jackson. 1982. Rowing performance and maximal aerobic power of oarsmen. *Scand J Sports Sci* 4 (1): 9-11.

Strømme, S.B., F. Ingjer, and H.D. Meen. 1977. Assessment of maximal aerobic power in specifically trained athletes. *J Appl Physiol* 42 (6): 833.

Young, V.R. Protein and amino acid metabolism with reference to aging and the elderly. *Prog Clin Biol Res* 326: 279-300.

Chapter 3

Jensen, K., L. Johansen, and N.H. Secher. 2001. Influence of body mass on maximal oxygen uptake: Effect of sample size. *Eur J Appl Physiol* 84 (3): 201-205.

Secher, N.H. 1993. Physiological and biomechanical aspects of rowing. Implications for training. *Sports Med* 15 (1): 24-42.

Chapter 4

McNeely, E. 2000. *Training for rowing.* Ottawa: Sport Performance Institute.

Chapter 5

Jensen, Nilsen, and Smith. 1990. Analysis of the Italian national training programme. *FISA Coach* 1(2): 1-5.

Chapter 6

Adam, K., H. Lenk, P. Nowacki, M. Rulffs, and W. Schröder. 1977. *Rudertraining.* [Training in Rowing.] Bad Homburg: Limpert.

Åstrand, P.O., and K. Rodahl. 1977. *Textbook of work physiology.* New York: McGraw-Hill.

Bueno, M. 1999. Die anaerobe Schwelle—von der Euphorie zur Vertrauenskrise. [Anaerobic threshold—from euphoria to a crisis of trust.] *Leistungssport* 1: 13-17.

de Marées, H. 1981. *Sportphysiologie.* [Sport Physiology.] Köln-Mühlheim: Tropon.

Fritsch, W. 1981. Zur Entwicklung der speziellen Ausdauer im Rudern. [Developing specific endurance in rowing.] In Rudern [Rowing], ed. W. Fritsch and V. Nolte. *Beiheft zu Leistungssport,* 4-32. Berlin: Bartels and Wernitz.

Fritsch, W. 1990. *Handbuch für das Rennrudern.* [Handbook for competitive rowing.] Aachen: Meyer and Meyer.

Fritsch, W. 1999. *Handbuch für den Rudersport.* [Handbook for rowing.] Aachen: Meyer and Meyer.

Fritsch, W. 2000. *Rowing: Training, fitness, leisure.* Aachen: Meyer and Meyer.

Hartmann, U., A. Mader, and W. Hollmann. 1997. Rudern von 8 bis 88 Jahren—wesensbestimmende Merkmale und Ausprägungsgrade einer lifetime-Sportart unter besonderer Berücksichtigung des physischen Aspekts. [Rowing from 8 to 88 years of age—quantitative characteristics and qualities of a lifetime sport with specific recognition of the physical aspects.] In *Rudern: erleben, gestalten, organisieren,* ed. W. Fritsch, 124-135. Wiesbaden: Limpert.

Heck, H., and P. Rosskopf. 1993. Die Lactat-Leistungsdiagnostik—valider ohne Schwellenkonzepte. [Lactate performance evaluation—more valid without threshold concepts.] *TW Sport & Med* 5: 344-352.

Mader, A. 1994. Die Komponenten der Stoffwechselleistung in den leichtathletischen Ausdauerdisziplinen—Bedeutung für die Wettkampfleistung und Möglichkeiten zu ihrer Bestimmung. [The components of metabolic capacity in the track and field endurance disciplines—The importance for competition and the possibilities of their determination.] In *Neue Tendenzen im Ausdauertraining,* ed. P. Tschiene. Informationen zum Leistungssport Bd. 12: 127-216.

Mader, A., and W. Hollmann. 1977. Zur Bedeutung der Stoffwechselleistungsfähigkeit des Eliteruderers im Training und Wettkampf. [The importance of metabolic capacity of elite rowers during training and competition.] *Beiheft zu Leistungssport* 3(9): 8-62.

Mader, A., H. Liesen, H. Heck, H. Philippi, R. Rost, P. Schürch, and W. Hollmann. 1976. Zur Beurteilung der sportartspezifischen Ausdauerleistungsfähigkeit im Labor. [The assessment of sport-specific endurance capacity in the laboratory.] *Sportarzt und Sportmedizin* 27: 80-88; 109-112.

Neumann, G. 1994. Anpassung und Belastungsgestaltung im Hochleistungstraining—Leistungsreserven aus sportmedizinischer Sicht. [Adaptations and loading in high performance training—performance reserves from a sports medicine point of view.] In *Neue Tendenzen im Ausdauertraining*, ed. P. Tschiene. Informationen zum Leistungssport Bd 12:97-116.

Neumann, G., A. Pfützner, and A. Berbalk. 1999. *Optimiertes Ausdauertraining*. [Optimal endurance training.] Aachen: Meyer and Meyer.

Neumann, G., A. Pfützner, and K. Hottenrott. 2000. *Alles unter Kontrolle*. [All under control.] Aachen: Meyer and Meyer.

Stegemann, H., and W. Kindermann. 1982. Comparison of prolonged exercise tests at the individual anaerobic threshold and the fixed anaerobic threshold of 4 mmol/l lactate. *Int J Sports Med* 105-110.

Weineck, J. 2000. *Optimales Training*. [Optimal training.] Balingen: Spitta.

Zintl, F. 1988. *Ausdauertraining*. [Endurance training.] München: BLV Verlagsgesellschaft.

Chapter 7

Acevedo, E.O., and A.H. Goldfarb. 1989. Increased training intensity effects on plasma lactate, ventilatory threshold, and endurance. *Med Sci Sports Exerc* 21:563-568.

Bompa, T.O. 1999. *Periodization: Theory and methodology of training*, 4th ed. Champaign, IL: Human Kinetics.

Bosch, A.N. et al. 1990. Physiological differences between black and white runners during a treadmill marathon. *Eur J Appl Physiol* 69:68-72.

Coertzer, P. et al. 1993. Superior fatigue resistance of elite black South African distance runners. *J Appl Physiol* 75:1822-1827.

Gaskill, S.E., R.C. Serfass, D.W. Bacharach, and J.M. Kelly. 1999. Responses to training in cross-country skiers. *Med Sci Sports Exerc* 31:1211-1217.

Hagerman, F.C., R.A. Fielding, M.A. Fiatarone, J.A. Gault, D.T. Kirkendall, K.E. Ragg, and W.J. Evans. 1996. A twenty-year longitudinal study of Olympic oarsmen. *Med Sci Sports Exerc* 28 (9):1150-56.

Hawley, J.A. 1993. State-of-the-art training guidelines for endurance performance. *NZ Coach* 2: 14-19.

Hawley, J.A., K.H. Myburgh, T.D. Noakes, and S.C. Dennis. 1997. Training techniques to improve fatigue resistance and enhance endurance performance. *J Sports Sci* 15:325-333.

Lindsay, F.H., J.A. Hawley, K.H. Myburgh, H.H. Schomer, T.D. Noakes, and S.C. Dennis. 1996. Improved athletic performance in highly trained cyclists after interval training. *Med Sci Sports Exerc* 28:1427-1434.

MacDougall, J.D., A.L. Hicks, J.R. MacDonald, R.S. McKelvie, H.J. Green, and K.M. Smith. 1998. Muscle performance and enzymatic adaptations to sprint interval training. *J Appl Physiol* 84: 2138-2142.

Mujika, I. 1998. The influence of training characteristics and tapering on the adaptation in highly trained individuals: A review. *Int J Sports Med* 19 (7): 429-46.

Rodas, G., J.L. Ventura, J.A. Cadefau, R. Cusso, and J. Parra. 2000. A short training programme for the rapid improvement of both aerobic and anaerobic metabolism. *Eur J Appl Physiol* 82: 480-486.

Stepto, N.K., J.A. Hawley, S.C. Dennis, and W.G. Hopkins. 1999. Effects of different interval-training programs on cycling time-trial performance. *Med Sci Sports Exerc* 31:735-741.

Tabata, I., K. Nishimura, M. Kouzaki, Y. Hirai, F. Ogita, M. Miyachi, and K. Yamamoto. 1997. Effects of moderate-intensity endurance and high-intensity intermittent training on anaerobic capacity and $\dot{V}O_2$max. *Med Sci Sports Exerc* 28:1327-1330.

Chapter 8

Hartmann, U., A. Mader, K. Wasser, and I. Klauer. 1993. Peak force, velocity, and power during five and ten maximal rowing ergometer strokes by world class female and male rowers. *Int J Sports Med* 14 (supplement 1): S42-S45.

Secher, N. 1975. Isometric rowing strength of experienced and inexperienced oarsmen. *Med Sci Sports* 7 (4): 280-283.

Chapter 9

Fiskerstrand, Å., and K.S. Seiler. 2004. Training and performance characteristics among Norwegian international rowers 1970-2001. *Scand J Med Sci Sports OnlineEarly.*

Houmard, J. et al. 1989. Effects of reduced training on submaximal and maximal running responses. *Int J Sports Med* 10:30-33.

Houmard, J., et al. 1994. The effects of taper on performance in distance runners. *Med Sci Sports Exerc* 26:624-631.

Johns, R. et al. 1992. Effects of taper on swim power, stroke distance and performance. *Med Sci Sports Exerc* 24:1141-1146.

Steinacker, J.M., et al. 1998. Training of rowers before world championships. *Med Sci Sports Exerc* 30:1158-1163.

Zarkadas, P., J. Carter, and E. Banister. 1994. Taper increases performance and aerobic power in triathletes. *Med Sci Sports Exerc* 26:34.

Chapter 10

Affeld, K., K. Schichl, and A. Ziemann. 1993. Assessment of rowing efficiency. *Int J Sports Med* 14:S39-S41.

Asami, T., N. Adachi, K. Yamamoto, K. Ikuta, and K. Takahaski. 1978. Biomechanical analysis of rowing skill. In *Biomechanics VI-B*, ed. E. Asmussen and K. Jorgensen, 109-114. Baltimore, MD: University Park Press.

Bachev, V., A. Tsvetkov, and K. Boichev. 1989. System for biomechanical study and simultaneous improving of the rowing cycle. In *Biomechanics in Sports V*, ed. L. Tsarouchas, J. Terauds, B.A. Gowitzke, and L.E. Holt, 245-255. Athens, Greece: Hellenic Sports Research Institute.

Baird, E.D., and W.W. Soroka. 1951. Measurement of force-time relations in racing shells. *Am Soc Mech Eng* 58:77-86.

Bompa, T.O., M. Hebbelinck, and B.Van Gheluwe. 1985. Force analysis of the rowing stroke employing two differing oar grips. *Can J Appl Sport Sci* 10 (2): 64-67.

Carter, A., T. Pelham, and L.E. Holt. 1993. Is the "big blade" better? *Av Can Row* 16 (5): 7-8.

Celentano, F., G. Cortili, P.E. di Prampero, and P. Cerretelli. 1974. Mechanical aspects of rowing. *J Appl Physiol* 36 (6): 642-657.

Dal Monte, A., and A. Komor. 1989. Rowing and sculling mechanics. In *Biomechanics of Sport*, ed. C.L. Vaughan, 53-119. Boca Raton, FL: CRC Press.

Duchesnes, C.J., R. Borres, L. Lewillie, M. Riethmuller, and D. Olivari. 1989. New approach for boat motion analysis in rowing. In *Biomechanics in Sports V*, ed. L. Tsarouchas, J. Terauds, B.A. Gowitzke, and L.E. Holt, 276-280. Athens, Greece: Hellenic Sports Research Institute.

Gerber, H., H. Jenny, J. Sudan, and E. Stuessi. 1987. Biomechanical performance analysis in rowing with a new measuring system. In *Biomechanics X-B*, ed. B. Jonsson, 721-724. Champaign, IL: Human Kinetics.

Hartmann, U., A. Mader, K. Wasser, and I. Klauer. 1993. Peak force, velocity, and power during five and ten maximal rowing ergometer strokes by world-class female and male rowers. *Int J Sports Med* 14:S42-S45.

Herberger, E. 1989. *Rudern.* [Rowing.] Toronto: Sport Books Publisher.

Hill, H. 2002. Dynamics of coordination within elite rowing crews: Evidence from force pattern analysis. *J Sports Sci* 20 (2): 101-118.

Ishiko, T. 1971. Biomechanics of rowing. In *Biomechanics II*, ed. J. Vredenbregt and J. Warternweiler, 249-252. Baltimore, MD: University Park Press.

Ishiko, T., S. Katamoto, and T. Maeshima. 1983. Analysis of rowing movements with radiotelemetry. In *Biomechanics VIII-B*, ed. H. Matsui and K. Kobayashi, 816-821. Champaign, IL: Human Kinetics.

Kleshnev, V. 1999. Propulsive efficiency of rowing. In *Proceedings of the XVIIth International Symposium on Biomechanics in Sports*, ed. R.H. Saunders and B.J. Gibson, 224-228. Canberra, Australia: Australian Institute of Sport.

Kleshnev, V. 2000. Power in rowing. In *Proceedings of the XVIIIth International Symposium of the Society of Biomechanics in Sports*, ed. R. Sanders, D.P. Johns, and Y. Hong, 663-666. Hong Kong: Chinese University of Hong Kong.

Kleshnev, V. 2001. Rowing biomechanics newsletter. Australian Institute of Sport 1(4).

Körndle, H., and V. Lippens. 1988. Do rowers have a particular "footwriting"? In *Biomechanics in Sport*, 7-11. London: Institution of Mechanical Engineers.

Loschner, C., R. Smith, and M. Galloway. 2000. Intra-stroke boat orientation during single sculling. In *Proceedings of the XVIIIth International Symposium of the Society of Biomechanics in Sports*, ed. R. Sanders, D.P. Johns, and Y. Hong, 66-69. Hong Kong: Chinese University of Hong Kong.

Lueneburger, C. 1995. A comparative analysis of Macon and big racing blades. *FISA Coach* 6 (2): 1-8.

Martin, T.P., and J.S. Bernfield. 1980. Effect of stroke rate on velocity of a rowing shell. *Med Sci Sports Exerc* 12 (4): 250-256.

Mason, B.R., P. Shakespear, and P. Doherty. 1988. The use of biomechanical analysis in rowing to monitor the effect of training. *Excel* 4 (4): 7-11.

McBride, M.E. 1998. The role of individual and crew technique in the enhancement of boat velocity in rowing. Doctoral thesis, University of Western Australia.

McBride, M.E., D.J. Sanderson, and B.C. Elliott. 2001. Seat-specific technique in pair oared rowing. In *Proceedings of the XIXth International Symposium of the Society of Biomechanics in Sports*, ed. J.R. Blackwell, 263-266. San Francisco: University of San Francisco.

Nolte, V. 1984. *Die Effektivität des Ruderschlages*. [The efficiency of the rowing stroke.] Berlin: Bartels and Wernitz.

Nolte, V. 1991. Introduction to the biomechanics of rowing. *FISA Coach* 2 (1): 1-6.

Nolte, V. 1993. Do you need hatchets to chop your water? *Am Rowing* 25 (4): 23-26.

Pannell, W.J. 1979. Mechanics of oar, boat, and body. *Sports Coach* 3 (4): 14-20.

Pelham, T.W., L.E. Holt, D.G. Burke, and A.G.W. Carter. 1993. Accelerometry for paddling and rowing. In *Biomechanics in Sports XI*, ed. J. Hamill, T.R. Derrick, and E.H. Elliott, 270-273. Amherst, MA: University of Massachusetts.

Pope, D.L. 1973. On the dynamics of men and boats and oars. In *Mechanics and Sport*, ed. J.L. Bleustein, 113-130. Detroit, MI: American Society of Mechanical Engineers.

Roth, W. 1991. Physiological-biomechanical aspects of the load development and force implementation in rowing. *FISA Coach* 2 (4): 1-9.

Roth, W., P. Schwanitz, P. Pas, and P. Bauer. 1993. Force-time characteristics of the rowing stroke and corresponding physiological muscle adaptations. *Int J Sports Med* 14:S32-S34.

Schneider, E., F. Angst, and J.D. Brandt. 1978a. Biomechanics in rowing. In *Biomechanics VI-B*, ed. E. Asmussen and K. Jorgensen, 115-119. Baltimore, MD: University Park Press.

Schneider, E., and M. Hauser. 1981. Biomechanical analysis of performance in rowing. *Biomechanics VII-B*, ed. A. Morecki, K. Kedzior, and A. Wit, 430-435. Baltimore, MD: University Park Press.

Schneider, E., F. Morell, and N. Sidler. 1978b. Long-time investigation in rowing by multiparameter telemetry. In *Biotelemetry IV*, ed. H.J. Klewe and H.P. Kimmich, 211-214. Basel, Germany: Karger.

Schwanitz, P. 1991. Applying biomechanics to improve rowing performance. *FISA Coach* 2 (3): 1-7.

Smith, R., M. Galloway, R. Patton, and W. Spinks. 1994. Analyzing on-water rowing performance. *Sports Coach* 17:37-40.

Smith, R., and C. Loschner. 2000. Net power production and performance at different stroke rates and abilities during pair-oar rowing. In *Proceedings of the XVIIIth International Symposium of the Society of Biomechanics in Sports*, ed. R. Sanders, D.P. Johns, and Y. Hong, 66-69. Hong Kong: Chinese University of Hong Kong.

Smith, R., and W. Spinks. 1989. Matching technology to coaching needs: On-water rowing analysis. In *Proceedings of the VIIth International Symposium of the Society of Biomechanics in Sports*, ed. W.E. Morrison, 277-287. Melbourne, Australia: Footscray Institute of Technology.

Smith, R., and W. Spinks. 1995. Discriminant analysis of biomechanical differences between novice, good, and elite rowers. *J Sports Sci* 13 (5): 377-385.

Smith, R.M., W.L. Spinks, and J. Moncrieff. 1988. The development of an automated analysis system for the on-water evaluation and enhancement of rowing capacity and skill. *Report to the Australian Sports Commission Applied Sports Research Program*, Canberra, Australia.

Spinks, W.L. 1996. Force-angle profile analysis in rowing. *J Hum Mov Stud* 31:211-233.

Wagner, J., U. Bartmus, and H. de Marees. 1993. Three-axes gyro system quantifying the specific balance of rowing. *Int J Sports Med* 14:S35-S38.

Wing, A.M., and C. Woodburn. 1995. The coordination and consistency of rowers in a racing eight. *J Sports Sci* 13:187-197.

Zatsiorsky, V.M., and N. Yakunin. 1991. Mechanics and biomechanics of rowing: A review. *Int J Sport Biomech* 7:229-281.

Chapter 11

Davenport, M. 1992. *The nuts and bolts guide to rigging*. Church Hill, MD: Mouse House Books.

Nolte, V. 1979. Über die Genauigkeit bei der Anlagemessung. [The precision of measuring the pitch.] *Rudersport* 26:627.

Nolte, V. 1985. *Trimmen von Booten*. [Rigging of rowing boats.] Ratheburg, Germany: Ruderakademie.

Piesik, S. 2000. *Individual rigging and adjustment of rowing boats*. Eberbach, Germany: Empacher.

Chapter 15

Csikszentmihalyi, M. 1975. *Beyond boredom and anxiety: The experience of play in work and games*. San Francisco: Jossey-Bass Inc.

Fritsch, W. 2000. *Rowing: Training, fitness, leisure*. Oxford: Meyer and Meyer.

Gerges, R. 1977. Der unbekannte Ruderschlag. [The mysterious rowing stroke.] *Rudersport* 9: vii-viii.

Kleshnev, V. 2003. Rowing biomechanics newsletter. Australian Institute of Sport (3) 3.

McLaughlin, S. 2004. A comparison of two methods for teaching beginners the sport of rowing. Masters thesis, University of Western Ontario.

Nolte, V. 1984. *Die Effektivität des Ruderschlages*. [The efficiency of the rowing stroke.] Berlin: Bartels and Wernitz.

Nolte, V. 1984. Rudertechnik. [Rowing technique.] In *Bericht zum* 13, ed. V. Nolte, 31-41. Minden, Germany: FISA-Trainer-Kolloquium.

Nolte, V. 2001. Coach boat view: Drills. *Row Can Aviron* 24 (2): 15-23.

Nolte, V. 2001. Drills from the experts. *Row Can Aviron* 24 (2): 19-23.

Nolte, V. 2002. Coach boat view: The biomechanics of rowing. *Row Can Aviron* 24 (3): 8-15.

Chapter 16

Atmanspacher, H., and G.J. Dalenoort, eds. 1994. *Inside versus outside: Endo- and exo-concepts of observation and knowledge in physics, philosophy, and cognitive science*. Berlin: Springer.

Christian, P., and R. Haas. 1949. Wesen und Formen der Bipersonalität. [Characteristics and types of the bipersonality.] *Beiträge aus der Allgemeinen Medizin* (7):1-65.

Conolly, K., and B. Jones. 1970. A developmental study of afferent-reafferent integration. *Brit J Psych* 61:259-266.

Cruse, H., J. Dean, H. Heuer, and R.A. Schmidt. 1990. Utilization of sensory information for motor control. In *Relationships between perception and action: Current approaches*, ed. O. Neumann and W. Prinz, 43-79. Berlin: Springer.

Csikszentmihalyi, M. 1975. *Beyond boredom and anxiety—The experience of play in work and games*. San Francisco: Jossey-Bass.

Csikszentmihalyi, M. 1990. *Flow: The psychology of optimal experience*. New York: Harper.

Csikszentmihalyi, M. 1999. *Flow in sports: The key to optimal experiences and performances*. Champaign, IL: Human Kinetics.

Court, J. 1995. Die Anthropologie, der Sport, und das Glück. [Anthropology, sport, and happiness.] *Sportwissenschaft* 25(3): 227-244.

Groeben, N. 1988. Explikation des Konstrukts "Subjektive Theorien." [Explication of the concept "subjective theory."] In *Forschungsprogramm Subjektive Theorien: Eine Einführung in die Theorie des reflexiven Subjektes* [Research program subjective theories: An introduction into the theory of the reflexive subject], ed. N. Groeben, D. Wahl, J. Schlee, and B. Scheele, 17-24. Tübingen: Francke.

Groeben, N., and B. Scheele. 2001. Dialogue-hermeneutic method and the "research program subjective theories." *Forum Qualitative Sozialforschung* 2, no. 1 (February), http//:qualitative-research.net/fqs/fqs-eng.htm [accessed January 3, 2002].

Hacker, W. 1994. Diagnose von Expertenwissen: Von Abzapf zu Aufbau Konzepten. [Diagnosis of the knowledge of experts: From broaching to (re-) constructing concepts.] Forschungsbericht der Technischen Universität Dresden, Institut für Allgemeine Psychologie und Methodenlehre, Band 15. [Research report from the Technical University Dresden, Institute for Psychology and Methodology, Volume 15.]

Hill, H. 2002. Dynamics of coordination within elite rowing crews: Evidence from force pattern analysis. *J Sports Sci* 20:101-117.

Kearney, A.R., and S. Kaplan. 1997. Toward a methodology for the measurement of knowledge structures of ordinary people: The conceptual content cognitive map (3CM). *Environ Behav* 29(5): L579.

Körndle, H., and V. Lippens. 1988. Do rowers have a particular "foot-writing"? In *Proceedings for the Congress: Biomechanics in Sport,* 7-11. London: Institution of Mechanical Engineers.

Lambert, C. 1998. *Mind over water.* Boston: Houghton Mifflin.

Lenk, H. 1985. *Die achte Kunst: Leistungssport—Breitensport.* [The eighth art: Performance sport—recreational sport.] Zürich: Interform.

Lippens, V. 1996a. Zum sportpädagogischen Modell einer transdisziplinären Bewegungshand-Lungsanalyse zwischen Kognition und Motorik. [Regarding the sport-pedagogical model of a transdisciplinaritory analysis of the movement performance from cognition to motion.] In *Bio-Mechanik. Bericht über die Tagung der dvs-Sektion Biomechanik 1995 in Herzogenhorn,* ed. A. Gollhofer, 89-97. St. Augustin: Academia.

Lippens, V. 1996b. "Die Stabilität des Bootslauf durch geschickte Variabilität sichern!" Zur zeitlichen und dynamischen Bewegungs-Synchronisation in (ungesteuerten) Riemen-Booten unter Trainings und Wettkampfbedingungen des Rudersports. ["Secure the stability of the run of the boat with a smart variability!" Regarding the temporal and dynamic synchronization of the motion in coxless sweep boats in rowing during training and competition.] In *Kognition und Motorik,* ed. R. Daugs, et al., 109-114. Hamburg: Czwalina.

Lippens, V. 1999. The temporal and dynamic synchronization of movement in coxless oared shells. In *Sport kinetics 1997: Theories of motor performance and their reflections in practice,* vol. 2, ed. P. Blaser, 39-44. Hamburg: Czwalina.

Meyer-Drawe, K. 1990. *Illusionen von Autonomie: Diesseits von Ohnmacht und Allmacht des Ich.* [Illusions of autonomy: On this side of the unconsciousness and superpower of the I.] München: Fink.

Newell, K.M., and D.M. Corcos, eds. 1993. *Variability and motor control.* Champaign, IL: Human Kinetics.

Runeson, S. 1977. On the possibility of "smart" perceptual mechanisms. *Scand J Psychol* 18:72-179.

Tamboer, J.E.J. 1988. Images of the body underlying concepts of action. In *Complex Movement Behavior: 'The' Motor-Action Controversy,* ed. O.G. Meijer and K. Roth, 439-461. Amsterdam: North-Holland.

Troitzsch, K.G. 1996. Individuelle Einstellungen und kollektives Verhalten. [Indiviudal behavior and collective reactions.] In *Chaos und Ordnung,* ed. G. Küppers, 200-228. Stuttgart: Reclam.

Vereijken, B., and H.T.A. Whiting. 1990. In defense of discovery learning. *Can J Sport Sci* 15: 99-106.

Zimmer, A.C., and H. Körndle. 1988. A model for hierarchically ordered schemata in the control of skilled motor action. *Gestalt Theory* 10:85-102.

Chapter 17

Nolte, V., J. Klauck, and A. Mader. 1983. Vergleich biomechanischer Merkmale der Ruderbewegung auf dem Gjessing-Ergometer und im fahrenden Boot. [Comparison of biomechanical parameters of the rowing motion on the Gjessing-ergometer and in the boat.] In *Sport—Leistung und Gesundheit,* ed. H. Heck, et al, 513-518. Köln.

Rekers, C. 1993. Verification of the RowPerfect ergometer. In *Proceedings of the A.R.A. Senior Rowing Conference.* London.

Chapter 18

Atkinson, W. 2000. Modeling the dynamics of rowing. Atkinsopht, www.atkinsopht.com/row/rowrpage.htm (accessed May 24, 2004).

Cameron, A. 1967. Some mechanical aspects of rowing. In *Rowing: A scientific approach,* ed. J. Williams and A. Scott, 64-80. Kingswood, UK: Kaye and Ward Ltd.

Dal Monte, A., and A. Komor. 1989. Rowing and sculling mechanics. In *Biomechanics of sport,* ed. Vaughan, C.L., 53-119. Boca Raton, FL: CRC Press.

Gerber, H., H. Jenny, J. Sudan, and E. Stuessi. 1987. Biomechanical performance analysis in rowing with a new measuring system. In *Biomechanics X-B,* ed. B. Jonsson, 721-724. Champaign, IL: Human Kinetics.

Hawkins, D. 2000. A new instrumentation system for training rowers. *J Biomech* 33:241-245.

Kleshnev, V. 1996. The application of computer technologies to management of special training in cyclic sports. In *Current research in sport sciences: An international perspective*, ed. V. Rogozkin and R. Maughan, 137-146. Plenum Publ.

Kleshnev, V. 1996. The effects of stroke rate on biomechanical parameters and efficiency of rowing. In *XIV ISBS Symposium Abstracts Proceedings*, ed. J. Abrantes, 321-325. Lisboa, Portugal: Edicoes FMH.

Kleshnev, V. 1997. The determination of total power during on-water rowing. *XVI Congress of ISB. Book of Abstracts*, 19. Tokyo: University of Tokyo.

Kleshnev, V. 1998. Evaluation of rowing efficiency. Unpublished.

Kleshnev, V. 2000. Power in rowing. *Proceedings of XVIII Congress of ISBS*, (2): 662-666. Hong Kong: Chinese University of Hong Kong.

Kleshnev, V. 2001. Racing strategy in rowing during Sydney Olympic Games. *Australian Rowing* 24(1): 20-23.

Kleshnev, V. 2001. Stroke rate vs. distance in rowing during the Sydney Olympics. 24(2): 18-22.

Kleshnev, V. 2002. Measurement of the point of force application at the handle and the blade during rowing in single scull. Unpublished.

Martin, T.P., and Y.S. Bernfield. 1980. Effect of stroke rate on velocity of a rowing shell. *Med Sci Sports Exerc* 12(4): 250-256.

Nolte, V. 1984. *Die Effektivität des Ruderschlages*. [The efficiency of the rowing stroke.] Berlin: Bartels and Wernitz.

Ozkaya, N., and M. Nordin. 1991. *Fundamentals of biomechanics*. New York: Van Nostrand Reinhold.

Secher, N. 1993. Physiological and biomechanical aspects of rowing. *Sports Med* 15 (1): 24-42.

Smith, R., and C. Loschner. 2000. Net power production and performance at different stroke rates and abilities during sculling. Coaches' infoservice, http://www.coachesinfo.com/category/rowing/79 (accessed May 18, 2004).

Wagner, J., U. Bartmus, and H. de Marees. 1993. Three axes gyro system quantifying the specific balance of rowing. *Int J Sports Med* 14:35-38.

Zatsiorsky, V.M., and N. Yakunin. 1991. Mechanics and biomechanics of rowing: A review. *Int J Sport Biomech* 7:229-281.

Chapter 19

Lenk, H. 1964-65. Konflikt und Leistung in Spitzensportmannschaft—Soziometrische Strukturen von Wettkampfachtern im Rudern. [Conflicts and performance in elite sport teams—Sociometrical structures of competitive eight crews in rowing.] *Soziale Welt* 307-343.

Lenk, H. 1977. *Team dynamics*. Champaign, IL: Stiper.

Rushall, B.S. 1987. *Handbook for understanding, interpreting, and using the tests contained in the sport psychology consultation system*. Spring Valley, California: Sports Science Associates.

Chapter 20

Klavora, P. 1980. Rowing racing strategy: Psychological considerations. *Oarsman* 12(1): 6-11.

Klavora, P. 1982. Racing strategy. In *Rowing 2—National coaching certification program*, ed. P. Klavora, 205-239. Ottawa, Canada.

Kleshnev, V. 2001. Racing strategy in rowing during Sydney Olympic Games. *Australian Rowing* 24 (1): 20-23.

Kollmann, W. 2000. Rennanalysen. [Race analysis.] *Rudersport* 21:782-785.

Schwanitz, P. 2000. Zeitprognosen vor Olympia. [Time prognosis before the Olympics.] *Rudersport* 5:218-221.

Chapter 21

Csikszentmihalyi, M. 1975. Play and intrinsic rewards. *J Hum Psyc*, 15(3): 41-63.

Doherty, K. 1964. *Modern training for running*. New Jersey: Prentice Hall.

Elgin, D. 1993. *Awakening earth*. New York: William Morrow Co.

Goleman, D. 2003. *Destructive emotions*. New York: Bantam.

Jackson, P. 1995. *Sacred hoops*. New York: Hyperion.

Jackson, P., and C. Rosen. 2002. *More than a game*. New York: Atria.

Kabat-Zinn, J. 1994. *Wherever you go, there you are*. New York: Hyperion.

McCluggage, D. 1983. *The centered skier*. New York: Bantam.

Mitchell, S., ed. 1988. *Tao te ching*. New York: Harper.

Morrow, A. Presentation at the eighth annual Joy of Sculling coaches conference, Saratoga, NY, December, 2000.

Tart, C.J. 2000. *Mind science: Meditation training for practical people*. Novato, CA: Wisdom Editions.

Wilber, K. 1997. *The eye of spirit*. Boston: Shambhala.

Note: The italicized *f* and *t* following page numbers refer to figures and tables, respectively.

A

Adam, Karl 3, 187
aerobic base, developing
    cross-training 54-61
    Fartlek training 49
    heart rate, determining 53, 53*f*, 53*t*, 54,
        54*f*
    importance of 49
    intensity levels of 50
    lactate concentration 51
    steady-state training 49-50
    training effectiveness, determining 51,
        52*f*, 53
    training intensity, controlling 50, 51
Ali, Muhammad 249
anaerobic threshold, improving
    anaerobic capacity and, examples 63-64
    conditions for improving 71, 72, 72*f*, 73,
        74*t*
    as control mechanism 64-65
    demands of 70
    increasing 68-69
    maximal oxygen consumption ($\dot{V}O_2$max)
    as reference point 65-66, 67, 67*f*, 68*f*
    measuring 65
    threshold testing 73, 75
    training, limits of 69-70
athletes' physiology, monitoring
    golden standard 26-27
    physical performance, optimizing 25
    quality training 29, 29*f*
    results, analyzing 28-29
    rowing training, applications 29-30
    sample training models 30
    test method, developing 26-27
Awakening Earth (Elgin) 257

B

back pain, mechanical 40
biceps tendinosis 36
biomechanical analysis
    biomechanical modeling 220, 220*f*, 221,
        221*f*, 222
    data processing 217, 218, 218*f*, 219*f*
    performance analysis 222, 222*t*
    statistical analysis and evaluation 218,
        219, 219*t*
biomechanical feedback
    direct feedback 224
    immediate feedback 224

    traditional feedback 222-223, 223*f*
biomechanical measurements
    contact and noncontact methods 210, 211*f*
    environmental parameters 217
    noncontact measurements (imaging tech-
        nology) 217
    rowing kinematics 211-213, 211*f*-213*f*
    rowing kinetics 213-216, 214*f*-216*f*
biomechanics of rowing
    assessment of 112, 113-115
    blade forces 116-119
    boat velocity 121, 122-123, 122*f*
    improved techniques, past 111
    oar force 119, 119*f*, 120, 120*f*
    oar motion 115 115*f*, 116
    rower's primary goal 111
    rowing stroke 112, 113*f*
    science of 111-112
blade forces
    drag force 116
    lift force 117, 117*f*, 118
    propulsive and transverse oar force 118,
        118*f*, 119
    resultant force 118, 118*f*
bladework. *See also* bladework exercises
    blade control 141
    blade shape 150
    body position and movement 147-149
    communication 153-154
    competitive rowing and 142-147
    performance and 141
    pitch 150-151
    stroke length 149-150
    swivel height 141-142
    work height 151
bladework exercises
    angle and speed of entry 151
    angle of entry 1 151
    angle of entry 2 151
    beginnings, finishes, and balance 153
    boat, balancing 153
    finish, strengthening 152
    quick entry 1 152
    quick entry 2 152
    rhythm and balance 153
    uniform depth, maintaining 152
boat velocity
    hydrodynamic drag 121
    maximum boat velocity 121, 122
    periods above mean value, extending,

study on 122-123
rowing shell velocity 121, 122
variations in 121
velocity oscillations 121, 122*f*
body position and movement
performance, maximizing 147-148
power phase 148, 148*f*, 149
recovery phase 149
Boitano, Brian 256
Boraska, Igor 237
Bürgin, Melch 129

C
Campbell, Neil 250, 258
catch. *See also* catch position
coaching 160-161, 161*f*
importance of 155
oar angles, setting 161-162, 162*t*, 163, 163*f*
power and recovery 155-156
preparation 156-159
catch position
blade entry 157, 158, 158*f*
correct catch position 156, 157*f*
end of catch 158, 158*f*, 159
no backsplash 159, 159*f*
perfect splash 159, 159*f*
sculling 156, 157*f*
in sweep boat 156
too much backsplash 159, 159*f*
Centered Skier, The (McCluggage) 253
competitive rowing and bladework
blade splash 144, 145*f*
boat speed, factors influencing 142-143, 143*f*
middle of stroke 145, 145*f*
puddle 146, 147*f*
recovery 147
stroke, beginning of 143-144, 144*f*
stroke finish 146, 146*f*
costochondritis 39
CoxBox 266, 268-269
coxing, advanced. *See also* coxing rowing technique
calling distance 266-267
calling place 267
calling time 266
motivation 267-268
positioning in shell 265-266
racing 268-269
weight requirements 269
coxing, basic responsibilities
basic commands 263-265
communication 262
steering 262-263
coxing rowing technique
angle of entry 270
balance 271-272
blade height and depth 271
body position and hand technique 271
preparation 269
rhythm and ratio 272-273
timing 270

coxswains 261, 262, 265, 266
crossover tendinosis. *See* intersection syndrome
cross-training
ball sports 61
cross-country skiing 55, 56, 57-58, 58*t*-59*t*
cycling 55, 56*t*, 57*t*
in-line skating 59-60
kayaking 60
reasons for using 54
running 59
windsurfing 61
Curtis, W.B. 195

D
DeQuervain's tendinosis 35
Doherty, Kenneth 254
doping control 48
Dreissgacker, Dick 196
Dreissgacker, Peter 196
drug notification 48

E
Elgin, Duane 257
energy systems, simulation of
energy supply during maximal performance 21, 21*t*
possible energy supply, distribution of 22, 22*f*
VLA (anaerobic lactic energy), influence of 21-22
ergometer, modern
body attachments 199
Concept2 Indoor Rower (C2IR) 196, 198
Gamut ergometer 196
Gjessling ergometer 15, 196, 197
model D 197
monitor 198
rower adjustments 199
RowPerfect 197
slide 198
ergometer technique. *See also* ergometer, modern
coaching rowers on 207-208
drills, rowing ergometer 203-204
maintaining ergometer 206-207
Narragansetts 195-196
pace, learning to 207
rowing machine, history and purpose of 195-196
stroke 199, 200*t*-201*t*, 201-202
workout plan, creating 204-206
workouts, beginning 202-203
Explosive Lifting for Sports (Newton) 93
Eye of Spirit, The (Wilbur) 256

F
forearm compartment syndrome 35-36
Foster, Tim 61

G
golden standard 26-27, 243, 243*t*
golfer's elbow. *See* medial epicondylosis
Gretsky, Wayne 256

H

Hagerman, Fritz 196
Haining, Peter 258
hip flexor tendinosis 41
Holmes, Andrew 141
high-intensity continuous exercise (HICE) 82, 84

I

injuries. *See* training, medical considerations
intercostal strain 38-39
intersection syndrome (crossover tendinosis) 35
intervertebral disk lesion 39-40
ischial bursitis 41

J

Jackson, Phil 249, 250, 251, 253, 256
Jordan, Michael 249-250, 251, 256

K

Karpinnen, Pertti 194
Karsten, Ekaterina 258
knee pain
    anterior 41-42
    posterior 42
Kolbe, Peter-Michael 194
Korzeniowski, Kris 238-239
Koven, Jamie 237

L

lateral epicondylosis (tennis elbow) 36
leaning 128, 128*f*
leg drive. *See also* leg drive phases
    description of 165, 166*f*
    drills for 174-175, 175*f*, 176
    sliding rigger and sliding seat 165, 166
    timing 165, 166
leg drive drills
    half slide 174
    legs down 175
    movement through catch 174
    moving ergometer 175, 175*f*
    part boat 174-175
    resistance rowing 175
    Russian catch 174
leg drive phases
    boat balance 168
    catch 166, 167*f*, 168, 168*f*, 169
    catch pressure 172
    drive 166, 167*f*, 169-171, 170*f*-171*f*
    finish 167*f*, 173, 173*f*
    recovery 167*f*, 174
    stroke length and power 173
Lucerne Regatta 4, 5, 31

M

McCluggage, Denise 253
McKay, Mike 61
McKinney, Steve 257
medial epicondylosis (golfer's elbow) 36
medical concerns
    competition considerations 48
    medical team, importance of 31
    postcompetition considerations 48
    precompetition considerations 45-47
    preparticipation examination 32
    training considerations 32-45
meditation techniques
    quiet sitting 252-253
    visualization 253-254
meralgia paresthetica 41
Miller, Bill 195
Mitchell, Stephen 257
Morrow, Al 256
Müller, Xeno 55, 59, 60, 237, 258
muscle fibers 14

N

Newton, Harvey 93

O

oar angles, setting
    distance from centerline of boat to pin 162, 162*t*
    importance of 161-162
    marking catch angle 162
    marking correct catch angle 163
    sculling 162
    setting finish angle 163
    sweep boat 162
    taping gunwale of boat 162, 163*f*
    using video 163
oar force
    force-angle graphs 119, 119*f*
    negative and positive oar angles 119
    oar force against oar angle 119
    research and force-time curves 120, 120*f*
    seat specific technique 120

P

physiological conditions
    anaerobic lactic and anaerobic alactic
    metabolic systems, energy from 11, 12-13, 12*f*
    maximal oxygen uptake ($\dot{V}O_2$max) 10, 11, 11*f*, 12*f*
    metabolic performance 10, 11*f*
piriformis syndrome 40-41
pitch
    inbuilt 138, 138*f*, 139
    inward 138
    lateral 127*f*, 138
    outward 138
Porter, Derek 194
precompetition considerations
    making weight 45-46
    staying hydrated 46-47
    travel-related illnesses, avoiding 47

R

race plans and tactics
    collecting information 242-243
    race plan, adapting to crew 238-240
    race preparation 240-242

realistic goals, setting 240
respecting competition 237
speed profile, factors 238
strategy and tactics 238
studying races 243-246, 243t-246f
recovery
  biomechanics 179, 180, 181
  drills 182-184
  hand movement during 181, 181f
  oarlock-force, boat-acceleration, and oar-angle 177, 178f
  practical applications 181-182
  recovery goals 177, 178
  recovery movements on stroke rate 180, 180f, 181
  rower-boat-oar system 179, 179f
  velocity of rower-boat-oar system 179, 180, 180f
Redgrave, Sir Steven 61, 141
Regatta, Henley 140
relaxation and focus. *See also* meditation techniques
  benefits of 249
  examples of 249-250
  flow 250, 257-258
  meditative practices 251-252, 252f
  relaxation techniques 254-257
  yearly plan 250, 250f, 251t
rib stress fracture 38
rigging
  boat measurements used in 126, 126f, 127f
  description 125
  footstretcher height 127f
  guidelines for 126
  importance of 128-130
  leaning 128, 128f
  longitudinal and lateral pitch of oarlock pin 127f
  oarlock height 127f
  rigging on boats, effects of 139
  rigging work to check boat 136
  special measurements 137-139, 137f, 138f
  sweep boat 126f
  total length, inboard, and outboard of oar 127f
  workthrough 127f
rigging principles
  accuracy 135
  basic measurement values 130-133, 131t-132t
  proper rigging tools 134, 134f, 135
  testing 135-136
  work in sequence 133, 133f, 134
Robinson, Rusty 49
rotator cuff dysfunction 37
rower's mind, inside. *See also* technology and technique training
  athletes and their motion 186-187
  athletes' subjective theories, finding 187-188
  movement, complex analysis of 185
  subjective theories, potential 194

synchronization strategies in coxless pairs 188-190, 189f, 190f
rowing, art of
  developments over years 3-4
  improvement predictions 7-8
  world-class rower, becoming 6-7
rowing biomechanics
  analysis of 217-222
  feedback 222-224
  measurements of 210-217
  methodological model of sport science 209-210
  pyramid model of applied science 210, 210f
rowing kinematics
  boat velocity and acceleration 212, 212f
  oar angle 211, 211f, 212
  other kinematic parameters 213
  seat and upper-body displacement 212-213, 213f
rowing kinetics
  footstretcher force 214-215, 215f, 216f
  force production 213
  handle and gate forces 213, 214, 214f
  other kinetic parameters 216
rowing machine. *See* ergometer technique
rowing performance
  energy production and efficiency, factors 5
  improvements over the years 4, 4f, 5
  standards, ever-improving 5
rowing physiology. *See also* rowing-specific energy, metabolic conditions
  body-size requirements 13, 13f
  demands of 9
  different energy systems, simulation of 21-22
  muscular requirements 14
  physiological conditions 10-13
rowing-specific energy, metabolic conditions
  aerobic capacity (endurance) and anaerobic capacity 17, 18-19, 18f
  alactic anaerobic expenditure 15, 15f
  anaerobic lactic energy metabolism 16
  fallacies 17
  glycolytic power 16, 17
  lactate work capacity 15
  maximal lactate formation 16, 16f
  metabolism during race 19, 20, 20f
  mitochondria volume 18-19
  overall power 15
  oxygen uptake during maximal load 19, 19f
  power output 15
rowing-specific program, designing
  maximum strength phase 95-96, 96t
  power-endurance phase 98, 98t
  power phase 96-97, 97t
  symmetry and hypertrophy phase 92-93, 94t, 95

S
selection of athletes and crews
  categories 230
  field tests 234-235

selection of athletes and crews *(continued)*
    health, physical characteristics, and physi-
        ology 230-232, 230*t*, 231*f*-233*f*
    height 229
    physical and psychological capacities 229
    psychology and sociology 233-234
    technique and biomechanics 233
speed training
    high-intensity continuous exercise (HICE)
        82, 84
    interval training 82-83, 84, 85, 85*t*
    interval training and HICE, combination of
        82
    recovery time and eating 85
    threshold training 83, 83*t*
spondylolithesis 39
sprint and speed work. *See also* speed training
    body's energy systems 77-79, 78*f*
    interval or HICE training 81*f*, 86, 86*t*
    metabolic systems (energy systems) 78
    physiological profiles of 79
    speed, acquiring 82-83, 83*t*, 84, 85, 85*t*
    sport, demands of 79-80
    training techniques 80, 81-82, 81*f*
Stones, Dwight 253
strength testing
    maximal strength testing (1RM) 88, 89-90
    predicted tests 90
    submaximal repetition testing 88
    test exercises: squat, bench pull, and
        deadlift 90-91, 91*f*, 92, 92*f*
strength training. *See also* strength testing
    rowing-specific program, designing 92-98
    strength demands of rowing 87-88, 89*t*
*Strength Training for Young Athletes, Second
    Edition* (Kraemer, Fleck) 93

T
Tao Te Ching (Mitchell) 257
technology and technique training
    applications for 192, 192*f*, 193*f*
    developments, further 192, 192*f*, 193*f*
    helping coach close gap 191, 191*f*
    intervention 190-191
tendinosis of long head of biceps 37-38
tennis elbow. *See* lateral epicondylosis
test method, monitoring physiological capacity
    average power 27, 27*f*
    four-day test series 26, 26*t*, 27, 27*f*
    golden standard 26
    physical characteristics 26, 26*t*
threshold testing
    in boat 75
    on rowing ergometer 73, 75

simple procedures 75
Tompkins, Jimmy 61
training, competitive phase
    designing 103-104
    duration and frequency 105, 105*t*
    intensity 105, 106
    major taper 105, 105*t*, 106
    minor taper 104, 104*t*
    special considerations 106
    taper percentage decreases in volume
        105, 105*t*
training, medical considerations
    back injuries 39-40
    elbow injuries 36-37
    environmental exposure 43, 44
    general hygiene and illness prevention
        42-43
    hip injuries 40-41
    knee injuries 41-42
    medical team 34
    overuse injuries 32-33, 33*f*, 34
    rib injuries 38-39
    shoulder injuries 37-38
    women's health 44-45
    wrist injuries 35-36
training periods per year. *See also* training,
    competitive phase
    breakdown, by phase and intensity 101,
        102, 102*t*
    precompetitive phase 102, 103
    preparatory phase 102
    transition phase 106-107
training plan, designing
    distributing training volume 100-101, 101*t*
    logical training periods per year 101-107
    periodization, description of 99
    training volume, determining 99-100, 100*t*
triceps tendinosis 36-37

V
$\dot{V}O_2$max
    contributions to total energy supply 10,
        11, 11*f*, 12*f*
    for determining aerobic energy production
        10
    metabolic performance 10, 11*f*

W
Wilber, Ken 256
Wolloner, Leo 140

Z
Zvegeli, Denis 237

about the editor

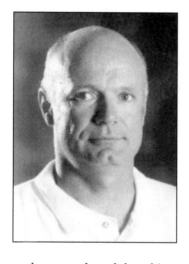

Dr. Volker Nolte is men's head rowing coach and assistant professor at the University of Western Ontario, where he teaches coaching and biomechanics. Since 1993, Nolte has led the men's rowing team to six Ontario University Athletics (UOA) Championships and repeated medal rankings at the Canadian University Championships. In addition, he was the lightweight men's national team coach with Rowing Canada from 1992 to 2000. His national team crews won an Olympic silver medal at the 1996 Atlanta Games, two world championship titles in 1993 and 2000, and several medals at world championships in recent years.

Nolte received both a physical education diploma (1976) and a civil engineering diploma (1979) from the University of Saarbrücken (Germany) and a PhD (1984) in biomechanics from the German University of Sport Sciences in Cologne. He is an internationally acknowledged expert in biomechanics. With his expertise in the coaching field, he presents frequently at scientific and coaching education conferences worldwide. His research includes coaching and biomechanics of high-performance sport, especially rowing. He is also a distinguished researcher in the field of sport equipment. He shares international patents for isokinetic training machines, and his developments range from special measurement tools to new boat designs in rowing. His research has produced many papers in refereed journals and articles in various publications.

Nolte is an experienced rower, representing his home country of Germany at several world championships. He is still a keen competitor in the Masters events.

Nolte lives in London, Ontario, Canada.

about the contributors

Marty Aitken is British International Rowing's chief coach for the lightweight and women's squads. He has coached Great Britain teams to three world championship bronze medals for men's eight and lightweight women's double (1989, 1991, and 2002). As chief coach for the Swiss national team in 1996 he was named Coach of the Year, taking his team to two gold medals and a silver in the Olympics, plus two gold, four silver, and four bronze medals in the world championships.

Dr. Richard Backus currently serves as both the medical director of Rowing Canada Aviron (RCA) and the chair of the RCA Medicine and Science Committee. He is a clinician and teacher of sports medicine in Victoria, British Columbia, as well as an adjunct assistant professor in the school of physical education at the University of Victoria. Backus has provided medical care for athletes at three Olympics and 13 world championships and was chair of athlete care at the Victoria Commonwealth Games (1994).

Dr. Declan A.J. Connolly is an exercise physiologist who has advised many Olympians over the past 20 years and has been invited to present for numerous athletic organizations, including USRowing, the Masters Rowing Association, NHL, and NFL, as well as professional teaching organizations and sports medicine groups. Connolly is currently a professor and director of the human performance lab at the University of Vermont. He is also a regular contributor to *Rowing News* and the *Journal of Competitive Rowing*.

Dr. Wolfgang Fritsch began as a successful international rower, competing in several German championships and winning the gold medal in the lightweight eight at the 1975 world championships. As a head coach in the German Rowing Association and lightweight squad leader of the Swiss Rowing Association from 1984 to 1990, he led teams to 6 gold medals and 14 overall medals at world championships. Fritsch is currently a lecturer in the department of sport science at the University of Konstanz, Germany.

Larry Gluckman is currently the varsity men's rowing coach at Trinity College in Hartford, Connecticut. He was a member of the 1976 U.S. Olympic team and the U.S. rowing team at the world championships in 1973 and 1975. He began his coaching career in 1969 as assistant rowing coach at Columbia University in New York, where he ultimately became head coach. Gluckman went on to coach heavyweight crews at Princeton and Dartmouth (1979-91) and the U.S. Olympic rowing team in 1980 and 1984.

Dr. Ulrich Hartmann monitored the German national rowing team from 1985 to 1992 with the aim of optimizing physiological effects at both sea level and high altitude, and in preparing teams for the 1988 and 1992 Olympic Games. He is a professor at the Technical University Munich and head of the department for theory and practice in sport. Hartmann has also authored and coauthored numerous papers and has lectured extensively around the world.

Kurt Jensen started rowing in 1968 and completed his thesis—a study on rowing during high-altitude training—at the August Krogh Institute, University of Copenhagen. He is currently responsible for the physiological testing of Denmark's elite athletes as a test coordinator for the Danish Elite Sport Federation at the University of Southern Denmark, Odense. Through his work, Jensen plays an instrumental role in the training programs of Denmark's Olympic champion lightweight rowers.

James Joy has enjoyed a distinguished career as an athlete, coach, and technical director for the Canadian Amateur Rowing Association (1980-89), which won more than 60 medals during his tenure. For the past 35 years, he has been a leader in coaching education through his Joy of Sculling coaching conferences. Joy specializes in mental training for coaches, training for flow, mental preparation for championship play, and integrative coaching.

Dr. Kristine Karlson was a world rowing champion in the late 1980s as well as a 1992 Olympian. In 1997 she went on to serve as team physician for USRowing. Currently, Karlson is assistant professor of community and family medicine and orthopedics at Dartmouth Hitchcock Medical Center in Lebanon, New Hampshire.

Dr. Valery Kleshnev began rowing at the age of 14 and has since evolved to become a world-class competitor and coach of the sport. He was the junior world champion in 1975, captured the silver Olympic medal in 1980, won bronze at the world championships in 1982, and earned five national championship titles. Kleshnev is currently a rowing biomechanist at the Australian Institute of Sport, Canberra.

Dr. Volker Lippens worked on the committee of biomechanics and science and teaching for the German Rowing Federation. Since 1996 he has been a private lecturer in sport science at the University of Hamburg, Germany, and is a substitute professor in the field for various other German universities.

Dr. Alois Mader was the physician for the German national rowing team from 1979 to 1988, where he helped guide the men's eight to Olympic gold in 1988. He is the former head of the institute of cardiology and sports medicine at the German University of Sport Sciences in Cologne. Mader's focus lies in the theory and practice of testing metabolic components of sport performance in rowing, running, swimming, and high-altitude training.

Dr. Margaret McBride was a member of the Canadian rowing team from 1985 to 1987, competing at both the world championships and Commonwealth Games. As a biomechanist at the Australian Institute of Sport from 1989 to 1997, she developed a system that allowed rowing coaches to instantaneously assess an athlete's performance on the water. McBride is currently a biomechanics lecturer at the Australian Catholic University in Sydney, Australia.

Ed McNeely has served as the physiologist and strength training consultant to Rowing Canada since 1992. He is also a consultant to many provincial rowing associations and U.S. colleges, as well as the U.S. Masters Rowing Association. He is a regular columnist for the *Rowing News* and the author of two books on rowing. McNeely is also a featured presenter at conferences across Canada and the United States.

Thor Nilsen is development director of the International Rowing Federation. From his start as an international competitor, Nilsen participated in 25 Norwegian championships, European championships, and Olympic Games. He went on to serve as the national rowing coach for Norway and Sweden and to develop national training centers in several countries. Nilsen has coached teams to more than 30 world championship gold medals and eight Olympic gold medals.

Brian Richardson, Rowing Canada Aviron's national team head coach, coached his native Australian national team to five medals in Sydney, including a silver for the men's eight. Richardson was head coach of the Canadian team before and during the 1996 Atlanta Olympics when the team won a gold, four silvers, and a bronze. Richardson was in the 1976 and 1980 Australian eights and on the team that secured Australia's 1983 America's Cup victory.

Mike Spracklen has more than 30 years of experience as a rowing coach in his native Britain as well as in Canada and the United States. He coached the Canadian men's eight to a gold at the 1992 Olympics and rejoined Canada's coaching staff in 2001, guiding the men's eight to two consecutive world championship titles (2002 and 2003). Spracklen was named the International Rowing Federation's Coach of the Year in 2002.

Mike Teti is men's head coach of USRowing. From 1997 to 1999, he coached the only men's eight to win three consecutive World Championship titles in U.S. history, which also garnered him three consecutive National Coach of the Year honors. As a competitor from 1977 to 1993, Teti won 24 national championships, a silver medal at the 1979 Pan American Games in the four, a bronze and a gold in the world championships in the eight (1985 and 1987), and a bronze at the 1988 Olympic Games in the eight.

Richard Tonks is head coach of Rowing New Zealand's high-performance program, where he is preparing a team for the 2004 Olympics in addition to coaching crews annually for other world events. From 1972 to 1975 Tonks represented the New Zealand elite team, which achieved their best result—silver medal—at the Munich Olympics in coxless four. From 1994 to 2003 he coached teams to numerous medals in the Olympic Games and world championships.

Lesley Thompson-Willie was a coxswain with the Canadian national women's rowing team from 1980 to 2000. She was named to six Olympic teams and is a four-time Olympic medalist, including a gold in 1992, as well as a multiple world medalist and world champion.